Epworth Commen

General Edito
Ivor H. Jones

The Epistle to the Ephesians

Albrecht Dürer's *Die Apokalypse* (1498): The Defeat of Satan by Michael and his angelic host. See Ephesians 6.12

The Epistle to the
EPHESIANS

LARRY J. KREITZER

EPWORTH PRESS

0 7162 0515 7

First Published 1997
by Epworth Press
20 Ivatt Way
Peterborough, PE3 7PG

Typeset by Regent Typesetting, London
Printed and bound in Great Britain by
Biddles Ltd, Guildford and King's Lynn

in loving memory of

Joy K. and Stanley R.
(† 15-2-1988 & 8-8-1988 †)

'O Spirit, as we gather'

1.
O Spirit, as we gather in this place,
Interpret to our waiting hearts
The signs that speak of grace.

2.
We need your touch of fire, your
touch of love,
We need the comfort and the power
That you alone can give.

3.
Be present with us here to make us
one,
That in his death and life we may
Be joined with Christ the Son,
Joined with Christ the Son,
Joined with Christ the Son.

4.
O Spirit, as we leave this sacred place,
Help us to see beyond the bars
Of gender, wealth and race.

5.
Grant us your strength, assistance from
above,
So that the way we live our lives
Will demonstrate your love.

6.
Be present with the church of Christ
the Son,
It is the mystery of grace
That all in him are one,
All in him are one,
All in him are one.

A Song for the Celebration of Baptism and Communion based on Eph. 1.9–13
and Gal. 3.27–28
Words by L. J. Kreitzer and D. W. Rooke; music by D. W. Rooke

CONTENTS

GENERAL INTRODUCTION

The *Epworth Preachers' Commentaries* that Greville P. Lewis edited so successfully in the 1950s and 1960s having now served their turn, the Epworth Press has commissioned a team of distinguished academics who are also preachers and teachers to create a new series of commentaries that will serve the 1990s and beyond. We have seized the opportunity offered by the publication in 1989 of the Revised English Bible to use this very readable and scholarly version as the basis of our commentaries, and we are grateful to the Oxford and Cambridge University Presses for the requisite licence. Our authors will nevertheless be free to cite and discuss other translations wherever they think that these will illuminate the original text.

Just as the books that make up the Bible differ in their provenance and purpose, so our authors will necessarily differ in the structure and bearing of their commentaries. But they will all strive to get as close as possible to the intention of the original writers, expounding their texts in the light of the place, time, circumstances, and culture that gave them birth, and showing why each work was received by Jews and Christians into their respective Canons of Holy Scripture. They will seek to make full use of the dramatic advance in biblical scholarship world-wide but at the same time to explain technical terms in the language of the common reader, and to suggest ways in which scripture can help towards the living of a Christian life today. They will endeavour to produce commentaries that can be used with confidence in ecumenical, multi-racial, and multi-faith situations, and not by scholars only but by preachers, teachers, students, church members, and anyone who wants to improve his or her understanding of the Bible.

Ivor H. Jones

FOREWORD

E. J. Goodspeed once described Ephesians as 'the Waterloo of commentators'. This is a delightfully ambiguous phrase which, since it
was penned by an American, cannot be assumed to be either pro-
French or anti-English. No doubt part of what he was indicating was
the fact that the letter to the Ephesians is maddeningly difficult to
pin down, with many scholars finding it either their greatest
triumph or their most humiliating defeat. It has the uncanny knack
of putting us in a situation in which, as it were, 'defeat is snatched
from the jaws of victory'. The impression that one has of the Apostle
Paul can be greatly affected by how one sees the epistle to the
Ephesians fitting within the Pauline corpus.

Like many others I have long been frustrated by the lack of a
credible scenario for the production of the letter. Goodspeed himself
did offer one over half a century ago, the 'covering-letter' hypothesis, which captured the imaginations of many, particularly in
the USA. However, it now seems rather dated and out of fashion,
especially given the fact that it was dependent upon a particular
reading of how Luke-Acts revived waning interest in Paul and his
letters and how Onesimus managed to gather together the Pauline
corpus and preserve an important tradition of the church. Both of
these ideas have been severely criticized and no longer command the
attention they once did. New solutions are needed to this long-
standing problem within Pauline studies, but they are few and far
between given the nature of the epistle itself.

I did not deliberately set out to attempt to offer a new scenario for
the historical circumstances which led to the production of the letter.
However, a fortuitous sabbatical visit to both Ephesus and the Lycus
Valley in June-July of 1995 planted some seeds of thought which
have come to fruition in this commentary. In particular, I made a
visit to the ancient city of Hierapolis in Phrygia, which was known
primarily to me as the home of both Epictetus, the former slave and
Stoic philosopher, and of Papias (circa 60–130 CE), the second bishop

11

of the city. As a NT tutor, Papias was the more familiar of the two to me since he is the source of the tradition that Mark was the interpreter of Peter and thus ultimately responsible for the suggestion that Petrine recollections underlie Mark's Gospel (as virtually every undergraduate essay on the topic I have ever heard in my ten years at Oxford relates!). I remember being struck by the view that one has of Hierapolis from the Lycus Valley below and the way in which the white calcium formations of Pamukkale, deposited over some 15,000 years, give the appearance of billowing clouds of heaven when set against the bright blue skies of Turkey. Based on this visit and the inspiration it provided for thinking about the geography of the region afresh, I was pleasantly surprised to discover in 4.8–10 (notably the probable allusion to the Plutonium of Hierapolis in verse 9), a key to the puzzle which seems, to my mind at least, to solve many of the interpretative difficulties of the letter. I hope that the suggestions I have offered here on the authorship, setting and date of the letter will be of interest to others and I would welcome comments about their worth (or otherwise!) in helping us to understand the epistle better. So much for the traditional features (author, date, setting, etc.) of the study offered here; a word about some of the other non-traditional features of the commentary is also in order.

For many people, including dedicated pastors, teachers and house-group leaders, commentaries remain closed books, both literally and metaphorically. I think that one of the reasons for this is that it is not immediately obvious to us what connection there is between the commentary and our everyday lives. I am convinced that commentaries must be written with an eye which is appreciative of the context in which Christian life is lived out: the complex and fast-paced world of the late twentieth century. Modern people are wide-ranging in their interests and perceptions of life and a commentary worth its salt must recognize that fact. Therefore I make no apology for using illustrations from literature, music, art and film in an attempt to make the message of Ephesians live for us today.

I am very conscious that the beliefs of many people are created and shaped more by the hymns and songs they sing than by anything they might read. In this regard, hymnody may be viewed as a spiritual resource which remains largely untouched by most NT commentators. I have tried to make amends for this oversight, in a small way, by incorporating discussion of some of the better known hymns and songs of the Christian faith at appropriate points within the commentary. It seems to me right and proper that the musical heritage of the church be given its due place. If Ephesians 5.19 is anything to go by, I rather suspect that the Writer of the letter would have agreed.

In summary, I would suggest that commentaries should be a resource for worship rather than a self-indulgent exploration of the biblical text. If I can persuade even one reader of the value of integrating the study of the scriptural text with his or her life, whatever it might contain in the form of personal and cultural attachments and interests, I will feel the effort of producing this commentary has been worthwhile.

The maps included in Appendix 1 are used with the kind permission of Inter-Varsity Press and are taken from the article on 'Hierapolis' by M.J.S. Rudwick and Colin J. Hemer in *The Illustrated Bible* (Volume 2, 1980), pp. 647–649.

A concluding word about translations might also be in order. As is consistent with the aims of the Epworth Commentary series, this volume takes as its starting point the Revised English Bible translation from 1989. It goes without saying that it might be useful, if not necessary, to have a copy of the REB to hand when using the commentary here offered. At the same time, I have tried to bring into discussion one or two other modern translations, some of which may not be as well known to the readership. Included among these are: F.F. Bruce's *The Letters of Paul: An Expanded Paraphrase* (Exeter: Paternoster Press 1965); Clarence Jordan's *The Cotton Patch Version of Paul's Epistles* (New York: Association Press 1968); and Eugene H. Peterson's *The Message: The New Testament in Contemporary English* (Colorado Springs, Colorado: NavPress 1993).

Larry J. Kreitzer
Regent's Park College, Oxford
Trinity Term 1996

ABBREVIATIONS

AB	Anchor Bible
AV	The Authorized Version
BCE	Before the Common Era
BJRL	*Bulletin of the John Rylands Library*
BS	The Biblical Seminar Series
BST	The Bible Speaks Today Series
CBQ	*Catholic Biblical Quarterly*
CE	Common Era
GNB	Good News Bible
GNS	Good News Studies
EQ	*The Evangelical Quarterly*
HTR	*Harvard Theological Review*
IC	Interpretation Commentary
JB	Jerusalem Bible
JBL	*Journal of Biblical Literature*
JSNT	*Journal for the Study of the New Testament*
JSNTSup	Journal for the Study of the New Testament Supplement Series
JSS	*Journal of Semitic Studies*
LXX	The Septuagint
NASB	New American Standard Bible
NCB	New Century Bible
NClB	New Clarendon Bible
NEB	New English Bible
NICNT	New International Commentary on the New Testament
NIV	New International Version
NovTSup	Supplement to Novum Testamentum
NRSV	New Revised Standard Version
NT	New Testament
NTG	New Testament Guides
NTR	New Testament Readings
NTS	New Testament Studies

Abbreviations

OT	Old Testament
PC	Proclamation Commentaries
REB	Revised English Bible
RevExp	*Review and Expositor*
RSV	Revised Standard Version
SNTSMS	Society of New Testament Studies Monograph Series
TZ	*Theologische Zeitschrift*
WBC	Word Biblical Commentary
WUNT	Wissenschaftliche Untersuchungen zum neuen Testament

COMMENTARIES AND KEY WORKS ON EPHESIANS

Fortunately the interested reader is spoiled for choice as far as commentaries and studies on the epistle to the Ephesians is concerned. Whether one wishes to tackle the monumental two-volume effort of Marcus Barth (a Herculean effort to have written, I am sure, and like one of the labours of Hercules to read!), or the splendid efforts by A.T. Lincoln and Rudolf Schnackenburg which bring one up to date with the latest scholarly investigations into the letter, or Martin Kitchen's exciting contribution in what promises to be a highly creative series entitled *Readings*, there is a variety of choice on the menu. Many good popular and less scholarly studies also abound, including John R.W. Stott's contribution in the *Bible Speaks Today* series which is a model of readability. With a little patience and careful attention one can readily find an appropriate level through which to explore the letter, whether it be a commentary requiring knowledge of NT Greek, a commentary based on a particular English translation, or a study which picks up a theme contained with the letter and uses that as the entry point. In my own experience, the following have proven to be of special note:

Commentaries requiring some knowledge of Greek

Markus Barth, *Ephesians* (AB nos 34 and 34A; Garden City, NY: Doubleday & Co 1974)

G.B. Caird, *Paul's Letters from Prison* (NClB; Oxford: Oxford University Press 1976)

Martin Kitchen, *Ephesians* (NTR; London: Routledge 1994)

Andrew T. Lincoln, *Ephesians* (WBC No. 42; Dallas: Word Book 1990)

Rudolf Schnackenburg, *The Epistle to the Ephesians: A Commentary* (Edinburgh: T. & T. Clark 1991)

Commentaries based on an English translation and general introductions to the epistle

C.E. Arnold, 'Ephesians, Letter to the' in Gerald F. Hawthorne, Ralph P. Martin, and Daniel G. Reid (eds), *Dictionary of Paul and His Letters* (Leicester: IVP 1993), pp. 238–249

Ernest Best, *Ephesians* (NTG; Sheffield: Sheffield Academic Press 1993)

G.B. Caird, *Paul's Letters from Prison* (NClB; Oxford: Oxford University Press 1976), pp. 9–94.

Raymond F. Collins, *Letters That Paul Did Not Write: The Epistle to the Hebrews and the Pauline Pseudepigrapha* (GNS no. 28; Wilmington, Delaware: Michael Glazier 1988), pp. 132–170

Nils Alstrup Dahl, 'Gentiles, Christians, and Israelites in the Epistle to the Ephesians', *HTR* 79 (1986) pp. 31–39

Victor Paul Furnish, 'Ephesians, Epistle to the' in David Noel Freedman (ed), *The Anchor Bible Dictionary, Volume 2* (New York: Doubleday 1992), pp. 535–542

Ralph P. Martin, *Ephesians, Colossians, and Philemon* (IC; Atlanta: John Knox Press 1991)

C. Leslie Mitton, *Ephesians* (NCB; London: Marshall, Morgan & Scott 1976)

J. Paul Sampley, 'Ephesians' in G. Krodel (ed), *The Deutero-Pauline Letters* (PC; Minneapolis: Fortress Press 1993), pp. 1–23

John Stott, *The Message of Ephesians* (BST; Leicester: IVP 1989)

Bonnie Thurston, *Reading Colossians, Ephesians & 2 Thessalonians: A Literary and Theological Commentary* (New York: Crossroad 1995)

Specialized studies relating to the epistle to the Ephesians

Clinton E. Arnold, *Ephesians: Power and Magic* (SNTSMS no. 63; Cambridge: Cambridge University Press 1989)

—— 'Jesus Christ: "Head" of the Church (Colossians and Ephesians)' in Joel B. Green and Max Turner (eds), *Jesus of Nazareth Lord and Christ: Essays on the Historical Jesus and New Testament Christology* (Grand Rapids: Eerdmans 1994), pp. 346–366

G.B Caird, 'The Descent of Christ in Ephesians 4, 7–11' in F.L. Cross (ed), *Studia Evangelica II* (Berlin: Akademie Verlag 1964), pp. 535–545.

Chrys C. Caragounis, *The Ephesian Mysterion: Meaning and Content* (Lund: G.W.K. Gleerup 1977)

W. Hall Harris III, *The Descent of Christ: Ephesians 4.7–11 & Traditional Hebrew Imagery* (Leiden: E.J. Brill 1996)

J.C. Kirby, *Ephesians: Baptism and Pentecost* (London: SPCK 1968)

Karl Georg Kuhn, 'The Epistle to the Ephesians in the Light of the Qumran Texts' in Jerome Murphy-O'Connor (ed), *Paul and Qumran: Studies in New Testament Exegesis* (London: Geoffrey Chapman 1968), pp. 115–131

Andrew T. Lincoln and A.J.M. Wedderburn, *The Theology of the Later Pauline Letters* (Cambridge: Cambridge University Press 1993)

Margaret Y. MacDonald, *The Pauline Churches: A Socio-historical Study of Institutionalization in the Pauline and Deutero-Pauline Writings* (SNTSMS no. 60; Cambridge: Cambridge University Press 1988)

Ralph P. Martin, *Reconciliation: A Study of Paul's Theology* (London Marshall, Morgan & Scott 1981), pp. 157–198

C. Leslie Mitton, *The Epistle to the Ephesians: Its Authorship, Origin and Purpose* (Oxford: Clarendon Press 1951)

Thorsten Moritz, *A Profound Mystery: The Use of the Old Testament in Ephesians* (NovTSup no. 85; Leiden: E.J. Brill 1996)

Franz Mussner, 'Contributions Made by Qumran to the Understanding of the Epistle to the Ephesians' in Jerome Murphy-O'Connor (ed), *Paul and Qumran: Studies in New Testament Exegesis* (London: Geoffrey Chapman 1968), pp. 159–178

Arthur G. Patzia, 'The Deutero-Pauline Hypothesis: An Attempt at Clarification', *EQ* 52 (1980), pp. 27–42.

W. Rader, *The Church and Racial Hostility: A History of Interpretation of Ephesians 2.1–11* (Tübingen: J.C.B. Mohr [Paul Siebeck] 1978)

A. Van Roon, *The Authenticity of Ephesians* (NovTSup no. 39; Leiden: E.J. Brill 1974)

J. Paul Sampley, *'And the Two Shall Become One Flesh': A Study of traditions in Ephesians 5.21–33* (SNTSMS no. 16; Cambridge: Cambridge University Press 1971)

References to Ignatius' *Epistle to the Ephesians* can be found in *The Apostolic Fathers*, Volume 1 (Loeb Edition). The same volume includes the texts of I Clement and Polycarp.

PRELIMINARY QUESTIONS

Three interlocking preliminary questions arise from any detailed study of the letter to the Ephesians, each of which has an important bearing on the interpretation which we give it. These are questions which concern matters of authorship, provenance and date: Who wrote the letter? To whom and for what purpose was it written? When was it written? We shall attempt to deal briefly with these matters in turn.

a. Authorship

There is little indication in the early church of a debate about Pauline authorship of Ephesians. The letter began to be quoted by other Christian writers at around the turn of the first century and they appear always to assume that Paul the Apostle was the writer. The Christian humanist Erasmus of Rotterdam (1466(?)–1536) in his *Novum Testamentum Annotationes* (1519) was one of the first commentators on Ephesians to question Paul's authorship of the epistle. This was done primarily on the grounds of style, the fact that Ephesians displays certain literary features which are at variance with those of much of the rest of the Pauline letters. With the rise of the historical-critical method at the beginning of the nineteenth century Ephesians came under more and more scrutiny. The debate about Pauline authorship continues to this day, although it has to be said that the majority opinion now is that Paul himself was not the author of the letter (probably about 80% of modern commentators would describe it as either *Deutero-Pauline* or *post-Pauline*). What is the reasoning behind such an assessment?

First of all, there is, as Erasmus rightly noted, the matter of literary style. The epistle contains several sentences which are exceedingly long and meandering, and which seem at times almost to run into the sand. The language is flowery and effusive, with many extra words and redundant phrases added for effect. It is almost as if the

21

writer of the letter has adopted the attitude: 'Why use one word when three will suffice?' The Greek text consists of approximately sixty-three sentences (depending on the textual edition used), sixteen or so of which have more than fifty words. Statistically, this is a higher percentage than occurs within most of the other Pauline letters (although it is not wildly out of line with what is found in Colossians). Likewise, in the undisputed letters of Paul, rhetorical questions are a standard means of advancing the argument; yet here in Ephesians there is only one such question put in the whole letter (4.9 – *'In saying, "He ascended," what does it mean but that he had also descended into the lower parts of the earth?'* (RSV)). Beyond that, there are approximately forty *hapax legomena* in Ephesians, alongside over fifty other words not used elsewhere in the Pauline corpus (although about half of these appear in Luke-Acts). In light of these various considerations, it is easy to see why recent stylistic studies have tended to confirm the non-Pauline authorship of Ephesians.

It is generally agreed that arguments for or against Pauline authorship which are based solely on style of writing are precarious. Indeed, debates along these lines over the authorship of literary works are by no means restricted to biblical documents. Did Homer write both *The Iliad* and *The Odyssey*? Or are the two works so different in style as to suggest a different author? Debates about whether Plato wrote all of the thirteen letters included in his corpus have long occupied classicists; indeed, there is hardly a major writer of the classical world who is not subjected to such scrutiny about the authorship of certain works within his corpus of writing. Likewise, is Shakespeare the real author of all of the works attributed to him, or might we reasonably attribute some of them to someone else, such as Francis Bacon? There are debates, for example, about Shakespeare's authorship of *Pericles*, which does not appear in the original 1623 folio publication of his work and clearly shows signs of different authorship (many Shakespearean scholars agree that George Wilkins had an important hand in the composition of the play). Similarly, most argue that the scenes involving the character Hecate in the play *Macbeth* once again exhibit signs of coming from a later hand.

To return to the Pauline corpus, could not the change in style evident in Ephesians be explained in some other way? Could it be due, for example, to a difference of circumstance, namely the imprisonment of Paul? Or perhaps the marked differences in style can be put down to there being a different pastoral reason for writing the letter, say the need to offer some reflections on the practice of baptism to a church newly emerging from paganism and badly in need of a theological grounding for their faith? Or perhaps the assistance of an amanuensis in the actual process of writing the letter is responsible for its change in style and phrasing? All of these suggestions have been put forward to try and account for the difference in style that is found in Ephesians.

However, differences in literary style and vocabulary are not the only reasons why most modern scholars doubt Pauline authorship of the letter. There are some notable differences in theological perspective as well, and many of these strike at the heart of key issues within Pauline thought. For example, in the undisputed letters of Paul the word 'church' almost always means a local congregation of Christian believers. In Ephesians the term never appears to carry that meaning; rather it is generally taken to mean the church universal, the church of all peoples, in all places. There is also a corresponding shift in the use of the metaphor of the 'body of Christ' in Ephesians. In the main, within the undisputed Pauline letters the church is described as the 'body of Christ' with individual members taking their part as eyes, ears, hands, feet, etc., thereby helping to constitute 'the body' (the classic example is I Corinthians 12.12–27). In Ephesians the 'body of Christ' metaphor is also used, but Christ himself is said to be 'the head of the Body', an addition which adapts the metaphor of the body and shows it being used in a slightly different way (the same adaptation occurs in Colossians 1.15, 18, which further complicates the issue since it therefore raises questions about the authorship of that letter). Similarly, the debate about the admission of Gentiles into the church and the related problems about whether or not adherence to the Jewish Law is required do not appear in Ephesians. Most take this to be an indication that the Jew/Gentile debate which so characterizes Galatians and Romans, for example, is now a thing of the past. The age-old 'circumcision divide' has been overcome and we are presented in Ephesians with a vision of a new Humanity which transcends the former antagonism of the two groups (see 2.11–22 in particular on this point). Again, it is somewhat unusual that Ephesians offers no advice on the Christian's attitude to the state (as in Romans 13.1–7), which might be construed as an indication that it comes from a later period when these matters are already settled. It is also worth mentioning that Ephesians does not contain any specific reference to the Lord's Supper, which could be said to distance it from another Pauline theme (albeit one which appears only in I Corinthians!).

23

Another point of contention concerns the eschatological perspective of Ephesians as compared with that of many of the Pauline letters. It is frequently argued that the realized eschatology of Ephesians represents a considerable development from that found in most of the rest of the Pauline corpus. Paul, so the argument goes, fervently believed in the imminent parousia of Jesus Christ, whereas in Ephesians this idea has given way to an understanding of eschatological matters which is wholly realized. Occasionally it is even stated that there are no future eschatological references at all in Ephesians. This is to overstate the case slightly, for there are some hints that belief in a future eschatological consummation is maintained, notably the description of the 'pledge of the Holy Spirit' in 1.13–14 and the mention of the 'day of liberation' in 4.30. However, it is certainly true to say that the delicate balance between realized and future eschatology, so carefully set forth in I Corinthians 15, for example, has decisively shifted in favour of the 'now' as opposed to the 'not yet'. In this sense, Ephesians seems to stand out among the rest of the Pauline letters. As Ernest Best puts it, cleverly adapting a well-known aphorism from T. S. Eliot.

> Ephesians does believe in a consummation of all things; if the world does not end with a bang the author certainly does not expect it to go out in a whimper.[1]

In short, there are a number of features of Ephesians which raise questions about accepting Paul the Apostle as the author of the letter. Not one of these features in and of itself is sufficient to prove that Paul is *not* the author of the work since alternative scenarios and extenuating circumstances can be brought forward to explain the various points of tension one by one. However, the *cumulative* effect of all of these matters is important to keep in mind and it is generally on this basis that most modern commentators feel that the letter was not written by Paul. In the face of all of these differences (in style, in vocabulary, in theological understanding, in conceptual imagery) it is unreasonable to suggest that Pauline authorship can still be entertained with anything like the degree of certainty that it was in the past. The case against Paul's authorship of the letter may not be proven, but the suspicion of a non-Pauline hand is beyond reasonable doubt.

If the Apostle Paul did not write the letter, who did? Several figures associated with the Apostle are regularly suggested as possible authors of the epistle. These suggestions are usually linked to reconstructions of the historical circumstances which might have occasioned its composition (see the discussion on Provenance below). One of the most celebrated proposals along these lines is that of E. J. Goodspeed, who suggests that Onesimus, later bishop of Ephesians (as mentioned in Ignatius, *Epistle to the Ephesians* 1.3; 6.2), was the author and that he wrote the work to serve as a covering epistle for the Pauline corpus. Goodspeed made this suggestion based in part upon his reconstruction of the history of the early church at the end of the first century. He assumes that the publication of Acts in circa 90 CE generated a resurgence of interest in Paul and his life. This, so Goodspeed continues, inspired Onesimus to gather together the extant letters of Paul which were held by the various congregations and make them available to the wider church. He wrote the covering letter we now designate as Ephesians as an introduction to the collection, including within it what he took to be the most salient features of Paul's thought. Part of this reconstruction hinges upon the fact that Onesimus would have known of both Colossians and Philemon since he was a member of the church at Colossae. One of the bonuses of this suggestion is that it does explain the heavy dependence of Ephesians upon Colossians. Goodspeed's theory has been widely influential, particularly in the United States, and it certainly stands as one of the most creative attempts to unravel what is a very complex question.

The 'covering letter' theory has some features to commend it, but it is not without its difficulties. For example, there are several key elements of Paul's thought which are not contained within this 'summary' of his thought, including a satisfactory discussion of the relationship between righteousness and the Mosaic law (which would have fitted nicely in 2.1–10), and a discussion of the Christian responsibility to the state along the lines of what we see given in Romans 13.1–7 (which would have fitted nicely in 5.22–6.9). Goodspeed's theory presumes that after Paul died there was a rapid loss of interest in the Apostle and his letters, a situation which he suggests was only set right by the publication of Acts. However, he does not say who and where those who lost interest lived (Rome? Corinth? Ephesus?). The suggestion about waning interest in Paul and his letters is made as a blanket statement and it is one for which there is no real evidence. In addition, one has to wonder how Ephesians might have been bundled together physically with the other Pauline epistles? Was it literally a covering letter, a 'cover sheet', so to speak? If so, this too presents something of a difficulty. While the placement of Ephesians within the order of the Pauline letters varies considerably in the manuscripts, it is never listed first (or last!) as Goodspeed's 'covering letter' theory requires. Moreover, the theory of a 'covering letter' distilling the essence of Paul's thought has been largely replaced by the recognition of the composite nature of the epistle as a whole. Recent investigations into the form and style of the letter suggest that it is more accurately described as a collage of phrases and materials which have been pasted together. Nevertheless, Goodspeed's suggestion that Onesimus was the author of the letter remains a real possibility, although there are others who appear more likely candidates for this honour.

C. Leslie Mitton accepted in large measure Goodspeed's idea of Ephesians as a covering letter to the works of Paul, but suggested that it was Tychicus, rather than Onesimus, who penned the epistle. Occasionally it is argued that Timothy was the author, generally based on the fact that he is known to have ministered and travelled alongside Paul during much of the so-called 'second' and 'third' missionary journeys. It may well be that Timothy was Paul's amanuensis since he is described as a co-author of several letters written by Paul (II Corinthians 1.1; Philippians 1.1; Colossians 1.1; I Thessalonians 1.1; II Thessalonians 1.1). Others, such as R.P. Martin, contend that Luke the physician was the author of the letter, partly because of stylistic and conceptual similarities between Ephesians and Luke-Acts. For example, of the forty or so words contained in Ephesians but not found elsewhere in the Pauline letters, twenty-five of these are used in Luke-Acts. In addition, the reference to Christ's exaltation to the right hand of God in 1.20–21 is often likened to the depiction of the ascension to heaven from the Mount of Olives on the road to Bethany outside the city of Jerusalem, a peculiarly Lukan idea (see Luke 24.51 and Acts 1.9–11). Similarly, the mention of Christ's 'descent to the lowest parts of the earth' in 4.9–10 could be taken as a veiled reference to Christ's descent in the form of the Holy Spirit at Pentecost and thus recall Acts 2.1–4.

One related matter needs to be addressed at this point: the connection between Ephesians and Colossians. Any attempt to identify the author of Ephesians must also provide a satisfactory explanation for the close relationship between the two letters. Clearly there is a literary dependence of one of the epistles upon the other; 73 out of 155 verses in Ephesians have some sort of parallel in Colossians. The most striking of these is Ephesians 6.21–22, which is virtually identical to Colossians 4.7–8. Understandably, this repetition of so long a passage has been taken by some to point to Pauline authorship of Ephesians on the grounds that no mere copyist would have plagiarized so unashamedly. Without a doubt there is a literary relationship between the two letters, but how might we try and explain it?

Another way of addressing this particular problem is to isolate those sections of Ephesians which have no parallel to Colossians and see if they might suggest an independent letter which underlies the present epistle, a 'first draft', to which the material from Colossians might have been added (by a subsequent, non-Pauline writer?). There are in fact seven different sections of Ephesians which have no parallel in Colossians: 1.3–14; 2.1–10; 3.14–21; 4.1–16; 5.8–14; 5.23–32; 6.10–17. Occasionally it is suggested that these together represent a baptismal catechism to which the material from Colossians has been added. It is an intriguing, but unproven suggestion. Occasionally the literary relationship between Colossians and Ephesians is said to run in precisely the opposite direction; that is to say that Colossians borrows from Ephesians. This has been argued particularly with regard to the ethical teaching contained in 5.21–6.9 (paralleled in Colossians 3.18–4.1). However, this suggestion is fraught with difficulties and has not been widely accepted.

Assuming for the moment that the writer of the letter was not Paul, what possible reason can there be for an author to invoke the Apostle's name and authority in his work? This brings us to consider the fascinating literary phenomenon known as pseudepigraphy (the issuing of documents under an assumed name).[2] There are four particular passages in Ephesians which are directly relevant to this issue. Two of them explicitly mention Paul the Apostle by name (1.1 and 3.1–13) and two of them allude to the tradition of Paul being imprisoned for his faith (4.1 and 6.21–22).

It is important that we view pseudepigraphy as a well-known first-century phenomenon and not impose our twentieth-century value judgments upon it. We must remember that the idea of literary copyright is fairly recent and would have been unknown in the ancient world. Pseudepigraphy should not automatically be equated with 'forgery' or 'fraud', and we should not assume that there was a deliberate intent to deceive underlying the production of all pseudepigraphical works. There is good evidence to demonstrate that some pseudepigraphical works were written as a means of honouring one's teacher and that they were recognized as such by the ancient readers. A good indication of this is found in the Muratorian Canon (dated to circa 200 CE) which describes the Wisdom of Solomon as a work not written by Solomon himself but 'by his friends in his honour' (line 70). Thus, some pseudepigraphical works were a sign of respect for a beloved teacher and as such no moral stigma should be attached to them as 'false' or 'misleading' documents. That is not to suggest that every pseudepigraphical work was issued with such a noble motivation in mind, however; the ancient world clearly had its own versions of 'Hitler's Secret Diaries' where the intention was financial gain on the part of an unscrupulous author. But it shows that there were a range of reasons for the production of pseudepigraphical works and that such writings were sometimes seen to be legitimate extensions of a deceased writer's thought.

There are numerous examples in our modern world where something approximating pseudepigraphy functions. We generally accept these as a matter of course, hardly raising an eyebrow over them. One could point to political speech writing, for example. Very few modern politicians actually write their own public addresses; instead an army of professional writers are brought in to do this job, applying rhetorical skills and well-researched slogans and such like in the process. Similarly there are many modern autobiographies which are produced by ghost-writers who put the ideas and thoughts of their subjects into a coherent form. We might also point to the way in which actors and actresses play the part of an historical figure in an attempt to bring that character to life as another instance of 'assumed identity', the idea which lies at the heart of pseudepigraphy. In none of these examples is the primary focus of our attention the questioning of these speeches or biographies as genuine products of their alleged author, nor do we automatically doubt the integrity of the actor as he or she attempts to portray a character on the screen. Indeed, it is precisely because Anthony Hopkins looks and sounds so much like former President Richard Nixon that his performance in Oliver Stone's film *Nixon* (1995) is so memorable. The greater the similarity between the actor and his subject in these matters the more believable the film becomes for us. No one would say that Hopkins is Nixon, for that is a nonsense. However, for the sake of the film he has become Richard Nixon and we recognize this as a necessary element in the fiction of the film. In that sense, the fact that Ephesians is made to sound and look as if it comes from the pen of Paul himself, notably in 1.1; 3.1–13; 6.21–22, is part of the literary device of pseudepigraphy which is used in the letter. Through the pseudepigraphical epistle Paul's voice can again be heard speaking into the life of the churches of Asia Minor. The modern parallels suggested here are not exact, of course, but they do serve to demonstrate a number of ways in which the essential idea of pseudepigraphy continues to flourish in our time.

Having given a brief overview of these complex and controversial matters it is time to lay my own cards on the table. Within this commentary I assume that Colossians was written by Paul the Apostle at around the same time that he wrote Philemon and that both letters were occasioned, in part, by the incident involving Onesimus the runaway slave in the church at Colossae. I take Tychicus to have been the person who delivered both of these letters to the church in Colossae and assume that he was a member of the congregation there. I also assume that whoever wrote the letter we now know as Ephesians had a copy of Colossians to hand when he composed his letter; he may have even been a member of the church at Colossae which would explain his familiarity with the region (see the discussion of Provenance below). I would also suggest that the many allusions to other Pauline letters contained in Ephesians point to the writer's familiarity with the core of the Pauline canon.[3] However, the differences in style and theological understanding suggests to me that the writer of Ephesians was not Paul himself, but a disciple of Paul who was very familiar with the Apostle's work. I do not think it is possible to identify the writer beyond that; the suggestions that he is Onesimus or Tychicus or Epaphras or Luke remain, to my mind at least, intriguing and plausible but unproven. My own guess is that the anonymous author of the letter came to Christian faith as a result of the Pauline mission to the region which was led by Epaphras.

Throughout the commentary I have chosen to call the person responsible for the letter 'the Writer'. I realize that this is cumbersome expression, and at times it becomes a bit tedious. Others have taken up the insights offered by narrative criticism and have used the phrase 'the implied author' and there is much advantage to this. However, it does necessitate going on to explain the relationship between 'the implied author' and 'the real author' and this too quickly becomes a barrier of terminological expression. It seems to me that 'the Writer' is less misleading than calling him 'Paul' (with deliberate speech marks), even though that is probably very close to how the Writer himself expected his audience to understand the situation. However, to use 'Paul' (even with the speech marks) in our modern, historical-critical era is to fudge the issue of pseudonymity and appears as if one is vacillating on the subject. I do not think it is possible in this instance 'to have one's cake and eat it'. I fail to see what is really gained by insisting on Pauline authorship of the letter beyond the fact that we can pat ourselves on the back and say that we are interpreting 1.1; 3.1–13; 4.1 and 6.21–22 *literally*. But the authority of the letter as part of the NT canon does not rest so much on who wrote it, as on who inspired it. Thus, I would suggest that the authority of the letter rests in the message that it conveys about Jesus Christ, for the risen Lord himself must stand as the sole and absolute focal point of our faith. In fact I would go so far as to say that something quite important is lost by straddling the very awkward fence of Pauline authorship and proceeding as if the matter was a legal trial. As one writer put the point:

> A man is innocent until he is proven guilty. Ephesians is Pauline until it is proven non-Pauline.[4]

I do not find such an approach helpful; it confuses the processes of the courtroom with those of reading and assessing a piece of literature. In fact, it can be positively counter-productive if our ultimate aim is the interpretation of the letter, rather than the mere establishment of the author of the letter. One could quite easily win the 'battle' over authorship and against all odds maintain that the letter is genuinely Pauline, only to find that the 'war' of interpretation is lost. An insistence on Pauline authorship means that we lose the ability to see how the Apostle's writings were creatively adapted to meet the needs of the next generation of believers. By issuing the letter in Paul's name our anonymous Writer strengthens the bonds between himself and the church. He builds upon the memory of Paul who was admired and respected among the church members, many of whom may have had personal acquaintance with the Apostle and may have come to faith, either directly or indirectly, through his ministry. In so doing the Writer keeps open various channels of communication which otherwise would have been closed and the on-going witness of Paul the Apostle continues unabated.

We turn now to consider the question of the provenance of the letter. What is the social and geographical setting of the letter? To whom was it written and why?

b. Provenance

If it is correct, as we suggest along with many others, that the epistle was written by a close follower of Paul, then it is not unreasonable to view this anonymous author as part of a 'school of Paul' dedicated to preserving their founder's vision of the Christian faith. The question then becomes, 'Where is the most likely place for such a school to develop and flourish?' The answer that is commonly given is Ephesus, based primarily upon the long association that Paul had with the city (some have suggested that Acts 19.9 hints at the foundation of such a school with its description of Paul's daily disputations in the hall of Tyrannus). Indeed, it may be that the connection between the Apostle and the city is ultimately responsible for the ascription of the letter as one addressed 'To the Ephesians'. There is one major problem to be overcome with the suggestion that the letter itself was directed to the church at Ephesus, which may be described as the proposal's "Achilles' heel". This concerns the lack of details about the church which are to be found within the letter itself, something which is quite inexplicable given that the church at Ephesus was one which Paul himself had founded and one in which he was intimately involved for several years. The fact that the Writer in 3.2 has to remind his readers of Paul's apostolic calling also militates against Ephesians as being the true destination of the letter, since we assume that such details would have been made known to the congregation by Paul himself long ago. Robert Scott puts his finger on the essential point here when he says.

> Are we to suppose that in his prison cell this bent and bruised apostle blossomed forth into a magnificent rhetorician and preacher, without a furrow on his cheek, without a rent in his body, without a pang in his heart; a rhetorician, in form systematic and regular, in language imaginative and eloquent, in conception profound and noble; a preacher who disdained the common incidents of life, the common feelings of brotherly connection while he soared loftily above his audience and set forth only the counsels of eternity? If this is Paul, he is transformed indeed.[5]

Thus, an increasing number of commentators point to other sites in Asia Minor as more likely candidates for the epistle's original destination. Two places in particular have been suggested, Laodicea and Hierapolis, both notable cities within the Lycus valley and both known to have Christian churches within them. In one sense, given the close geographical proximity of the two cities (they were only about six miles apart as the crow flies), it matters little whether one or the other is chosen as the original recipient of what we now know as Ephesians. We can assume that the social concerns and interests of the two cities were pretty much identical and that the dynamics of the congregations within the cities would have been virtually indistinguishable. Indeed, the latest full-bodied commentary on the epistle, that of Andrew T. Lincoln (1990), argues that the original destination was the *churches* in Laodicea and Hierapolis, a suggestion which is based partly on an imaginative reconstruction of the awkward syntax of the Greek text of verse 1.1.[6] Several secondary arguments may be marshalled to support the suggestion that the epistle was intended for a congregation in the fertile Lycus valley (see Appendix 1 for a map of western Asia Minor and the Lycus region).

First, there is the tradition of Marcion (circa 140 CE) which associated the letter we now know as Ephesians with the city of Laodicea, building upon the intriguing reference contained in Colossians 4.16. The close literary connection between Colossians and Ephesians also comes into play here, especially since Colossians 4.16 suggests that the apostolic letters to the two churches (at Colossae and Laodicea) were to be shared between the two congregations and read in public worship. Incidentally we can assume that any letter to nearby Hierapolis would also have been shared with the churches in Colossae and Laodicea in similar fashion.

Second, we have to reckon with the person of Tychicus as the common bond between Colossians and Ephesians (noting Colossians 4.7 and Ephesians 6.21). We know that Tychicus was from Asia Minor (see Acts 20.4), and beyond this there is also a later tradition of him being sent by Paul to the church in Ephesians (II Timothy 4.12). Perhaps this later tradition arises as a direct result of the publication of Ephesians which links him to the city in 6.21. Clearly Tychicus was closely associated with the church at Colossae and there is good reason, as suggested above, to take him to be the courier of both Colossians and Philemon.

It is sometimes suggested that the letter of Paul to Philemon is in fact the lost 'letter to the Laodiceans' mentioned in Colossians 4.16. If this is so, then we might be tempted to view Ephesians as originally addressed to the church in Hierapolis, if for no other reason than it means that all three of the major sites in the immediate geographical area have a letter within the Pauline corpus dedicated to them. Is there anything within the text of Ephesians which might be said to support this idea and allow us to move a step further than Lincoln's suggestion and choose between Laodicea and Hierapolis as the original destination of the letter? Assuming for the moment that the epistle was intended for the church in Hierapolis, we can find an explanation for the curious references to Christ's 'descent into the lowest level' (4.9) and his 'ascent far above the heavens' (4.10) within the geography of the city itself. Two particular features of the ancient city of Hierapolis need to be kept in mind at this point (see Appendix 1 for a map of the city).

First, just next to the south side of the Temple of Apollo in the centre of the city there was a cave which emitted poisonous gases and was thought to be an entrance to the underworld. This subterranean cavern was known as the Plutonium, named after the god Pluto, Ruler of the Underworld (the Greek travel-writer Strabo mentions the site in his *Geography* 12.8.17 and 13.4.14 as do Pliny *Natural History* 2.208; Dio Cassius *Roman History* 68.27.3; and Ammianus Marcellinus *History* 23.6.18 [7]). The 'descent to the lowest level' may be a veiled reference to this well-known characteristic of the city of Hierapolis, with the author making a christological point which would have been immediately recognized by his intended readership, even if it is somewhat obscure to us today.[8] Christ might be said to 'descend' into the very bowels of the earth through the Plutonium before ascending in his victory over death (see Appendix 2 for the ancient texts dealing with the Plutonium).

Second, the city is situated on the north bank of the Lycus and it sits on an impressive terrace which rises some 525 feet or so above the base of the surrounding plain. The site was built around hot springs whose waters flow down the terrace and over the centuries have created a spectacular display of cascading pools set against white lime deposits. The medicinal springs gush forth 38,000 litres of hot water (at places it is over 40° Celsius!) per minute which deposits about twenty cubic metres of limestone sediment each day.[9] The modern Turkish name of the site, Pamukkale, reflects the dream-like beauty of this natural wonder of the world; it means 'Cotton Castle' (most good guide books of Turkey contain pictures of the limestone formations). Given this natural setting it is understandable that Hierapolis (literally the 'Holy City') has long been a site for religious worship, including local Phrygian gods such as the snake-like Sabazios (worshipped under the name of Echidma), and the Anatolian goddess Cybele (worshipped under the name of Leto).

The cliffs of Hierapolis, together with their geological showcase, dominate the area and can be seen for miles around. It is certain that inhabitants of the cities of Colossae and Laodicea in the valley below would have known of the site; in fact, the inhabitants of Laodicea would be reminded of it every time they looked across the river Lycus to the north side of the valley. In view of this, could we not take the 'descent *to the lowest level*' to be an indication that the Pauline mission was brought to the cities of the valley floor before coming to the city of Hierapolis itself? According to Colossians 2.1 Paul himself was not known personally by the churches of the Lycus valley and in this sense he was not their founder; that honour probably goes to Epaphras (as Colossians 1.7–8; 4.12–13 suggests). Nevertheless, Paul describes Epaphras as a 'fellow-slave' (Colossians 1.7) and a 'fellow-prisoner' (Philemon 23) and in this sense we can view the churches of the Lycus valley as falling within the orbit of the Pauline mission. There is an ancient tradition associating the Apostle Philip with the city of Hierapolis, but it appears unlikely that he was responsible for the establishment of Christian churches in the region (see Eusebius *Ecclesiastical History* 3.31.3–4; 3.39.9; 5.24.2 for mention of Philip and his four daughters, two of whom are said to have been buried in Hierapolis; this may represent a confusion with Philip the Evangelist who is mentioned in Acts 21.8–9). Legend has it that Philip died in Hierapolis and there are ruins of an ancient fifth century church dedicated to his memory on a hill behind the city's amphitheatre.

Let us assume for the moment that the city of Colossae was the first to which Epaphras brought the Christian message, a suggestion which is supported not only by the several references to him recorded within both Colossians and Philemon, but also by the fact that the traveller coming to the area from the east (Lycia and Pamphylia) would naturally follow the Roman road which paralleled the Lycus river into the region. From Colossae the gospel message was then taken to Laodicea, ten miles away and still within the lower valley, and only after that was it taken to the city of Hierapolis on the cliffs and hills above. The same basic point pertains if we assume that Epaphras was sent by Paul to the Lycus valley from the west (maybe even from the city of Ephesus) where again the Roman road follows the course of the Menander river, passes through the cities of Magnesia and Tralles before coming to

Laodicea. Perhaps at this point Epaphras continued along the road in order to get to Colossae (perhaps it was his home-city) before eventually taking another road which runs from Colossae northward to Hierapolis. Either scenario works as far as our basic suggestion is concerned.

The essential point is that, as far as the proclamation of the gospel is concerned, Christ first had to 'descend' to the cities of Laodicea and Colossae before he could 'ascend' to the heaven-like heights of Hierapolis. Thus, we could describe the church in Hierapolis as a 'daughter-church' of either Colossae or Laodicea, and take the references to 'dear children' in 5.1 and 'children of the light' in 5.8 to be extensions of this familial metaphor. In this regard the Writer's citation of Zechariah 8.16 in 4.25 also makes perfect sense. The exhortation to 'Speak truth, each one *to his neighbour*' is a natural way of expressing the hope that the two neighbouring congregations might get on well together and keep the lines of communication open. The suggestion that either Colossae (or Laodicea) was the 'mother-church' to the congregation at Hierapolis also helps makes sense of 4.20 where the Writer gently reminds his readers that 'you did not learn Christ in this way'. We could easily take the implied sense of the verse to be 'you did not learn Christ in this way *from us*', and reinforce the suggestion that the very existence of the church in Hierapolis was historically, and no doubt financially, dependent on one or the other congregations in the valley below. We could also add at this point that Laodicea was the wealthier and more prosperous of the two valley cities and as such would have had the financial resources to fund the establishment of a 'daughter-church' in Hierapolis. Laodicea was well-known as a centre for wool-dyeing and served as the business hub for the region (Strabo, *Geography* 12.8.16 and Cicero, *Letters to Atticus* 5.15 testify to this). Indeed, something of the financial self-sufficiency of Laodicea can be seen by how the city was able to recover following a devastating earthquake in 60 CE. Tacitus, *Annals* 14.27.1 tells us that Laodicea was 'rebuilt from its own resources without any state assistance from Rome'. Other indications of the wealth of the city comes from Cicero, who alludes to an incident in 62 BCE when the Roman governor of the region, Flaccus, seized the annual contributions of the Jewish population of the area which were intended for the temple in Jerusalem. According to Cicero, some twenty pounds of gold (calculated as the contributions of 7,500 adult males) were commandeered from the inhabitants of Laodicea alone (*Pro Flacco* 68). Cicero also mentions in passing that Laodicea held gladiatorial contests (*Letters to Atticus* 6.3.9) which could be taken to be a sign of civic pride and wealth (stone reliefs from the city's amphitheatre depict scenes of gladiatorial contests). Indeed, one is tempted to wonder if the city of Laodicea had anything to do with the construction of this Roman amphitheatre in Hierapolis, one of the largest theatres in the province of Asia Minor and capable of seating approximately 15,000 people.

Perhaps too the geography of the area, with Hierapolis 'above' and Laodicea and Colossae 'below', helps explain the Writer's use of the word 'heavens' (*ouranōn*) in 4.10, which stands in contrast to the phrase normally associated with Christ's ascension in this epistle, namely 'in the heavenly realms' (*en tois epouraniois*). In other words, we must question whether 'heavens' is equivalent to 'in the heavenlies' within the epistle. The word 'heaven' (as opposed to 'the heavenlies') is used three other times in the letter: in 1.10, 3.15 and 6.9. However, two of these instances are clearly dependent upon their parallel in Colossians; 1.10 being a reflection of Colossians 1.20 and 6.9 being a reflection of Colossians 4.1. This leaves us with 3.15 as the only other instance beyond 4.10 where 'heaven' is used by the Writer in a passage which is not ultimately derived from the twin-epistle Colossians and thus probably stands as one of his own compositions. The meaning of 3.15 is difficult to determine precisely, particularly with the mention of 'the Father from whom every family in heaven and on earth takes its name'. Generally this is taken to mean that God is the Father of angelic beings in the heavens as well as human beings on earth. However, this is somewhat artificial and forced and sounds either as if it states the blindingly obvious or promotes the blatantly absurd (do angels have families in heaven?). What if we were to take 'every family in heaven' to refer to the Christian families in Hierapolis and 'every family on earth' to refer to the Christian families in the cities of Laodicea and Colossae down below in the valley? Perhaps what we are seeing in 3.15 is an echo of the way in which the people of the region themselves made a distinction between those who lived 'above' and those who lived 'below'; the citizens of Hierapolis were inhabitants of 'the Heavens Above' and the citizens of Laodicea and Colossae were inhabitants of 'the Land Below'.[10]

All of this means that the curious ascension/descension motif in 4.9–10, a passage which is inserted into the chapter and interrupts the flow of the argument which runs from 4.1–7 to 4.11–15, might be taken as something of a double, or even triple-entendre. It is not only a theological declaration of Christ's exaltation to the heavenly realms following his triumphant resurrection from the dead, but is also a coded double-reference to the geography of Hierapolis. In other words the language simultaneously operates on three interlocking levels; our Writer is painting in mental pictures deliberately designed to invoke the imagination of his readers. He builds upon what they know about their own local geography and challenges them to apply the idea of an ascension/descent to the realms of theology. The Writer is making a theological point about Christ's descent (incarnation as a human being) and his ascension (to the heavens); he is also making a point about the mission of Epaphras in bringing the message of the gospel to the region, first to the *lower* regions of the valley (Laodicea and Colossae) before *ascending* to the heights of Hierapolis; and he is making a point about Christ's *descent* into the underworld of the Plutonium before *ascending* to claim the city as conqueror. This last point would have been particularly significant for the inhabitants of the city of Hierapolis which was renowned in the ancient world for its vast numbers of tombs known as the Necropolis (some 1,200 tombs have been identified). In each instance the importance of the 'ascent' is made all the clearer by reference to a prior 'descent'. In any event, the suggestion, based as it is on these few tantalizingly obscure references, that Hierapolis was the original destination of the letter must remain speculative, even if it does seem to unlock many mysteries surrounding the interpretation of the letter.

With regard to the social make-up of the congregation to which Ephesians is addressed, it is commonly thought that the Christians were from a predominantly Gentile background but that there was a significant minority of Jewish-Christians within the fellowship. Both 2.11 and 3.1 appear to point in this direction. However, Thorsten Moritz has recently suggested that the balance was likely to have been in the other direction and that there was a larger Jewish contingent within the congregation than is generally thought. He suggests that the church at Laodicea was the original recipient of the letter and that the epistle is a deliberate rewriting of Colossians which takes into account this social mix.[11] It is an interesting theory but one which has not yet commanded wide acceptance, although it does give due weight to the fact that there was a considerable Jewish population in the city of Laodicea. Nevertheless, the majority of interpreters take the letter to be written to a congregation which is made up predominantly of Gentile-Christians.

If, as seems likely, the church was largely made up of Gentile-Christians this helps provide a clue as to the reason why the letter was penned. The Writer wishes to exhort his readers to live up to their calling as Christians and not lapse back into the pagan attitudes and heathen practices they had prior to their discovery of Christ. In short, it is a deep and abiding pastoral concern which drives the Writer to produce what is in effect an 'Open Letter' to his readers about living in a manner distinct from the world. At the same time the Writer is seeking to offer guidance to the church about how she can establish suitable structures and develop an organizational framework to carry on now that Paul, her apostolic anchor, has passed from the scene. As Margaret Y. MacDonald describes it in an important study of the social dynamics of pseudepigraphy, the church is engaged in 'community-stabilizing institutionalization'.[12] This is quite a helpful way to assess the purpose of the letter and it suggests that the social setting of the church is a second generation of believers who are seeking to build upon and consolidate the work of their founders. It also suggests that attempts, such as those of Ernst Käsemann[13] and Peter Stuhlmacher[14] which argue that the reason for writing the letter was to issue a challenge to the Gentile-Christians not to forsake their *Jewish* roots, are somewhat misguided.[15] This assumes that Gentile converts have Jewish roots, as if they undergo a pre-conversion to Judaism before moving on to a conversion to Christianity. Such readings of the letter presume a tension, not to say a hostility, between Jewish-Christians and Gentile-Christians which does not appear to be central to the thought of the letter.

One final point is worth noting briefly on the matter; it concerns what we know about the Jewish community of Hierapolis. Unfortunately, the witness of the most famous citizen of ancient Hierapolis is of limited assistance on this point. The freed-slave and Stoic philosopher Epictetus was born in Hierapolis in about 50 CE and might well have been familiar with the size and influence of the Jewish population within the city. In fact, Epictetus does mention 'Jews' by name once within his *Discourses* (2.9.19–21). Yet his statement is not clear for he goes on immediately to allude to their baptism, and one is never quite sure if he means by this Jews who have become Christians and been baptized or not. That he means Christians appears a likely reading of the situation since he does refer to 'Galileans' at another point in the *Discourses* (4.7.6). The problem with Epictetus' testimony on this point is that we do not know from where his experience and knowledge of Judaism and Christianity come. We know that he was born in Hierapolis, but we do not know how old he was when he moved to Rome with his slave-master Epaphroditus. We know that he was later made a freedman and that he moved to Nicopolis on the Aegean coast where he lived until he died, but we do not know when this manumission and relocation occurred. In other words, his knowledge of Judaism and Christianity might have come from any of the three places (Hierapolis, Rome or Nicopolis). In all likelihood, Epictetus would have been hard-pressed to distinguish between Jews and Christians; many Greeks and Romans of the period had the same difficulty. He probably would have viewed them as a single group. But even in its own way this may speak obliquely to the Writer's message which lies at the heart of the letter – that both Jews and Gentiles have been brought together to form one new humanity.

What else do we know about Judaism within the city of Hierapolis? It is commonly agreed that there was a thriving Jewish community in the city, one which was involved in the lucrative wool-dyeing industry of the area and may have even formed their own trade-guild. The numerous inscriptions which have been discovered and catalogued by archaeologists over the years, many of which come from the tombs of the Necropolis areas of the city, offer some information which may be of interest to our study. One of the most celebrated of these inscriptions mentions a fine being levied against someone for having illegally buried a body in (what was presumably) an inappropriate place, probably a Jewish tomb.[16] The fine is to be paid to 'the settlement (*katoikia*) of Jews who dwell (*katoikountōn*) in Hierapolis.' What is striking about this inscription is that it may suggest the official status of the Jewish population of the city as a 'settlement' (*katoikia*), a term which we can assume served as a Jewish self-designation. What is more important for our purposes is the fact that it is the exact same language that the Writer uses to describe the Christian community he addresses (in 2.22 and 3.17). Could it be that the Writer is deliberately alluding to the position that the Jewish members of the congregation held within the city of Hierapolis itself, gently reminding them that they carry the same residency status of resident aliens in the church as they hold in the city, and indeed share it with the Gentile members of the congregation? Perhaps this is another small piece of the jigsaw puzzle labelled 'the provenance of the letter', one which points us again to the city of Hierapolis as the original destination of the epistle.

Assuming that this hypothetical reconstruction is at least a viable

possibility, then we may have a new way of resolving the
long-standing debate about how 'I' and 'we' language fits together
with 'you' and 'your' language in the same epistle. This 'question of
the pronouns' presents one of the most protracted interpretative
debates of the letter and has been the subject of an intense, not to
say acrimonious, discussion. Traditionally, the matter is often
interpreted either as an indication of the 'Jew versus Gentile' debate,
or as an 'old-convert versus newly-baptized' debate. In the former
scenario, the author is thought to write from the perspective of a
Jewish-Christian and when he says 'we' he means 'the Jews', as
opposed to 'the Gentiles' whom he describes in 'you' language (as in
2.1 and 3.1 for example). In the latter scenario, the author is thought
to write from the perspective of a person who was converted to faith
long ago and as such is part of the 'we' of the Christian faith. This is
in contrast to those new converts who are just entering the faith and
making this public through the act of baptism; these people the
author designates as 'you'.[17]

However, the interpretative debate is taken in a completely
different direction if we accept that what underlies the use of
the personal pronouns in the letter is not a two-fold contrast
either between the 'Jewish-Christians' and the 'Gentile-Christians'
within a single congregation, or between 'older Christians' and
'newer converts' within a single congregation. Rather, the linguistic
contrast implied by the use of 'we' and 'you' pronouns is between
the church in Hierapolis and the other two churches in the
area, namely Laodicea and Colossae. At times the Writer sets the
'daughter-church' of Hierapolis over against the 'mother-church' by
means of 'you' and 'we' language; in other words, 'you' and 'your'
refers to the church at Hierapolis and 'we' and 'our' refers to the
church at Colossae. It follows then that when the Writer uses 'I'
language he means himself as a member of the church at Colossae,
even though it is highly unlikely that he was writing *from* the city.[18]
At the same time, the Writer also uses 'we' and 'our' language to
include the 'daughter-church' as an equal partner with the congregations at Laodicea and Colossae. On this reading of the situation
whether the membership of any of the three churches is predominantly of Jewish or Gentile background is of secondary importance.
The result is that the rather futile debate about Jewish/Gentile rela-
tions in the epistle can be safely by-passed.

Let us attempt to separate out the various uses of the personal
pronouns in Ephesians, together with other phrases, such as 'the

saints', which might be taken to support the proposal being made here (for the most part we can skip the ethical teaching given in 5.22–6.9 since it is directed to individuals). Note the following table (the NASB phrasing is used here since it follows the Greek word order rather strictly):

'You' and 'Your' (Daughter-Church in Hierapolis)	'I', 'We' and 'Our' (Mother-Church in Colossae)	'We' and 'Our' (All Three Churches in the Lycus Valley)
to the *saints* (1.1)		
grace to *you* (1.2)		
		our Father (1.2)
		our Lord Jesus Christ (1.3)
		who has blessed *us* (1.3)
		he chose *us* (1.4)
		we should be holy (1.4)
		he predestined *us* (1.5)
		bestowed on *us* (1.6)
		we have redemption (1.7)
		our trespasses (1.7)
		lavished upon *us* (1.8)
		made known to *us* (1.9)
		we have obtained (1.11)
	we who were the first (1.12)	
you also (1.13)		
your salvation (1.13)		
you were sealed (1.13)		
		our inheritance (1.14)
	I too, having heard (1.15)	
among *you* (1.15)		
your love (1.15)		
	for the *saints* (1.15)	
for *you* (1.16)		

my prayers (1.16)

our Lord Jesus (1.17)

to *you* (1.17)
your heart (1.18)
you may know (1.18)

in the *saints* (1.18)

toward *us* (1.19)

you were dead (2.1)
your trespasses (2.1)
you formerly walked
(2.2)

we too all formerly
lived (2.3)
our flesh (2.3)

he loved *us* (2.4)
we were dead (2.5)
our trespasses (2.5)
made *us* alive (2.5)

you have been saved
(2.5)

raised *us* up (2.6)
seated *us* (2.6)
toward *us* (2.7)

you have been saved
(2.8)
not of *yourselves* (2.8)

we are his (2.10)
we should walk (2.10)

you, the Gentiles (2.11)
you were separate
(2.12)
you who formerly
were (2.13)

he is *our* peace (2.14)
reconcile *us* both
(2.16)
we both have (2.18)
our access (2.18)

you are no longer
(2.19)

you are fellow
citizens (2.19)

with the *saints* (2.19)

together (2.21)

you are being built
(2.22)

together (2.22)

I, Paul the prisoner (3.1)

you Gentiles (3.1)
you have heard (3.2)

to *me* (3.2)

for *you* (3.2)

to *me* (3.3)
I wrote before (3.3)

when *you* read (3.4)
you can understand
(3.4)

my insight (3.4)

(*you*) Gentiles (3.6)

fellow heirs (3.6)
fellow members (3.6)
fellow partakers (3.6)

I was made (3.7)
to *me* (3.7)
to *me* (3.8)
of all the *saints* (3.8)

(*you*) Gentiles (3.8)

our Lord (3.11)
we have boldness
(3.12)

I ask (3.13)
my tribulations (3.13)

on *your* behalf (3.13)
they are *your* glory
(3.13)

I bow *my* knees (3.14)

family in *heaven*
(3.15)

on *earth* (3.15)

he would grant *you*
(3.16)

in *your* hearts (3.17)
you, being rooted
    (3.17)

                       with all the *saints* (3.18)

you may be filled
    (3.19)

                                           we ask (3.20)
                                         within *us* (3.20)

                     I, therefore, the
                         prisoner (4.1)

entreat *you* (4.1)
(*you*) walk (4.1)
you have been called
    (4.1)

                                         one body (4.4)

you were called (4.4)
your calling (4.4)

                                         one baptism (4.5)
                                         of *us* (4.7)
                                         of the *saints* (4.12)
                                         we all attain
                                            the unity of faith
                                            (4.13)
                                         we are no longer (4.14)
                                         we are to grow (4.15)

                     I say (4.17)

you walk no longer
    (4.17)
you did not learn
    (4.20)
you have heard him
    (4.21)
your former manner
    (4.22)
you lay aside (4.22)
you be renewed
    (4.23)

your mind (4.23)
(*you*) put on (4.24)
(*you*) lay aside (4.25)

(*you*) speak truth (4.25)

we are members
   of one another (4.25)

(*you*) be angry (4.26)
(*you*) do not sin (4.26)
(*you*) do not give (4.27)
(*you*) do not let (4.29)
your mouth (4.29)
(*you*) do not grieve (4.30)
you were sealed (4.30)
(*you*) let (4.31)
(*you*) be kind (4.32)
(*you*) be forgiving (4.32)
Christ forgave *you* (4.32)
(*you*) be imitators (5.1)
(*you*) walk in love (5.2)
Christ loved *you* (5.2)

(Christ) gave himself
   up for *us* (5.2)

(*you*) do not let (5.3)
among *you* (5.3)

among *saints* (5.3)

you know (5.5)
deceive *you* (5.6)
(*you*) do not be (5.7)
you were formerly (5.8)
you are light (5.8)
(*you*) walk (5.8)
(*you*) try to learn (5.10)
(*you*) do not participate (5.11)
(*you*) expose them (5.11)
you walk (5.15)
(*you*) make the most (5.16)
your time (5.16)
(*you*) do not be foolish (5.17)
(*you*) understand (5.17)
(*you*) do not get drunk (5.18)
(*you*) speak (5.19)
(*you*) sing (5.19)
(*you*) make melody (5.19)
with *your* heart (5.19)

(*you*) give thanks
   (5.20)

our Lord Jesus (5.20)

(*you*) be subject (5.21)

we are members
   of his body (5.30)

(*you*) be strong (6.10)
(*you*) put on (6.11)
you may be able
   (6.11)

our struggle (6.12)

(*you*) take up (6.13)
you may be able
   (6.13)
(*you*) stand firm (6.14)
(*you*) having girded
   (6.14)
your loins (6.14)
(*you*) having put on
   (6.14)
(*you*) having shod
   (6.15)
your feet (6.15)
(*you*) taking up
   (6.16)
you will be able
   (6.16)
you take (6.17)
(*you*) pray (6.18)
(*you*) be on the alert
   (6.18)

for all the *saints* (6.18)
my behalf (6.19)
to *me* (6.19)
my mouth (6.19)
I am an ambassador (6.20)
I may speak (6.20)
as *I* ought to speak (6.20)

you may know (6.21)

my circumstances (6.21)
how *I* am doing (6.21)

to *you* (6.21)

              I have sent him (6.22)

to *you* (6.22)
you may know
  (6.22)

             about *us* (6.22)

your hearts (6.22)
(*you*) brethren
  (6.23)

                     all who love (6.24)
                     our Lord Jesus (6.24)

It comes as no surprise that the majority of the passages in the table which come from 4.1–6.24 are addressed to the 'daughter-church' in Hierapolis. This is in line with what we might expect from a Writer who is a concerned member of the 'mother-church' in Colossae, someone who may have been given special responsibility over the church-plant in Hierapolis. It is also striking that references to the 'mother-church', either in the form of 'we' or 'I' passages, are virtually non-existent in 4.1–6.17, while they do appear quite regularly in 1.1–3.21. This suggests that a gentle reminder about the nature of the relationship between the two congregations underlies the discussion which is found in the first half of the epistle. Only in 6.18–22 does the Writer again bring himself and the church at Colossae back into the discussion, and then only after he has been attempting to enlarge the sense of participation in the larger Christian witness within the Lycus region by using 'we' language in 4.20–6.12. When the Writer does bring himself back into the discussion in 6.18–22 it is under the cloak of pseudonymity. In this sense, when addressing the church at Hierapolis he is their 'Paul', and exhibits all of the fatherly care and concern that the Apostle did when writing to the church at Colossae. The Writer thus emulates Paul, following his master's advice to imitate him (see I Corinthians 4.16; 11.1; Philippians 3.17; I Thessalonians 1.6 and II Thessalonians 3.7, 9). Indeed, the exhortation to 'imitate God' which is issued in 5.1 may be seen as an indication not only of the Writer's genuine modesty, but of the esteem in which he held Paul. Now that the Apostle has passed from the scene the church, in one sense, can no longer 'imitate Paul' and the Writer is too modest to suggest that they 'imitate' him in the same way. He therefore adapts the 'imitation' idea and appeals to the church in Hierapolis to 'imitate God'.

47

Similarly, the Writer's curious statement in 3.8 about being 'less than the least of the saints' builds upon Paul's declaration in I Corinthians 15.9 and establishes the relationship between pupil and master. Rather than viewing the verse to be an illustration of self-inflated praise or arrogance, we should perhaps view it as an indication of reverential modesty. In other words, once again the Writer may be demonstrating a crisis of self-confidence; he sees himself as a follower of Paul, but one who is conscious of the unworthiness of his position. If Paul is 'the least of the apostles', then the only position the Writer can adopt with due consideration and respect is to be 'less than the least of the saints'. Therefore, in 3.8 he creates a grammatical oddity in order to make precisely this point. It may well be that the shift from 'apostles' to 'saints' between the two verses is due to the fact that the Writer uses 'saints' as a way of describing the members of the church at Colossae.

In conclusion, I take the letter we now know as Ephesians originally to have been one intended for the church in the city of Hierapolis. This congregation was a 'daughter-church', and was probably founded in circa 52–55 CE by Epaphras as part of the Pauline mission to the Lycus valley. It is likely that Epaphras was a member of the church in nearby Colossae and that he was well-known and respected in Hierapolis. This suggests that Epaphras' home-church in Colossae was the 'mother-church', although financial assistance from the wealthier congregation in Laodicea cannot be ruled out. The congregation in Hierapolis probably consisted of both Jewish-Christians and Gentile-Christians, with the latter being in the majority. The Writer addresses the church primarily in order to offer them some practical advice on how to live as Christians in a socially-changing world where the temptation to lapse back into pagan ways was ever present.

c. Date

Traditionally Ephesians is said to have been written by Paul from Rome in about 62–64 CE while he was in prison during the reign of the Emperor Nero. However, if one does not accept Pauline authorship of the epistle, a credible alternative to this date is required. What clues do we have for establishing a possible date for the Deutero-Pauline letter? One of the most important pieces of evidence in this area concerns the quotations and allusions to Ephesians which appear in other early Christian writings. These help to establish the latest possible date that the letter might have been composed.

There is some evidence that Ephesians was known by other writers of the NT documents. For example, it is likely that I Peter 3.22 echoes Ephesians 1.22 and this suggests a date no later than 100 CE (presuming that we date I Peter before the end of the first century). The same holds true for the allusions to a baptismal liturgy which appear in I Peter 3.3–5 and Titus 2.11–14; 3.3–8 and may reflect the influence of Ephesians 2.1–10 and 5.25b–27. Similarly, it is sometimes suggested that the author of Revelation had a copy of Ephesians before him when composing his apocalypse. Closeness of expression between Ephesians 2.6 and Revelation 3.21; Ephesians 1.13 and 4.30 and Revelation 7.2–3; Ephesians 5.11 and Revelation 8.4; and Ephesians 6.23–24 and Revelation 22.21 are said to point in this direction.

Other important early Christian writers also cite and allude to Ephesians and give us an indication as to the widespread acceptance of the letter within Christendom; invariably the assumption is that it is from the hand of Paul the Apostle. Included among these are: Clement of Rome in circa 96 CE (who appears to allude to Ephesians a number of times, most notably in his use of 4.4–6 in I Clement 46.6–7); Ignatius of Antioch in circa 110 CE (who alludes to 5.25 in his *Letter to Polycarp* 5.1 and to 3.17 in his *Letter to the Smyrnaeans* 1.1); Polycarp of Smyrna in circa 140 CE (who alludes to 2.8 in his *Letter to the Philippians* 1.13); the anonymous author of the Shepherd of Hermas in circa 140 CE (who alludes to 4.3–6 in *Similitude* 9.13.5; 9.17.4; 9.18.4); Tertullian of Carthage in circa 208 CE (who mentions the letter in his refutation of the heretic Marcion in *Against Marcion* 5.11.12 and 5.17.1); Origen of Alexandria in circa 250 CE (who cites numerous examples in both his *De Principiis* and *Contra Celsum*),[19] Irenaeus of Lyons in circa 185 CE (who cites 5.30 in *Against the Heretics* 5.2.3); Clement of Alexandria in circa 200 CE (who cites 5.21–25 in *Stromateis* 4.65; 4.13–15 in *Pedagogue* 1.18; and 2.12 in *Exhortation to the Greeks* 2.20); the Muratorian Canon in circa 200 CE (which lists Ephesians as one of the letters by Paul addressed to seven different congregations).[20] The letter was also known to Egyptian Gnostic circles of the second and third centuries as the use of 6.12 in *Hypostasis of the Archons* II.86.20–25 and *Exegesis of the Soul* II.6.131, two texts from Nag Hammadi, indicates.

Taken together this evidence suggests a date for Ephesians

which is no later than 90–95 CE since this seems to be the time at which it is beginning to be quoted and alluded to by other writers. What about the earliest possible date for the letter? Undoubtedly one of the most traumatic episodes of the first-century world of which the new-born Christian faith was a part was the destruction of the temple in Jerusalem in 70 CE. Is there any internal evidence within Ephesians which might assist us in plotting the composition of the epistle against this historical backdrop? There is only one verse which may be taken as an important clue in this regard: the destruction of the 'middle wall of partition' mentioned in 2.14. It is frequently argued that this is a veiled reference to the destruction of the Jerusalem temple wherein the balustrade separating Jews and Gentiles was torn down as part of the conquest of the city by the Roman legions. If this is so, and if one accepts the traditional view that Paul was martyred in about 64 CE during the Neronic persecutions, then the pieces of the puzzle begin to fit into place and the non-Pauline authorship of the letter is established. This is precisely the line taken by Martin Kitchen in his recent commentary on the letter.[21] Assuming non-Pauline authorship, Kitchen sees the events of circa 70 CE as a catalyst for the Writer to reflect theologically about the death of Christ and the destruction of the temple and to forge a theological connection between the two events. In effect this means that the destruction of the 'dividing wall' is interpreted by the Writer as a vindication of his master's teaching, perhaps even as something of a rebuke against Christians who inadvertently had a hand in the Apostle's death.

If we assume that a short time is needed for the impact of the destruction of the temple of Jerusalem to make itself felt and for a theological response to be generated, say a period of five to ten years or so, then there is no real reason why Ephesians cannot be dated between 75–80 CE. Most commentators tend to date it slightly later than this, at around 90 CE. This is to allow time for distribution of the letter to occur and helps explain why the letter is known and loved by writers as far away as Antioch in Syria (Ignatius), Rome (Clement), Gaul (Irenaeus), Alexandria (Clement and Origen), North Africa (Tertullian), and Egypt (the Nag Hammadi materials).

COMMENTARY

Greetings
1.1–2

1. The opening words of the letter clearly place it within the Pauline tradition, boldly declaring that it is an epistle coming from *Paul, by the will of God an apostle of Christ Jesus*. We need not rehearse the debate about pseudepigraphy at this point, although it is worth noting that the name of the apostle is given both here and in 3.1. The introductory greeting contained in verses 1–2 is very similar to that found in other (undisputed) letters of the Pauline corpus (notably Romans 1.1, 7; I Corinthians 1.1–3; II Corinthians 1.1–2; Philippians 1.1–2; cf. Colossians 1.1–2) and conforms readily to the style of letters within the Graeco-Roman world of the day. The reference to Paul being an apostle *by the will* of God is reminiscent of Galatians 1.1–17 and may well reflect the ongoing debate about the legitimacy of his apostleship in the early church.

There is some debate about whether the words at Ephesus are original to the letter. They are missing in some important early manuscripts, including P⁴⁶ (which probably dates to circa 200 CE), ℵ, and B, and it appears that Origen, Basil, Marcion and Tertullian did not have the phrase in their texts. Somewhat mysteriously, one or two manuscripts follow the lead of Marcion (circa 140 CE) and read 'at Laodicea' at this point (probably under the influence of Colossians 4.16). The syntax of the Greek is awkward and has given rise to a number of hypothetical reconstructions, none of which has commanded overall support but several of which have demonstrated scholarly ingenuity. All of this suggests that the association of the letter with the city of Ephesus may have been rather late, a fact which figures significantly in discussions about the authorship, provenance and date of the epistle (see the discussion on pp. 21–50 above).

Most problematic for those wishing to argue in favour of Ephesians as a genuine letter from the apostle Paul is the fact that, according to 1.15, 1.32, the congregation is one with which the Writer is unfamiliar. This is difficult to reconcile with traditions intimately associating Paul with the city of Ephesus and the church located there (see especially Acts 18–20). Indeed, Paul's farewell speech to the leaders of the church in Ephesus as he prepares to depart for Jerusalem from the port of Miletus is perhaps the most personal section of the material dealing with Paul's life and ministry within the book (see Acts 20.17–35). This suggests an intimacy and affection for the church in Ephesus which is altogether lacking in Ephesians. Thus, the modern interpreter is virtually forced to decide between a Pauline authorship which is based on the traditions associating Paul with the church at Ephesus, and a non-Pauline authorship which makes sense of the text of the epistle as we now have it.

Occasionally commentators have attempted to distinguish between the two groups implied by the terms translated as *people* and *faithful*, suggesting that the former refers to Jewish-Christians and the latter refers to Gentile-Christians. However this is improbable given the use of *God's people* (*hagioi*) elsewhere in the letter as a general reference to the 'saints' of God without reference to their ethnic status (notably 1.15, 18; 3.8, 18; 4.12; 5.3 and 6.18; the only possible exception to this is found in 2.19 on which see below). Rigid distinctions between the Jewish-Christian and Gentile-Christian components within the congregation here addressed (whether it be in Ephesus, Hierapolis or elsewhere in Asia Minor) are ill advised. It is best to take the letter as addressed to a mixed congregation consisting of both Jewish-Christians and Gentile-Christians and not try to read too much into the terms *people* and *faithful* (see the note on 1.13–14 below). G.B. Caird makes an interesting observation on the word *hagioi*, frequently translated as 'saints':

It is noteworthy that Paul never uses the word in the singular. Christians are saints only as members of the holy community.[22]

This is a salutory word for Christians today who live in a world which is preoccupied with individual rights and private concerns at the expense of the communities of which they are a part.

2   The references to *grace* and *peace* are terms sometimes said to be associated with greetings common in Greek and Jewish letters respectively. Here the standard Greek greeting *chairein* has been

replaced by the noun *charis*, 'grace', while the Hebrew greeting *shalom* has been translated as 'peace'. The pairing of the words is found in introductory greetings of all of the letters within the Pauline corpus (Romans 1.7; I Corinthians 1.3; II Corinthians 1.2; Galatians 1.3; Philippians 1.2; Colossians 1.2; I Thessalonians 1.1; II Thessalonians 1.2; Titus 1.4; Philemon 3; the additional term 'mercy' is added in I Timothy 1.2 and II Timothy 1.2). The same two words are used at the conclusion of the letter (6.23–24), although they are reversed in order. Thus, the epistle begins and ends on a note of God's grace (an effect often called an *inclusio*).

The Blessing of God's Salvation through Christ
1.3–14

This section of Ephesians is frequently described as 'The Great Eulogy' of the epistle. One of its most striking features is lost in virtually all English translations – the fact that it is one continuous sentence in Greek.[23] The REB divides it into eight sentences spread over two paragraphs, following the trend of most English translations which attempt thereby to make it more intelligible. This in itself stands as some indication of the difficulty in translating the flowery, effusive style of the language in the section, filled as it is with redundant expressions and repetitive phrases which are piled one upon the other. So lofty and soaring is the thought here that it is at times difficult to see where the Writer is heading in the argument. The paragraph gives the impression that here he puts everything he holds dear in the shop window and that there is little attention to clarity of presentation. In the words of J. Armitage Robinson:

> The twelve verses . . . baffle our analysis. They are a kaleidoscope of dazzling lights and shifting colours: at first we fail to find a trace of order or meaning.[24]

The paragraph might be described as a theological cross-roads, with many important ideas and key terms of the Christian faith intersecting within the course of the argument contained in the verses. Here we find such themes as God's election, redemption, sacrifice, the adoption as children, the forgiveness of sins, and the mystery of divine revelation; all are given brief expression in the space of a few crowded verses. The section is a veritable treasure-trove of theological richness and serves as an introduction to the epistle as a whole. It has been described as the interpretative 'key' to the letter, giving advance notice of many of the themes which follow in the body of the work. The fact that the paragraph is followed by a second introductory thanksgiving (in 1.15–16) has led to the suggestion that 3–14 originally had an independent existence. Thus it is sometimes described as a *berakah*, a prayer beginning with the exclamation 'Blessed be You, O God!'. There are many examples of such Jewish prayers from antiquity, including several of the *Eighteen Benedictions*. In addition, precisely the same introductory formula is regularly used in the *Siddur Lev Chadash*, a new prayerbook produced for the Union of Liberal and Progressive Synagogues in 1995.

Many attempts have been made to identify the language and structure of verses 3–14, and thereby recover the original liturgical hymn upon which the present passage is based. It is not unusual to find commentators dividing the passage up into a hymn of three, or four, or even six strophes. Texts from the Qumran community, notably *The Hymns Scroll* (1QH), are often cited as containing phrases and ideas remarkably similar to the eulogy of 1.3–14. However, there has been no consensus of opinion on the matter and a bewildering number of formal analyses remain on offer. Somewhat surprisingly, the JB is one of the few modern translations to acknowledge the hymnic nature of verses 3–14 and set the passage out in verse; one might have expected that such a presentation would be more common than it is in modern translations. Many see the influence of Colossians 1.3–23 on the passage since many of the phrases and ideas contained in that earlier epistle are found here, suitably adapted to reflect the Writer's viewpoint and purposes.

God the Father is the major actor on the overcrowded stage and he is clearly the initiator in the drama of redemption here described, although Christ the Son is the agent through whom it is accomplished and in whom it is embodied. This christological dimension is seen in the dozen or so references to *in Christ* (or equivalent expressions such as *in him* or *in his beloved*) within the passage. Indeed, many interpreters have argued for a trinitarian formula of salvation within these verses, emphasizing the *election of* God the Father (verses 4–5), *redemption through* Jesus Christ (verse 7), and the *sealing in* the Holy Spirit (verse 13). Such an interpretation is perhaps within the bounds of the thought of the Writer of Ephesians as long as it is recognized that the salvation here expressed does not set Jesus Christ *against* God the Father in the process. The crucial point is that Jesus Christ, God's Son, is the means whereby reconciliation is effected; the two (Father and Son) are not at logger-heads one with the other; rather they are working in harmony to effect the redemption of humankind.

The three-fold use of the phrase 'to the praise of his glory' in verses 6, 12 and 14 is striking. Unfortunately from the standpoint of recognizing the continuity of expression, the REB does not translate the phrase consistently in the three instances and offers a paraphrase instead. The repetition of the phrase ties together sections of the paragraph much as a refrain brings together various stanzas of a hymn or song. This is all the more significant when it is noted that the subject in the verses is respectively God the Father, Jesus Christ and the Holy Spirit. As noted above, the expression has lent itself to trinitarian exposition at various stages in the history of Christianity, although it is anachronistic to suggest that the author intended such a credal affirmation here. The phrase does, however, hint at the liturgical nature of the paragraph and is one of the reasons which has led some to speculate that it originally existed as an independent prayer, perhaps as part of a early Christian baptismal rite (more on this below in connection with 1.13 and 4.30).

3   Here we first encounter one of the phrases so characteristic of the epistle as a whole: *in the heavenly realms*. This occurs five times in Ephesians (1.3, 20; 2.6; 3.10; 6.12) and is somewhat different from the phrase normally used elsewhere in the Pauline letters.

Part of the difficulty in interpreting the meaning of *en tois epouraniois* lies in the fact that the Writer of Ephesians uses it in two distinct ways. In 1.3, 20 and 2.6 the phrase refers to the dominion of God and/or Christ; while in 3.10 and 6.12 it refers to the dominion of the evil rulers and authorities which oppose the purposes of God and against which the people of God struggle. In other words, *in the heavenly realms* has both a positive and a negative side to it. It is impossible for a modern reader to enter into exactly the same conceptual framework of a first century person; our cosmological understanding is radically different, and we find it difficult to locate God in the heavenly realms which lie 'up there' or 'out there'. Nevertheless, we perhaps get closest to the meaning of the phrase if we think of it as speaking of a spiritual dimension of existence, one in which the forces of good and evil conduct a campaign for the hearts and minds of people. The Christian is called to live recognizing that there is a spiritual demand upon her or his life, and that obedience to such a demand necessarily requires an allegiance beyond that normally given to the earthly, human realm.

The REB consistently adds the word *realms* to the five occurrences of the phrase in an attempt to make sense of what is in fact an ambiguous expression in Greek; the plural adjective does not have a noun following it. This means that *en tois epouraniois* in verse 3 could mean heavenly *things* (referring to the blessings which the verse maintains God has showered upon his people) as well as heavenly *places* (referring to the abode of God). The latter sense is generally agreed to be the intent here, although the interpretation of *en tois epouraniois* as referring to spiritual blessings has a long line of advocates, including John Chrysostom and Martin Luther. The expression here communicates the idea of the unseen spiritual world which stands above and beyond the material, earthly realm where affairs are conducted according to human values and viewpoints. In so far as it speaks of the *position* of the believing community as one incorporated in the person of Christ, it is reminiscent of the language used in Colossians 3.1–4. Indeed, it may well be that the Writer of Ephesians is building upon the earlier letter at this point in his argument. The passage from Colossians offers an important clue as to the meaning of the phrase, by providing an eschatological context in which the idea of 'the heavenlies' is to be understood. Having stressed the believers' union with Christ, who sits at the right hand of God in heaven, Colossians 3.4 boldly states: 'When Christ, who is our life, is revealed, then you too will be revealed with him in glory.' The verse clearly has the awaited parousia of Christ in view, and stands as the only unambiguous reference to futuristic eschatology in the epistle. And yet, this assurance of the future revelation of glory is seen as the fulfilment of the life that the believing community presently enjoys in heaven with Christ. In effect, *in the heavenly realms* becomes a shorthand expression for Christian existence, including within it the eschatological tension which characterizes it. That is to say, life in the heavenly realms is both 'now' (in so far as our participation in the risen Lord Jesus Christ is ongoing) and 'not yet' (in so far as a future consummation is still to be awaited).

4–5 The blessings of God spoken of in verse 3 are here spelled out in terms of his choosing a people for himself. As a way of stressing the fervour of that choice the Writer declares that this decision was made *before the foundation of the world*. The point is that God's plan of bringing his church into being was not something that was cobbled together at the last minute; rather it was the divine intention all along. A number of similar terms and expressions in the rest of the paragraph convey this divine initiative in selecting his people. The Writer asserts that what had been conceived in eternity has now become realized in time. The language of predestination and calling pervades here as it does elsewhere in Paul's letters (notably Romans 8.28–29), and yet, quite astonishingly, the Writer here takes the idea a step further when he explicitly states that such election is accomplished *in Christ*. God's care and compassion for those he loves is demonstrated by the way in which we are made to share in the life of his own Son. To make this explicit the Writer turns in verse 5 to another powerful metaphor, that of adoption into the family of God. This is a familiar image from Paul (see Romans 8.15, 23; 9.4; Galatians 4.5). The background for such an idea lies within the Roman legal system, and there are enough examples of people enjoying new-found position within an adoptive family to suggest that the image would have been a powerful one in the minds of the readers. The classic example, which would have been widely known in the first century, is the adoption of the young, ambitious Octavian by his great-uncle Julius Caesar in 44 BCE. The adoption was publicly revealed when Caesar's will was read and made Octavian, better known to us as the Emperor Augustus, Caesar's legal heir with all of the rights and privileges of a natural-born son. Octavian, as the adopted son, assumed Caesar's name and rank and forfeited all legal claims to his old family. It is not hard to see the opportunities which the image of adoption offered for both Paul and the Writer of Ephesians.

Nevertheless, due care should be taken over the potentially sexist assumptions underlying the idea of adoption. The word translated as 'adoption' is *huiothesian*, a term which is linguistically related to the word for 'son' (*huios*), and speaks of the male-centred system of Roman law (in the NT period only males were formally adopted). To use 'son' language (as the RSV, the GNB, the NIV, the NEB, the JB, and Moffatt all do here) grates on the sensitivities of many modern people in so far as it reflects the cultural setting of the NT which was often patriarchal and did not recognize the equality of the sexes. The REB has attempted to resolve this somewhat by translating the Greek term *huiothesian*, which in terms of the first-century context was gender-inclusive in much the same way that 'man' was until recently, as *to be adopted as his children*.

7   The word translated as release is *apolutrōsis*, a term rich in meaning within the ancient world and one which has as its heart the idea of a transfer of possession or ownership by means of payment. Unfortunately, the OT does not help us much in understanding the root meaning of the image. The noun occurs only once in the Septuagint, in Daniel 4.34 where it refers to the recovery of Nebuchadnezzar from a seven-year long illness. The basic meaning in the NT is 'freed by ransom', and thus, by extension, 'redemption'. Occasionally the word is used in this sense by ancient Greek writers.

A good example is found in Plutarch *Pompey* 24.2 which speaks of daring pirates holding captured cities to ransom during the period of the Mithridatic war.

The idea of sacrifice as the means whereby such freedom is obtained is never far away from discussion of the theme, as in this verse where it is explicitly linked to *the shedding of his (Christ's) blood*. Modern equivalents of *apolutrōsis*, which convey something of the theological wealth involved without getting ensnared in the details of the sacrificial imagery, or bogged down in the mechanics of how financial transactions are accomplished (who pays what to whom; what is the cost and who pays the price?), might include 'emancipation' and 'liberation'.

The idea of *apolutrōsis* as 'release' or 'emancipation' is particularly important in the Deutero-Pauline epistles (Colossians 1.14; Ephesians 1.7, 14; 4.30) and may ultimately have as its basis the so-called 'ransom' saying of Jesus recorded in Matthew 20.28/ Mark 10.45. There may also be a connection to Romans 3.24–26, particularly if, as is commonly asserted, this paragraph in Romans contains early, pre-Pauline ideas which are being picked up by the Apostle.

Because of the institution of slavery in the ancient world such ideas of 'release' or 'emancipation' were undoubtedly much more evocative in the first century world than they are in our time. Nevertheless, there are many living today who would welcome the note of liberation from a slave-like existence that the term *apolutrōsis* implies. Release necessarily implies freedom, and there can be little doubt that for countless millions around the world, lives are characterized not by freedom but by bondage to political and economic and ecclesiastical structures. Rigid distinctions between 'personal' liberation, 'socio-economic' liberation and 'political' liberation often fail to appreciate that people are wholistic beings who are personally involved in both political and socio-economic spheres. One cannot help but recall the words of the Revd Dr Martin Luther King, Jr, proclaimed from the steps of the Lincoln Memorial in Washington DC on 28 August 1963 as part of the so-called *Freedom March* on the capital city. These words, forming part of the famous 'I Have a Dream' speech, go far in helping us to grasp the social implications of what release through the shedding of Christ's blood on the cross can, and should, mean for us today.

When we let freedom ring, when we let it ring from every village and every hamlet, from every state and every city, we will be able to speed up that day when all of God's children, black men and white men, Jews and Gentiles, Protestants and Catholics, will be able to join hands and sing in the words of that old Negro spiritual, 'Free at last! Free at last! Thank God almighty, we are free at last!'

9   In this verse God is said to have *made known to us his secret purpose*. The term rendered here as *secret purpose* is *to mustērion*, something of a technical expression within the mystery religions of antiquity, such as those associated with the Eleusinian or Mithraic cults. Not surprisingly, a great deal of investigation into the conceptual background of the word has been undertaken in recent years. The growing consensus is that *to mustēriōn* is closely related to the thought-world of Jewish apocalypticism and is best interpreted against that religious movement. As a result, the earlier attempts to relate 'mystery' to the thought-world of Hellenism or Gnosticism are suspect and have been judged by many to be positively misleading.

The Writer does not here mean to suggest that 'the mystery' is something which has been revealed to one group and withheld from another; to know God's secret purpose is not intended to be a means of exerting privilege over others or of pulling rank on them. It is not 'secret' in the sense that Masonic rituals and passwords are secret, only to be understood by the 'insider', one of the initiated. We are not a spiritual Sherlock Holmes seeking to unravel a puzzling case. Rather the focus is on the *revelatory dimension* of the mystery, that God has unveiled something which hitherto remained unknown to, or hidden from, us. The point is that the secret is now known, 'the cat is out of the bag', as we like to say. In this regard we are more like the audience watching an episode of *Colombo* who know what the mystery is; we watch knowing the truth of the situation and delight in the fact that what we know to be the truth is finally revealed for all to see. But what is this revealed secret? Fortunately, the matter is given a great deal of attention within the Pauline corpus generally, as well as having special prominence in Ephesians (*to mustēriōn* occurs in 3.3, 4, 9; 5.32 and 6.19). When these are taken together one begins to see how ecclesiastical the idea of the secret purpose of God is for the author of the letter.[25] In short, the secret is that God's plan is to unite both Jews and Gentiles into one people, so as to form one united church. At the same time, there is a conceptual link to another term in verse 10, one which is loaded with theological significance and which sets this aim of establishing a united people against the backdrop of God's wider purposes in creation.

10   The reference to God putting into effect his divine plan *when the time was ripe* again asserts the Creator's guiding hand in the course of all things. The phrase is reminiscent of Galatians 4.4, although the focus in Ephesians is not so clearly Christ-centred and incarnational. It is in verse 10 that we encounter the central point of the paragraph. Indeed, we might well describe the declaration here made as the crown jewel of the Writer's thought in so far as it serves as the focal point of the argument in the eulogy. The REB renders the crucial verb *anakephalaiōsasthai* as *might be brought into a unity*. The verb is an unusual one (occurring only here and in Romans 13.9 in the NT) and carries with it the sense of everything being 'summed up' in Christ. The word was one used by classical rhetoricians in connection with a 'summary argument', much in the same way that we use it today to describe a lawyer's final speech at the conclusion of a courtroom trial.

We should, at the same time, relate the idea of such a 'summing up' to that of 'restoration' or 'renewal'. In Christ the whole of the created order (*ta panta*), or as we might say using the words of Douglas Adams, *Life, the Universe, and Everything*, finds its purpose and realizes the goal from which it had previously been deflected. The cosmic implications of Christ's redemptive act on the cross are central here and it is hardly surprising that the verse has long been used to promote the idea of universalism. We can easily leap forward to the next paragraph of the letter where Christ is proclaimed as the reigning head (*kephalē*) over all things (see 1.22). Interestingly, the verb *anakephalaiōsasthai* becomes important in later Greek and Latin writers, notably Irenaeus of Lyons (circa 190 CE) whose doctrine of 'recapitulation' (the Latin translation equivalent of the verb) is built on it.[26]

One might well ask: when does this 'consummation' take place? When is it that this unification of all things might be said to occur? Is it a wholly futuristic event, a point sometime off in the distant future? This seems unlikely given the stress throughout the epistle on the present realities which have taken effect in Christ. There is a sense in which the summation of all things in Christ has already occurred, that the exaltation of the risen Lord has already effected a change in reality which is in the process of working itself out in practice. The fact is that the 'secret mystery' of God, uniting both

Jews and Greeks into one new humanity, has already been revealed. The assertion that this unification was accomplished through Christ's death on the cross (verse 7), points firmly in the direction of a realized perspective on the part of the Writer of the letter.

11–14   The reference to the *seal of the promised Holy Spirit* in verse 13 is often taken to be a veiled allusion to Christian baptism. A similar expression occurs in 4.30 but it is by no means certain that water baptism is meant in either instance (related language is used in II Corinthians 1.22 and 5.5). It is true that language describing one as being sealed by the Holy Spirit occurs in connection with passages which are sometimes taken to be baptismal in character (notably II Corinthians 1.21–22). And it is clear that some early Christian writers do come to describe baptism in terms of it being a 'seal' (II Clement 7.6; 8.6 is a classic example). However, it appears that the declaration made here is essentially one about the presence of the Holy Spirit in the life of the believers. Water baptism as a sign or mark of that gift of the Spirit has to be read into the verse; it is an inference at best. Nevertheless, many interpreters do precisely this and appeal to 1.13 as a key text in their attempts to see Ephesians as a baptismal homily itself, or perhaps as a letter containing liturgical material which was originally associated with the rite of Christian baptism. Several other curious features of 1.3–14 are said to support this idea, including the use of 'adoption' in verse 5 (recalling that the divine voice at Jesus' baptism specifically addresses him as son); the use of 'the Beloved' in verse 6 (again, a term is uttered by the heavenly voice at the Lord's baptism); and the reference to the 'forgiveness of sins' in verse 7 (echoed in many passages dealing with baptism including Acts 2.38).

Interestingly, in verses 13–14 we encounter a shift in the use of personal pronouns. In verses 3–12 it was 'we' which prevailed; here it is 'you'. This can easily be overplayed and lead to an interpretation whereby a distinction is made between Jews ('we') and non-Jews ('you') which may not be at all intended. As we suggested above on pp. 40–48 it is more likely that the fluctuation between 'we' and 'you' language has to do with the relationship between the 'daughter-church' in Hierapolis and the 'mother-church' at Colossae.

Occasionally, attempts are made on the basis of something as tenuous as the prefix of the participle in verse 12 (*tous proēlpikotes*) to argue for a Jewish contingent of 'early-hopers', as over against Gentile believers who come rather late on the religious scene and could be classed as 'no-hopers' (2.12!). This should likewise be abandoned since the reference to 'we who believed *before*' probably refers to the fact that the Writer was from the church at Colossae which was responsible for the planting of the church in Hierapolis and naturally would be described as having come to faith earlier.

Thus, the shift to 'you' in verses 13–14 may be nothing more innocent, and indeed nothing less profound, than the author demonstrating a pastoral concern by stressing the inclusion of his *Christian* audience in Hierapolis as recipients of God's redemptive purposes in the world. The members of the church at Hierapolis are being reminded that they too are in possession of the Holy Spirit which stands as a *pledge of inheritance*, as it had done to the saints in Colossae before them, and as it will to others who succeed them. They are the latest beneficiaries in a long line of those who have been so graced by God.

Pledge is a term which is used elsewhere in the Pauline letters; the Greek word is *arrabōn* and, in addition to the reference here, it appears in II Corinthians 1.22; 5.5.[27] It is noteworthy that the term in all three instances is associated with the granting of the Spirit of God to the believers. The word is a Semitic loan-word which comes from the realm of commerce and finance. It is often translated as 'deposit', or 'down-payment' or 'earnest', meaning that it stands as a promise to fulfil an obligation. Thus, the metaphor perfectly illustrates an eschatological perspective in which the present possession of the Spirit guarantees that God will, in the future, make good on his promise to redeem humankind. A related image, that of 'firstfruits' drawn from the world of agriculture, is similarly used in the Pauline letters, not only with reference to the gift of the Holy Spirit (as in Romans 8.23), but also with reference to the resurrection of Jesus Christ (as in I Corinthians 15.20).

Verse 14 finishes off the image of financial transaction by describing how God will come *to redeem what is his own*. This attempts to translate what is a very awkward expression in Greek. The idea is that one day God will come to take full possession of his property, a property which has become legally his by means of the *pledge* of the Holy Spirit. The focus of the complex metaphor is thus not so much on *our possession of the pledge* of the Holy Spirit as it is on *God's possession of us* by means of that pledge.

A Thanksgiving, an Intercession and a Credal Fragment
1.15–23

This section can be divided into three distinct but interlocking parts. It consists of a thanksgiving prayer (verses 15–16), which is followed by an intercessory prayer (verses 17–19), to which is joined an early liturgical set-piece extolling the resurrection and exaltation of Christ to the right hand of God (verses 20–23). The liturgical section may well contain material which was used as a credal affirmation, possibly in connection with Christian baptism. Strictly speaking, in terms of form, the opening thanksgiving runs through to 2.10 (or perhaps even to 2.22!) in that throughout these verses the Writer praises God for the joy of salvation as part of his introductory remarks within the letter. The Greek consists of either one or two sentences (depending upon the textual edition used), which the REB expands into five.[28]

15–16 *Because of all this* links this thanksgiving with the eulogy contained in 1.3–14. The verses hint at the Writer's insight into the life of the fellowship without giving specific details; they are vague and generalized and suggest hearsay evidence. Given the lack of concrete information here divulged it is hardly surprising that the association with the church at Ephesus has been called into question, particularly as the letter purports to be from the hand of Paul the Apostle (a similar question arises in connection with 3.2). All of the references to *you* in both verses are plural and suggest that the whole of the congregation in Hierapolis is being praised for its *faith* and *love*. The Writer rejoices that their faith has blossomed into love and concern for others. Such love is said to have been demonstrated to *all God's people*, which may refer to the 'mother-church' in Colossae and reflect a situation in which the 'daughter-church' in Hierapolis has been about to demonstrate her thankfulness for all that had been done for her. Some manuscripts omit the word *love* here, probably due to an error on the part of an early copyist.

17 *I pray* is added here (and in verse 18, as well as in 3.1) to make the thought more understandable (the whole of 1.15–23 is one sentence in Greek). The Writer prays that God may grant *wisdom and vision* to them, describing these gifts as *spiritual* so as to emphasize

the role of the Holy Spirit in bringing the recipients to maturity in such matters. The word for *vision* here is *apocalupsis*, a term which is used elsewhere to describe the revelation of God's actions in Christ (see 3.3, 5). The phrase *the all-glorious Father* (literally 'the Father of glory') is found only here in the NT.

18–19   The substance of the Writer's intercessory prayer for the church is continued here. It has three main points which are set out in a highly stylized fashion. The vast resources and power of God are called to mind and his divine initiative in calling a people to himself is asserted. The Writer outdoes himself in piling up four words for 'power' in verse 19 (possibly reflecting the influence of a related declaration in Colossians 1.11). The grammar of the phrase (*so*) *that your inward eyes may be enlightened* is very difficult and it is hard to see clearly how it connects with what precedes. One possibility is to take the eyes to be a second object of the verb *confer* in verse 17, meaning that the Writer prays for God the Father to confer both spiritual gifts and enlightened eyes. A literal translation such as 'the eyes of your heart having been enlightened' shows something of the difficulties involved in translating the perfect passive participle in the phrase. Physiologically such an idea is, of course, impossible for contemporary people to accept, but metaphorically the image powerfully communicates the idea of spiritual perception among those who have received the Holy Spirit (verse 17). In short, the prayer on the part of the Writer is that his readership might be graced with spiritual illumination.

20–21   Here we have the first reference in the letter to the resurrection of Christ from the dead. What is significant here however is the use to which that reference is put, namely as an assurance of the power and might of God which is extended to the believers. The point is that it is in the resurrection of Christ from the dead that the power of God is most clearly revealed and that this source of strength is available for Christian living. Somewhat surprisingly the future resurrection of the believers themselves is never made explicit in Ephesians (as it is in I Corinthians 15). The closest we get to a discussion along these lines is in 2.6 where the believers are said already to have been united with Christ in his resurrection and exaltation.[29] The Writer's thought here races forward, pausing only to concentrate on the resurrection for a moment before moving on to

Christ's glorious exaltation. It is this theme which occupies the rest of the chapter.

There is a sense in which Christ's death on the cross can be viewed as a surrender and his resurrection/exaltation as a vindication. What we should not fail to appreciate is the way that Christ's willingness to submit to death paves the way for his elevation which follows and all that that implies in terms of all things being subjected to him. To surrender is to discover the means to unity once again. This truth is one of life's most profound paradoxes.

Enthroned him at his right hand is an allusion to Psalm 110.1, the OT passage which is explicitly quoted more often than any other in the NT. Many feel that the psalm was associated with the messianic coronation and thus readily lent itself to Christian exegesis interested in filling out the meaning of Christ's life, death and resurrection. The exaltation to God's right hand is a symbol of honour, power and authority. The reference to *in the heavenly realms* helps us to understand the theological implications of the exaltation for the Writer by offering a glimpse of his eschatological perspective. As Andrew T. Lincoln remarks.

> Christ's exaltation to heaven means that a shift in the center of gravity from the realm of earth to that of heaven has taken place, for the central figure in the drama of salvation has been moved from the setting of earth to that of heaven, where he now is (cf. 6.9). This is crucial for understanding the writer's perspective in this letter. It is not that Christology has been swallowed up by ecclesiology, but rather that what has happened to Christ becomes determinative for the Church in its relation to the heavenly realm.[30]

A similar idea is found in Hebrews 4.14 where Christ the high priest is said to have 'passed through the heavens' to his place of exaltation where he intercedes for the church. Or again, in 7.26 where the same high priest is said to be 'exalted above the heavens.'

The rule of the exalted Christ is said to extend *far above all government and authority, all power and dominion, and any title of sovereignty that commands allegiance.* In other words, no figure of authority, no power structure in existence, is beyond its reach. The various terms used to describe the hostile forces are probably drawn from Colossians 1.16 but we should not attempt to set them in any sort of hierarchical arrangement. The Writer is merely ransacking his vocabulary in order to make a christological point. There has been much recent debate concerning the meaning of these 'principalities and powers' (to use a phrase from the Geneva Bible of 1560 which has passed into common parlance). Were they impersonal forces or evil spiritual beings? (see the discussion on 6.12 below for a fuller treatment of this topic).

Not only is the Writer careful to stress the comprehensiveness of Christ's rule but he is eager to assert how sweeping it is in terms of time, declaring that he reigns *in this age but also in the age to come*. The two-fold division of time is perfectly in keeping with Jewish tradition and is one of the few instances in the letter where a futuristic note is maintained. The Writer shows remarkable agility of thought here in how he presents his understanding of Christian existence. Life must be lived out with an awareness not only of two realms (earthly/heavenly), but of two ages (present/future). While it is true that the Writer prefers to use the spatial metaphor, we see here that he is not beyond using the temporal one when it suits his purpose.

22–23 Verse 22 opens with an allusion to a line from Psalms 8.6, a proof-text frequently used by early Christians to proclaim the messiahship of Jesus (see I Corinthians 15.27; Philippians 3.21 and Hebrews 2.8). The Writer declares that *He (God) put all things in subjection beneath his (Christ's) feet*. The text of the OT psalm has been slightly reworked, probably under the influence of I Corinthians 15.27. The effect of this is to enlarge the meaning of *all things* to include the whole of the created order, thus giving another voice to the chorus of cosmic redemption which resounds elsewhere in the letter (notably in 1.10).

The precise meaning of *head* is a matter of considerable debate. Does it mean headship in the sense of 'ruler' or 'overseer'? Is the sovereignty of Christ what is being asserted here? Or do we need to look forward to the next verse to detect the Writer's meaning and see it as an extension of the somatic metaphor which is used for the church? The REB provides a fairly literal translation of the Greek word order when it says *(God) gave him as head over all things to the church which is his body*. The text suggests three separate but related things: (1) Christ was made head over all things; (2) as head over all things he was given to the church; (3) the church is the body of Christ. Our natural tendency is to conflate the three ideas, no doubt under the influence of the body metaphor so central to Pauline writings (Romans 12.4–5; I Corinthians 6.13–20; 10.16–17; 12.12–31). We mix together the head and body metaphors and conclude that the verse speaks of Christ as the head of the body. This is perhaps to miss something of the subtle delicacy of thought here and may over-look the note of sovereignty *over all things* which is sounded. The same language of Christ as the head of the church is taken up later in the epistle (4.15; 5.23). The term for *church* (*ekklēsia*) is used frequently in the epistle (3.10, 21; 5.23, 24, 25, 27, 29, 32), always to signify the church universal, God's people in all places and at all times. The description of the universal church as the body of Christ is probably reliant upon Colossians 1.18, part of an early Christian hymn (also note the related declaration made in Colossians 1.24). The body metaphor was widely known in the ancient world, and was applied to everything from city-states to armies to the human race. Given this prevalence, together with the fact that it is an immensely adaptable metaphor, it is not surprising to find it applied to the church.

Yet, this vision of the universal church offers a slightly different emphasis from the more congregational understanding found in most of the other Pauline letters which use the body image (see the references above). Such a congregational (as opposed to a cosmic) understanding of ecclesiology arises out of greater sense of the idea of 'Christ-mysticism' (as it has often been described) and stresses participation in the body of Christ. This Ephesians appears not to do, for here Christ is the head of his body, the church, whereas in most of the undisputed letters of Paul the church is the *whole* of the body of Christ and there is no mention of Christ as head. In practice this means that the ecclesiology of Ephesians is generally taken to be a development of Pauline thought, one which reflects a later historical date and a different setting. If this is so, then the declarations of Christ as the head of the church contained in Colossians 1.18, 24 could be said to serve as the bridge between genuine Paul and the Deutero-Pauline followers. On which side of that divide one places Colossians is a long-standing debate which need not detain us here.

The easy-flowing English prose of verse 23 conceals a number of interlocking grammatical difficulties which exist in the Greek. Chief among these is a debate about the precise meaning of the word translated as *fullness* (*plērōma*); is it to be taken in an active sense ('that which fills') or in a passive sense ('that which is filled')? The word can carry either sense and whether we take it to be active or passive in meaning depends largely on what we see as its relationship to *his body* (the church). Is the point here that the church is the fullness of Christ, or should we go further back to verse 22 to find the antecedent of *plērōma* and take the reference there to *him* to mean Christ as the fullness of God. At first glance the difference may not seem all that significant, but the crucial point is sometimes put in the form of a provocative question: is the fullness of Christ somehow lacking, so that the church must be wheeled on to the scene so as to bring about the fulfilment? Many would say that the answer to this question is 'No!' and insist that Christ himself is the fullness described here, especially since this interpretation coincides well with the declaration made in Colossians 2.9 that 'it is in Christ that the Godhead in all its *fullness* dwells embodied' (REB). Be this as it may, it is quite illegitimate to go on to argue that the church has no role to play in the process of the outworking of God's purposes through Christ. Rather it suggests that this role is one which flows from, rather than being determinative for, the fullness of God which is found in him. Thus, it is possible to see the church's contribution in bringing fullness as *complementing*, rather than *competing with* that of her Lord. This may offer the most productive way forward for an interpretation of what is a very compressed couple of verses and enable one to avoid falling into the trap of a false contrast in which the church is set over against Christ, as if she completes something lacking in him. For the church to carry on the work of Christ her head is not to reveal a deficiency in him, but a dedication in her. The church serves as the instrument of salvation in the world and she demonstrates the sovereignty of her Lord in the process. In so far as she discharges her responsibilities the church can legitimately be called the fullness of Christ; it is principally through her that his rule over the cosmos is actualized.

The famous prayer of St Teresa of Avila (1515–1582) entitled 'Christ's Body' may help us to grasp the theological truth expressed here.

Christ has no body now on earth but yours;
yours are the only hands with which he can do his work,
yours are the only feet with which he can go about the world,
yours are the only eyes through which his compassion can shine
   forth
upon a troubled world,
Christ has no body now on earth but yours.[31]

In verse 23 the REB adds the word *him* (which is implied by the participle *tou plēroumenou*) but wisely leaves it unspecified. Is it God or Christ *who is filling the universe in all its parts*? It is impossible to decide absolutely although there is something to be said for taking God as the subject since he is the one who is said to have *raised*, and to have *seated* Christ (verse 20), as well as the one who *subjected* all things to Christ and who *gave* him to the church (verse 23). The fact that 3.19 speaks of the 'fullness of God' while 4.13 refers to the 'fullness of Christ' (REB 'the full stature of Christ') suggests it is foolhardy to be dogmatic on the issue. Whichever is in mind, the point is that *the universe* is not governed by an impersonal force which has chaos theory at its heart. There is a divine order, a godly purpose at work and God (Christ?) will bring everything to completion in its time. The bottom line for the church being addressed here (be it in Ephesus, Hierapolis or somewhere else in Asia Minor) is that Christ reigns supreme. Far from thinking themselves to be an insignificant, inconsequential item on the cosmic agenda, they are to realize that as part of the body of Christ they have pride of place.

Brought to Life, Raised and Enthroned with Christ
2.1–10

There are several features of this passage which suggest that it has suffered in the process of transmission. It is not immediately clear how verses 4–7 follow on from verses 1–3 (the whole of 1–7 is a single, tangled sentence in Greek). In addition, odd phrases are repeated in such a way that they break up the flow of thought (the most important example being the seemingly unnecessary duplication of *it is by grace that you are saved* in verse 5).

Nevertheless, it is possible to detect a certain logic in the argument here in which the Writer picks up several of the themes already introduced in 1.20–21 and elaborates upon them in 2.1–7. Having accomplished that, he then moves on in the second paragraph of the section (2.8–10) to draw out some practical implications for Christian living. Here he reiterates our response in faith to God's act of grace and undermines any suggestion that salvation can come from human will and intentions, however noble they may be.

The paragraph is one of the most memorable within the letter, partly because it was seen by the Protestant Reformers of the sixteenth century as a summary statement of the Pauline doctrine of salvation. The slogan *sola gratia, sola fide* is derived in part from the ringing declaration made in 2.5, 8.

1–2   The Writer begins by offering an assessment of life without Christ. Humankind, he says, is *dead*, scarred by sin and wrecked by wickedness. For some strange reason the REB transposes the conventional translation of two common words here: *sins (paraptōmata)* and *wickedness (hamartiai)*. The use of the plural *hamartiai* is at variance with normal Pauline usage (the apostle uses it in the singular) and has been seen by some to hint at non-Pauline authorship of our letter. It seems likely that *you once were dead because of your sins* is borrowed from Colossians 2.13, although there it is filled out by reference to *uncircumcision* rather than to *wickedness*.

There is a curious fluctuation of expression between verse 1, *you once were dead because of your sins and wickedness*, and the comparable line in verse 5, *we were dead because of our sins*. Some would see lying behind this the Writer's recognition of the mixed nature of the congregation he is addressing. Effectively this means it is possible to argue that verse 1 uses 'you' language because it refers to Gentile-Christians, while verse 5 uses 'we' language because it has Jewish-Christians in mind (we presume the Writer was a Jewish-Christian). However, this distinction is forced and artificial and creates some theological difficulties. As a result some have suggested that Colossians 2.13 is responsible for the use of 'you' in verses 1–2 and that the Writer later switches to 'we' language in verses 3–10 in order to express his own sense of inclusion in the sinful state of humankind. A more likely explanation for the change from 'you' to 'we' is the fact that the Writer is a member of the 'mother-church' in Colossae who were responsible for the setting up of the church in Hierapolis to whom the letter is addressed. On this reading the 'you' of verses 1–2 refers to the congregation in Hierapolis, the 'we' of verse 3 refers to the church of Colossae, and the 'we' of verses 4–10 refers to all three of the churches of the Lycus region. Thus the Writer first addresses the readers in Hierapolis based upon the historical relationship between that church and his own home-church, before moving on to include the congregation of Laodicea in his declaration of what God has done for them all in Christ. The advantage of such a reading of the passage is that it avoids the difficulties of a 'Jew' verses 'Gentile' interpretation in as much as it assumes that all three churches of the area were mixed congregations made up of both Jewish-Christians and Gentile-Christians.

Because the human condition is one characterized by sin and death, it is also one in which spiritual forces are engaged in battle. Satanic forces are at work in the world, and although specific mention is not made of Satan himself, the meaning of *the commander of the spiritual powers of the air* seems obvious. The phrase suggests a personal centre of evil and is in keeping with the ideas of the ancient world. Perhaps a close cultural equivalent to this tendency to personify evil is found in the mythology first made popular by Bram Stoker's novel *Dracula* (1897). These ideas have persisted over the intervening century and are enjoying a new flush of popularity as the recent film adaptation of the story, Francis Ford Coppola's *Bram Stoker's Dracula* (1992), and the phenomenally successful novel by Anne Rice entitled *Interview With the Vampire* (1977) both testify. It is quite common to have language drawn from Ephesians 2.2, 'the Prince of the spiritual powers', or 'the Prince of Darkness', applied to the Dracula figure in such popular re-tellings of the myth. In most novels and films about vampires the plot revolves around a struggle of good versus evil, if not of God versus Satan. It is a spiritual battle, against a foe who is an incarnation of evil, which captures our imaginations. Verse 2 hints at such a mythological world-view and anticipates a more extensive discussion of spiritual warfare which is given later in 6.10–20.

The phrase *God's rebel subjects* (retained from the NEB) avoids sexist language, but adds a reference to 'God' which does not appear in the Greek and can only be inferred; the RSV gives it as 'the sons of disobedience'. Exactly the same translation is used in the REB for the repeat of the phrase in 5.6.

3–4   The details and motivations of sin are here spelled out, as are their consequences. Human sin is described in terms which are both internal and external, both individual in focus and universal in scope. A modern way of expressing this is to say that we struggle with 'the world, the flesh and the devil'. There is a traitor within, as well as a tyrant without, not to mention a social territory in which they co-exist, and all three have to be accounted for if we want to understand the depths and despair of the human situation apart from Christ.

Natural condition is best seen as an indication of the tendency to rebelliousness and sin within human beings rather than as a state of original sin as classically conceived (from Augustine onwards). The problem with using terms like 'state' or 'condition' in describing human behaviour is that they imply an inherent flaw or defect within people which cannot be helped. If care is not taken one quickly loses sight of the individual as we search to explain the reasons for human actions. Yet, human wickedness and ultimate destruction are not the final words on the matter because God is said to be *rich in mercy* and to demonstrate his *great love* to us. What we were by nature has been overcome by what we can be by God's *mercy* and *love* (verse 5), his surpassing *kindness* (verse 7), and his bountiful *grace* (verse 8).

5–6   These two verses are distinguished by three compound verbs which are quite difficult to translate into English. The REB renders them as *brought us to life, raised* and *enthroned*. Common to all three is the fact that they all have the prefix *sun* attached to them. This has the effect of associating the action of the verb with that performed on another subject, namely Christ Jesus himself. A good means of communicating the thought here would be to translate the three as *jointly brought to life, co-raised* and *co-enthroned*.[32] The essential point is that our existence is intimately tied up with Christ's; what God has done for Christ he has also done for the believers. Thus, the Writer stresses the present salvation of the people of God with the resurrection of Jesus Christ from the dead and his exaltation in the heavens, events which have already taken place and which are firmly established in the past. One common way of describing the solidarity between Christ and his followers which is implied by this trio of *sun* verbs is to describe them as expressing the idea of a corporate personality, based either on OT conceptions of the nation Israel or on the Pauline understanding of Christ as Second Adam (as in Romans 5.12–21; I Corinthians 15.20–22, 45–48; Philippians 2.6–11).[33] A similar trio of *sun* words, this time nouns instead of verbs, is found in 3.6 (see also the comments on 4.3 and 5.7, 11).

The declaration *it is by grace that you are saved* at the end of verse 5 is one of the best-known phrases of the letter. The exact same phrase is contained in verse 8 and although there is no textual evidence which suggests that it is a later interpolation into verse 5, it should probably be viewed as such (many translations, including the AV, the RSV, the NASB and the NRSV, bracket the words). Its presence breaks up the three *sun* verbs (see above) which are at the heart of the paragraph. The REB does recognize the difficulties posed by the intrusive phrase and sets them off by means of a semi-colon. Unfortunately this means that verse 6 then is made to start a new sentence, which again forces a mental break between *jointly brought to life, co-raised* and *co-enthroned*. The three actions are meant to be seen as a three-part harmony and it is best if we recognize them as such. The placement of the phrase *when we were dead because of our sins* in the REB is also unfortunate since it too breaks up the connection between the three crucial *sun* verbs. In the Greek the phrase commences the sentence, forging an effective parallel to the style of verse 1. It is a restatement of the thought with which the passage began before the Writer proceeds to hammer home the message of being brought to life in Christ. Once we were dead, but no longer!

7   The words *so that he might display* carry with them the idea of a public demonstration, such as in a courtroom setting. On the strength of this Markus Barth suggests that what we have here is the church being caught up in 'the great cosmic lawsuit of God'.[34] The mention of *ages to come* is but another brief glimpse of the futuristic eschatology to which the Writer gives passing acknowledgment in the course of the letter (see 1.21).

8   This verse might be described as the 'jewel in the crown' of the letter; it is sometimes said that the verse distills the theological argument of Romans 3–8 into a single verse. Thus, 2.8 is frequently taken to be *the* summary statement of Pauline theology, although it is language of *salvation*, as opposed to the language of *justification* (so characteristic of Paul's thought in Romans and Galatians) which dominates here. This may indicate that the debate between Jewish-Christians and Gentile-Christians about the validity of the Mosaic law as a foundation for Christian living is no longer a hot topic of discussion. Given the obvious reliance in Ephesians upon the central planks of Paul's thought, it is odd that there is no mention of the cross of Christ as the means whereby this salvation is achieved (the only reference to 'cross' in the letter is found in 2.16 in connection with the reconciliation of Jewish-Christians and Gentile-Christians).

The words *you are saved* contain within them a wealth of theological truth which can be easily missed or misunderstood. The Greek is *este sesōsmenoi* and three important features of the words are worth noting: they are in the plural; the participle concerned is in the passive voice; the participle is in the perfect tense.[35] All of which is to say that salvation is something which is collectively experienced, it is something which is done for us and not something we do for ourselves, and it is something which began in the past and continues into the present. G. B. Caird uses a delightful illustration, involving the noted Greek scholar and commentator B. F. Westcott, which may help us to appreciate the significance of the Greek here.

There is a story told of a former Bishop of Durham that he was accosted one day by a member of the Salvation Army, who asked him: 'Are you saved?' To which the bishop replied: 'That depends on whether you mean σωθείς, σωζόμενος, or σεσωσμένος. If you mean σωθείς, undoubtedly; if you mean σωζόμενος, I trust so; if you mean σεσωσμένος, certainly not.' Σωθείς is an aorist participle, denoting a single act in the past, and it refers either to the finished work of Christ on the Cross or to the baptism in which the Christian has once for all embraced his salvation. Σωζόμενος is a present participle, and describes an ongoing process of salvation, the journey of the Christian from the City of Destruction – or, perhaps we should say, from the Cross, where he felt the burden of sin slip from his shoulders – to the gates of the Celestial City. Σεσωσμένος is a perfect participle, and denotes a final consummation, the sounding of the trumpets on the other side, the disclosing of the salvation which is ready to be revealed at the last time. We may, then, paraphrase the bishop's answer as follows: if you mean 'Did Christ die for me?', undoubtedly; if you mean 'Are my feet firmly set upon the highway of salvation?', I trust so; but if you mean 'Am I safe home in the blest kingdoms meek of joy and love?', certainly not.[36]

Although Caird's story sets the discussion in the singular, we can readily see how its application to the plural declaration found in 2.8 can be made. The truth of salvation as being not only a past event, but a present experience, as well as future hope is not to be missed.[37] Yet it is quite striking that nowhere else in the Pauline epistles is salvation spoken of in the perfect tense. Rather salvation is something which is on-going, it is a process which continues throughout life, as I Corinthians 1.18 illustrates so well ('to us who *are being saved*. . .'). Likewise, in Romans 13.11 Paul notes that salvation is nearer than it once had been, but nowhere suggests that it has already arrived. The nearest equivalent to Ephesians 2.8 in the undisputed Pauline letters is Romans 8.24, but even here the futuristic note is sounded by the inclusion of a note of eschatological caution 'for *in hope* we have been saved.'

The stress in the phrase *God's gift* falls on the first word; it is *God's* gift. There are some things in life which are so precious that they can never be bought or earned; they must be given.

9–10   Here the ethical demands of Christian existence are asserted. Boasting is seen as something foreign to a life in Christ, not so much because it exalts the accomplishments of the one doing the boasting but because it detracts from the actions of Christ on our behalf. It is important to see the way in which 2.9–10 completes the thought begun in 2.8, moving the reader to consider the implications of his or her salvation. It might help if we set out the various phrases of 2.8–10 as a logical syllogism.

Premise 1 (The Positive):	You are saved by grace through faith (2.8a) It is a gift of God (2.8c) You are God's handiwork (2.10a)
Premise 2 (The Negative):	Salvation is not of yourselves (2.8b)

It does not come by works (2.9a)
There are no grounds for personal
   boasting (2.9b)

Therefore (The Results):   Having been created in
                                  *Christ Jesus, Produce good
                                  deeds!* (2.10b)

The assumption throughout is that, although *good deeds* cannot bring about salvation, they are the fruit of the new creation which is in Christ Jesus (see II Corinthians 5.17). The REB renders the first part of verse 9 as *not a reward for work done*; literally the phrase is much simpler and consists of only three words in the Greek: 'not of works'. It is commonly thought that the unqualified 'works' indicates that the Writer has moved beyond a situation where adherence to the demands of the Jewish Law was a point of contention within the church. In other words, the fact that he has universalized 'works', and no longer describes it in Jewish terms as *'works of the Law'*, means that *anyone*, Jew or Gentile alike, who thinks that human effort (works!) can please God is being challenged to reconsider the situation. Such a perspective hints at a date of circa 90 CE for the epistle since by that time the debate over the validity of the Mosaic law within the life of the church would have been largely over. The casual assumption that *how we act as Christians* has nothing to do with *who we are in Christ* is forcibly dismissed in verses 8–10. Orthopraxy and orthodoxy are not mutually exclusive dimensions of Christian life, but rather are inextricably welded together in an authentic existence.

The REB misses an important connection to verse 2 by its rendering of the final phrase of the paragraph as *for the life of good deeds*. In fact the same verb is used in the opening sentence to describe a previous pattern of 'living' (or was it 'death'?) in which one *followed the ways of this present world order*. The image of contrast which is set up by the opening and closing thoughts of the paragraph is remarkable. We all recognize that following a way of life is part of what it means to be alive. In such matters neutrality is not an option and allegiances must be declared. The question to be decided is whether we march to the tune of a dead and dying regime, or walk freely as part of God's new creation in Christ. The Writer picks up this idea of an ethical way of life, a Christian lifestyle, in 4.1, 17 and 5.2, 8, 15.

The church is here described as *God's handiwork*, which F.F. Bruce explains as 'His work of art, His masterpiece'.[38] This is a wonderful image and invites us to consider the artistic hand of God filling a fresh canvas with an original portrait of redeemed humankind, or carving out of rough stone a new presentation of people in Christ his Son.

Charles Wesley's well-known hymn 'Love Divine, all loves excelling' (first published in 1747) builds on the imagery contained in 2.10 (as well as 5.27 and II Corinthians 3.18–4.6!) and goes far in expressing the truth of God's saving activity in Christ. The fourth stanza of the hymn runs.

> Finish then thy new creation,
>   Pure and spotless let us be;
> Let us see thy great salvation,
>   Perfectly restored in thee.
> Changed from glory into glory,
>   Till in heaven we take our place,
> Till we cast our crowns before thee,
>   Lost in wonder, love, and praise! [39]

Making One New Humanity via the Cross
2.11–18

It is clear that one of the most important social and theological problems faced by the first generations of Christians concerned how Jewish-Christians and Gentile-Christians were to live together and be united within the fellowships of which they were a part. It is this complex issue which preoccupies the mind of the Writer throughout this section of the epistle. Ultimately he resolves the matter by vigorously asserting that reconciliation between the two groups has already been bought by Christ's death on the cross (2.13). However, in working up to the formulation of that crowning idea there are a number of important topics to which the Writer turns his attention. These all revolve around that central, governing thought like planets circling the sun. Each in its own way contributes to our understanding of the difficulties which faced congregations consisting of both Jewish-Christians and Gentile-Christians as they took up the challenge of life in the new Humanity.

The section falls into three parts: a description of the predicament in which Gentile-Christians found themselves prior to their life in Christ (2.11–13); a proclamation of what has been accomplished by Christ on the cross (2.14–16); a summary declaration of the access to God which is made available to both Jewish-Christians and Gentile-Christians (2.17–18). The discussion here is preparatory for what follows in 2.19–23 where a variety of images are applied to the people of God.

The passage consists of four sentences in the Greek which the REB expands into seven.

11–12 These verses, with their clear distinction between uncircumcised Gentiles and circumcised Jews, together with the contrast between life within the community of Israel and life outside of the covenant, offer the most important clues as to the social make-up and identity of the church to which the letter is addressed. Largely on the basis of them it is commonly assumed that the church predominantly consisted of Gentile-Christians, together with a not insubstantial number of Jewish-Christians. As we have already noted, it is likely that the Writer is addressing the church of Hierapolis in which the Gentile-Christians were the majority (see the discussion on Provenance on pp. 31–48 above). For this reason he

79

addresses them as 'uncircumcised Gentiles', although he is careful not to slip into confrontational language at this point by contrasting this with 'we circumcised Jews'. Rather the contrasting phrase the Writer uses is much more subtle, as if he is aware of the inappropriateness of calling attention to the former Jew-Gentile divide in the context of life in the church. He puts the contrasting phrase in the passive, 'by *what is called* the circumcised' (the addition of *themselves* at this point within the REB is unfortunate and runs roughshod over the thought).

Remember then links the passage with what was said in 2.10 and encourages the readers to ponder afresh their situation. *By birth* is a translation of a phrase (*en sarki*) which is more often than not used in the Pauline materials in a (negative) ethical sense, meaning 'fleshly' or 'carnal'. But as the REB here suggests, *sarx* can denote either physical descent or simple humanness (Romans 1.3 and II Corinthians 5.16 are classic examples of it bearing these senses with reference to the person of Jesus). While we can infer from *you* and *your* that the Writer was himself of Jewish extraction, this is not the essential issue. Rather, from the Writer's standpoint distinctions between circumcision and uncircumcision are, in one sense, no longer valid. They are an insufficient basis upon which to assess what it means to be in Christ. The days of the bitter and acrimonious debate over circumcision (as reflected in such passages as Romans 2.25–29; 4.1–12; Galatians 2.3–5; 5.6; Philippians 3.1–7) have passed and a new era of joint inheritance has dawned in the life of the church.

Two expressions drawn from the world of politics and nationality are here applied to the (predominantly) Gentile-Christians of the church in Hierapolis. The first is that they were *excluded from the community of Israel*; the second that they were *strangers to God's covenants and the promise*. We catch a bit more of the sting which lies behind these words if we translate the two key words *excluded* and *strangers* as 'outsiders' and 'foreigners' respectively. In other words, the charge in the past was that the Gentiles did not *really* belong; they were resident aliens as far as God's plans for his chosen people were concerned. This is not unlike the central point of Philippians 3.20 where Paul says, in effect, that Christians are resident aliens as far as the cities of the world are concerned (see also I Peter 1.1 and 2.11 for similar ideas). Here Moffatt's translation of Philippians 3.20 describing Christians as 'a colony of heaven' helps us to catch the essential point. Interestingly, the only other time that the word *excluded* occurs in the NT is in 4.18 where it describes those who are *alienated* (the REB changing its term) from a life with God.

Language of strangers and refugees, of exclusion and of alienation is quite familiar to us and we can conjure up many examples of it in our mind's eye. The novel *The Outsider* (1942), by the Nobel-Prize winning author Albert Camus, is a good example of this. Camus presents us with the disturbing story of Mersault, a clerk living in Algiers who is forced to live his life there as an outsider, one who is never quite able to integrate himself within his surroundings. He goes about his life, to be sure, but there is always a feeling of alienation, of distance, which pervades his existence.[40] This is not unlike the sense of 'otherness' which is hinted at by our Writer in 2.11–12.

Moreover, the metaphor of a stranger or pilgrim on a journey to (or from!) heaven has yielded a rich harvest in classic works of literature over the centuries. Works as diverse and as separated in time as Augustine's *The City of God* (circa 425), Dante's *The Divine Comedy* (circa 1308), Langland's *Piers the Ploughman* (circa 1380), John Bunyan's *The Pilgrim's Progress* (1678), and Robert Heinlein's science-fiction classic *Stranger in a Strange Land* (1961), all employ the image.

The plural *covenants* suggests the sequence of agreements made with Noah, Abraham, Isaac, Jacob, and David and focusses the discussion on the level of history rather than on the level of an abstract covenantal theology. This allows the Gentile-Christians of Hierapolis to gain a better sense of what their place is *now* within the purposes of God; there was more than one covenant and they are *now* participants in the *fulfilment* to which all these covenants pointed. By looking back to the past in this way the people of the new Humanity are encouraged to an historical self-consciousness, to gain a sense of who they are and where they have come from.

13   So lyrical is the thought of 2.13–18 that it has been suggested that an earlier hymn underlies it, possibly a Christian midrash based on selected verses from Isaiah 9, 52 and 57. If this is so, it is now impossible to recover the original hymn, so thoroughly has it been reworked into a piece of prose. Slightly more promising are attempts to see the christological hymn of Colossians 1.15–20 exerting its influence upon 2.14–18. There are several linguistic and conceptual parallels which support this and the reliance of Ephesians upon Colossians is almost universally agreed. Such an idea does assume that what was essentially a cosmological hymn (Colossians 1.15–20) has been transposed into ecclesiological prose (Ephesians 2.14–18),

but such transposition was certainly not beyond the abilities of our
Writer.

The shedding of Christ's blood is presented as the means by which
those who were *far off* (presumably the Gentile-Christians) *have been
brought near*. Brought near to what? To God? To the Jewish-
Christians? To each other? To the other churches in the Lycus area?
We need not feel compelled to choose between these various
options, for there is a sense in which all are true. Christ's death
affects us in all of the dimensions of our lives. The communion
which it brings about touches our relationship with the Father as
well as our relationship with each other, creating a wholeness not
unlike Jesus' picture of a reintegrated family provided by the
'Parable of the Two Lost Sons and their Loving Father' (to offer an
alternative to the traditional title of 'The Prodigal Son') in Luke
15.11–32.

It is somewhat surprising that Christ's *death*, as such, is never
mentioned in Ephesians, only the theological interpretation of it as
a sacrificial shedding of blood. Neither does the verb 'to crucify'
appear in the epistle. Mention of the cross as the instrument of his
death is found in 2.16, and that is a reworking of Colossians 1.20
which is followed by an explicit reference to Christ's death in 1.22.
The trinity of cross-death-blood, so familiar to our way of thinking
about Christ's crucifixion, has lost one of its members in our letter.

14–16   These verses are crowded, filled with many overlapping
images. Once again we have one wild, unruly sentence in Greek, the
argument of which is at times difficult to follow. The REB attempts
to tame it somewhat by dividing it into three sentences (two contained in verses 14–15 and one in verse 16). Before we move on to
discuss these verses in more detail we would do well to take a step
back and attempt to see the larger picture. The easiest way to do this
is to pay attention to various actions of Christ Jesus which are
described within them.

The series of verbs and participles in these verses suggests
decisive action on the part of Christ. It is quite striking that a
deliberate juxtaposition of tenses is made here, one which may provide the key to unlocking the purpose of the tangled phrases. The
passage begins with an emphatic declaration that (*Christ*) *is himself
our peace*, a statement which has echoes reverberating through the
whole of the sentence in 2.14–16. We are not to lose sight of who is
active here, as the phrases *in his own body of flesh and blood* (verse 14);

in himself (verse 15); and *in (his own?) single body* (verse 16), all serve to illustrate. Following this introductory declaration there are six aorists in the two verses, and each of them provides a separate snapshot of what was accomplished by the death of the Messiah (verse 13). By means of the death on the cross Christ is said to have:

Made (poiēsas) the two one;
Broken down (lusas) the barrier;
Annulled (katargēsas) the law;
Created (ktisē) a single new humanity out of the two;
Reconciled (apokatallaxē) the two into a single body;
Killed (apokteinas) the enmity.

We should not try to impose a rigid sequence upon these actions asking which is the most important, and in which order they were carried out. They are not to be viewed as sequential actions. Rather, they stand together as something of a theological montage, which attempts (however imperfectly) to give expression to the tremendous significance of the death of Christ. By using aorist verbs, participles and constructions in this way the Writer concentrates our attention on the death of Jesus Christ on the cross as the decisive event in the past, the turning point in the history of the new Humanity. At the same time, we must not miss the counterpoint to this essentially backward–looking exercise. There is embedded within the midst of these aorist constructions *one* present tense participle which, like the sword of Alexander the Great cutting through the Gordian knot of grammar in the verses, compels us to look *forward* from the cross to the here and now. This occurs at the end of verse 15 where the REB quite rightly (in my opinion) picks up the overall logic of the argument and renders the crucial present tense participle and its object as *thereby making peace.* We could even bring out the durative force of the participle and translate it *thereby continually making peace.* In effect, this invites us to consider that (from the Writer's perspective and indeed from our own as well) the peace process is ongoing, that it continues even now. We turn now to consider the various phrases in more detail.

Gentiles and Jews, he has made the two one provides notice of what was at times a serious social division in the early church, namely, the bitter division between two groups of believers, those coming from a Jewish background and those who did not. The REB identifies the two factions as *Gentiles and Jews*; the Greek is much less specific, and is perhaps more accurately translated, as it is in verse 18, as 'both'.[41] In any event, we can infer from the larger context that these two categories (Jewish-Christians and Gentile-Christians) were intended. The Writer proclaims the union which Christ forges between the two groups and the REB does not mislead us by its rendering. However, the distinction between the two groups should not be used to support a rigid interpretation of the prepositions 'you' and 'we' in the rest of the letter (see the discussion on Provenance on pp. 39–47 above).

Let us assume that the Writer means to assert that Jewish-Christians and Gentile-Christians are now united. How is union like this achieved? Shelby Foote, the eminent historian of the American Civil War (1860–1865), provides a wonderful illustration which may help us to answer the question. He notes how at the beginning of the conflict, both in the Union States of the north and in the Confederate States of the south, identities were separately conceived. The natural tendency was to align oneself with one side or the other; a person was either a Yankee or a Rebel. However, one of the outcomes of the Civil War was that all the states of the restored Union began to think of themselves as a single nation. An intriguing shift in language took place which reflected this difference of perception. Prior to the war plural verbs were used in connection with 'the United States'; one would say 'the United States *are*'. Following the war, however, singular verbs began to be the norm; one said 'the United States *is*'. In effect, the trauma of the war created a new sense of understanding in which, as Shelby Foote puts it, 'we' (Rebels) and 'you' (Yankees) became transformed into 'us' (Americans).[42] The same sense of new-found unity in Christ is declared here in Ephesians 2.14–16 with reference to Jews and Gentiles. The two sides, hitherto separated by both religion and culture, found that through the trauma of the spiritual war which was fought out on the cross at Calvary, a new union was created in Jesus Christ. There are hints in the undisputed Pauline letters of this perspective of two groups being made into a new one, notably I Corinthians 1.22–23 where Paul declares that '*Jews demand signs, Greeks* (representing the Gentile world) *look for wisdom, but we* (Christians) *proclaim Christ*'; and I Corinthians 10.32 where Jews, Greeks *and the church* are mentioned in a single breath. However the Writer of the epistle to the Ephesians gives this idea greater emphasis and force. To suggest, as Markus Barth does for example, that Gentiles are simply *added* to Jews as the people of God is to misconstrue the central thought of the Writer on this point.[43] We cannot impose the olive-tree/branch imagery from Romans 11.11–24 on the thought of Ephesians 2.14–16 without damaging the thought of the latter text in the process.

Broken down translates a verb which is often used in connection with violent action. This is the only time in the NT where it is used to refer to the destruction of a racial and religious barrier. Such destruction is presented as something already accomplished rather than something yet to be achieved. What is it that is destroyed? Nothing less than *the barrier of enmity which separated them*. The REB here is economical in its use of vocabulary, bringing together two different images in the single term *barrier*. The first of these is the term *to mesotoichon*, meaning 'the middle-wall', and the second is the word *phragmos* meaning 'hedge' or 'fence'. No one is quite certain about how the two architectural terms fitted together in the Writer's mind or what sort of building he was drawing upon in his imaginative use of them. The AV renders them by the well-known phrase 'the middle wall of partition'. Part of the difficulty arises from the fact that *to mesotoichon* occurs here and nowhere else in the NT.

One suggestion that has been made is to take 'the middle-wall' to be a dividing wall between the earthly and the heavenly spheres, a barrier which Christ breached in coming down from his place in the heavens with God. Needless to say, this 'spatial' understanding of the term goes hand in hand with interpretations of the epistle which see its Writer actively engaging with Jewish Gnosticism. On the other hand, many argue for what we might describe as a 'social' understanding of the term and see the wall separating Jews from Gentiles in the temple of Herod at Jerusalem as the source of the image. It is known that a temple balustrade separated the Court of the Gentiles from other sections of the temple complex which were reserved for the use of Jews (Josephus *Antiquities* 15.11.5; *Jewish War* 5.5.2; 6.2.4, and Philo *Embassy to Gaius* 31 all mention it, although they use different terms to describe the structure than those contained in Ephesians 2.14).

By sheer luck, several fragments of this structure in the temple have survived, including a large section found in 1871 by the French archaeologist M. Clermont-Ganneau. This piece was found in the debris of the temple complex in Jerusalem and is now housed in the Archaeological Museum in Istanbul, Turkey. The limestone slab (86 × 36 cm) is inscribed in Greek capital letters and gives a warning to anyone threatening to breach the barrier illegally. It reads: 'No foreigner is to enter within the balustrade and embankment around the temple. Whoever is caught will have himself to blame for his death which follows.'[44] Rather ironically, Acts 21.27–30 records how Paul himself was nearly killed by some who supposed that he had brought the Ephesian Trophimus with him into the temple precinct. As a symbol of division and separation it is hard to imagine a better ancient example than this temple barrier in Jerusalem (for the suggestion that the Berlin Wall is something of a modern equivalent, see below pp. 198–200).

Although it is occasionally suggested, it is unlikely that the tearing of the veil of the temple (mentioned in Mark 15.38/Matthew 27.51 and alluded to in Hebrews 10.20) is what the Writer has in mind here. It does offer an interesting point of speculation, particularly if one is persuaded by the 'spatial' understanding of 'the middle-wall' discussed above. The rent of the temple veil *'from top to bottom'* then becomes a point in favour of the interpretation. Similarly, attempts to see rabbinical traditions about the need to 'build a fence around the law' (*Pirke Aboth* 1.1; *Letter of Aristeas* 139–142) as the basis of the image here, while possible, do not seem to be what the Writer intends.

What this barrier was precisely is not known, but its effects are patently obvious. It is said to produce *enmity*, or perhaps we might translate the word as 'hatred' or 'feud'. Precisely the same term is used again at the end of verse 18 where it is said to have been *killed* by the death of Christ on the cross (Moffatt captures the idea by saying the feud has been dealt a 'death-blow'). We tend to view the cross as the instrument of Christ's death, and so it is. But it is much more besides and the Writer of Ephesians helps us see this. While he chooses not to speak (as Paul himself does) of the cross as the place where the believer also dies, our Writer nevertheless takes the idea in a new direction. He speaks of the cross as the instrument of the death of hostility and hatred among his people. This is the flip-side of Christ's role as the embodiment of peace (verse 14) who is responsible for promoting peace among God's people. True peace-making involves, indeed requires, enmity-killing.

For he annulled the law with its rules and regulations is one of those phrases which spurs on the modern translator's creativity. Thus, Eugene H. Pederson's *The Message* (1993) gives it as 'He repealed the law code that had become so clogged with fine print and footnotes'. It is a provocative theological statement to make and a difficult one to interpret, not least because it seems to fly in the face of Romans 3.31 (not to mention Matthew 5.17). Indeed, he *annulled* may not be strong enough to communicate the Writer's thought here; the Greek word *katargēsas* implies, as we said above, a violent and decisive action. Does it mean that Christ has *abolished* the Mosaic law and all that it represented? Is the dominant chord being struck here one of a *discontinuity* between Christianity and the Judaism which gave it birth? Or, alternatively, could it be that the ceremonial, as opposed to the moral, parts of the Mosaic law are the ones that have been cast aside? Is there a veiled reference to a distinction between the written law (the rules) and oral traditions based upon it (the regulations) contained here? The fact that P[46], one of the oldest and most important texts of the Pauline letters, does not contain the words *and regulations* has been used to advance just such an interpretation. These are some of the ways of trying to make sense of the Pauline teaching with regard to the Mosaic law which has attracted a number of advocates over the years. In this case, we could say that the dominant chord being struck is one of a *continuity* between Christianity and the Judaism out of which it sprang. After all (so the argument would go), we keep what is good and valuable and proper, while jettisoning the rest. We need not throw the baby out with the bath water!

The two groups, Jewish-Christians and Gentile-Christians, are brought together *so as to create out of the two a single new humanity.* This in itself is not all that surprising, but what sets it apart is the fact that it is said to be achieved by Christ *in himself*, a phrase which is somewhat enigmatic here (how does he create a body 'in himself'?). Perhaps the phrase is a pointer to a very similar one in 5.27 which is much easier to understand. There Christ the bridegroom prepares his bride so that he might present her to himself in the union of marriage. In any event, similar 'creation' statements are found in 1.10 and 4.24. We are perhaps not too far adrift if we follow through the implications of the imagery and think of the ethnic groups of Jews and Gentiles as the equivalents of sperm and egg, both of which must be united if the creation of a new human being is to take place. This anthropological image is immediately followed up by a somatic one whose basic thought is the same, *to reconcile the two in a single body.* The complex idea of reconciliation has been widely discussed over the years and the discussion shows no signs of abating. This is as it must be, so central is the idea to much that is distinctive in Christianity. Interpretations vary greatly as to the extent to which the concept of reconciliation was central to Christian theology in the NT period. Clearly it is an idea closely associated with Pauline thought. Astonishingly, *all* of the occurrences of both *katalassein* and the related compound verb *apokatalassein*, as well as the noun *katallagē* are contained in the Pauline letters. The relationship between reconciliation and Christian ministry is clearly set out in II Corinthians 5.18–21, a passage which stresses the initiative of God in the reconciliatory process ('God was in Christ reconciling the world to himself' – verse 21). Meanwhile the connection between peace and reconciliation is brought out powerfully in the other major passage in Paul given over to discussing the theme, namely Romans 5.1–11. Both of these emphases (the divine initiative in reconciliation and the securing of peace through reconciliation) are important to any interpretation of Ephesians 2.16. It is likely that the reference to reconciliation here is dependent upon the similar declarations made in Colossians 1.20–22. There, as here, reconciliation is said to have been achieved *through the cross* (or, as is the case in Colossians 1.22, *by Christ's death in his body of flesh and blood*). One additional feature of the statement in verse 16 is also worth noting; the reconciliation is said to be *to God*. In this sense the circle is completed; God initiates reconciliation, and its goal is a new-found relationship with him.

We may summarize the thought on the idea of reconciliation in the form of a series of questions: As to the question, 'Who needs to be reconciled?', the answer comes back, 'Both Jews and Gentiles!' As to the question, 'Who does the reconciling?', the reply is given, 'Christ himself!' As to the question, 'To whom is the act of reconciliation directed?', the rejoinder provided is 'To God!' As to the question, 'What is the effect of this reconciliation?', the response is given, 'A new humanity is created!' As to the question, 'By what means is it accomplished?', the proclamation is, 'By the cross of Christ!'

17–18   Language of nearness and distance is again employed here, as it was in verse 13. It has frequently been suggested that the debates surrounding Jewish proselytism (i.e. non-Jews who were 'far off' wishing to 'draw near' to God by converting to Judaism) are at root here and that these are responsible for the overall language and imagery of our verses. It is impossible to say whether this is the case or not, although there are some intriguing rabbinic parallels to support the contention. In any event, we can presume that the Gentile-Christians were the ones *who were far off* and the Jewish-Christians were the ones *who were near*. However, what is added to the description here is the proclamation of peace to both groups; the Writer makes his point by creatively using Isaiah 57.19 (together with echoes of 9.5–6). This reiterates the reference to Christ as *the peace* which was given in verse 14, and yet somehow enlarges upon it by suggesting that he (Christ) is also the peace-*maker* between two hitherto-divided groups. This reconciliation is said to be *the good news*, a perfect summation of the message of the gospel. It results in both groups having (joint!) access to God the Father via *the one Spirit*, a thought which appears again in 3.12. Given the temple imagery which is contained in the next paragraph (2.19–23), it seems most probable that the access here described is cultic in derivation. If we accept that the 'middle-wall of partition' mentioned in verse 14 is ultimately based on the physical arrangements of the temple complex in Jerusalem, then we can see the idea of access as part and parcel of the same metaphor. Paul does make a similar statement about access to God in Romans 5.2 and our Writer may be reliant upon that passage here (the fact that Romans 5.1 speaks of the *peace* we have in Christ also suggests such reliance).

The REB misleads us slightly by the way it renders the end of verse 18, concluding as it does with the reference to the Holy Spirit. In fact the final words in the Greek are *to the Father*, which is in keeping with the theocentric sentiments of the Writer elsewhere in the letter. This alteration of phrasing in the REB is probably simply a matter of style, designed to avoid separating the phrase 'to the Father' from 'having access'.

Each succeeding generation must wrestle with similar matters which arise out of the complexities of their own time and situation. The task of the church in every new age and in every modern setting is to make real the truth of union and harmony in Christ the Lord. The church must continually be in the process of seeking out modern equivalents to the Jew/Gentile divide which characterized much of the first century thought-world and tackle them in the name of the risen Lord. This also means that the way in which the message of the NT is presented needs to be continually updated and made relevant. In this sense we can rejoice that new translations and paraphrases of the scriptures continue to appear. One of the more exciting examples I can think of in this regard is the *Cotton Patch Version of the New Testament* (1968) by Clarence Jordan. Jordan sought to provide a translation which spoke into the setting of the Deep South of the United States at a time when civil rights issues were very much at the forefront of the social, political and ecclesiastical agenda.[45]

His translation of Ephesians 2.11–16 is a classic example of bringing a theological truth to bear on a modern issue and serves as a model for making the NT message relevant to a new setting. Understandably, given Jordan's own intended audience, the Jew/Gentile debate is given a fresh twist. The passage, though somewhat long, sparkles with fresh insight.

> So then, always remember that previously you Negroes, who sometimes are even called 'niggers' by thoughtless white church members, were at one time outside the Christian fellowship, denied your rights as fellow believers, and treated as though the the gospel didn't apply to you, hopeless and God-forsaken in the eyes of the world. Now, however, because of Christ's supreme sacrifice, you who were once so segregated are warmly welcomed into the Christian fellowship. He himself is our peace. It was he who integrated us and abolished the segregation patterns which caused so much hostility. He allowed no silly traditions and customs in his fellowship, so that in it he might integrate the two into one new body. In this way he healed the hurt, and by his sacrifice on the cross he joined together both sides into one body for God. In it the hostility no longer exists.

Yet even here the danger is that such a translation has passed its sell-by date, that it is so culturally encapsulated as to become irrelevant. To borrow a useful image from Victor Paul Furnish, we need to take constant care that the message of Christ which we proclaim to the contemporary world is never allowed to become either a 'sacred cow' or a 'white elephant'.[46] The church must ensure that she is neither dismissed as too holy to be questioned nor too old-fashioned to be relevant. This leaves us to face the aweful challenge of making the message of reconciliation meaningful for our day. There are plenty of issues which can serve as entry points in this endeavour: the Anglo-Irish question in the United Kingdom; the continuing tension within South Africa between blacks and whites in a post-apartheid setting; the conflict between Palestinians and Israelis in the Middle East; the struggle between nationalists and neo-communists in the former republics of the USSR; the bitter conflict between Serbs and Croats in the former Yugoslavia; and the open hostility between Tutsi and Hutu tribes in Rwanda and surrounding regions. These are just representative examples of a very real, and very human phenomenon; the list could, and must, go on and on and the church's commitment to addressing such human divisions continues unabated. The mythology of fear which brings about the divisions between peoples can only be overcome by the miracle of grace which brings about harmony between them. To be able to celebrate our differences yet live together in peace, is to be able to consecrate our unity and proclaim Christ as Peace.

Citizenship; God's New Temple
2.19–22

In 2.19–22 we are confronted with what is yet another(!) long and complicated sentence in Greek. Nevertheless, this one is slightly more manageable, largely because it revolves around two overlapping images, citizenship and temple-building. The REB divides this single Greek sentence into four, which coincidentally follows the traditional versification imposed upon the Greek text. Many commentaries discuss 2.11–22 as a single unit and it is easy to detect ways in which what was said in 2.11–18 is further elaborated upon here. The argument proceeds from the vantage-point of what is true for all believers in Christ, whether they happen to come from a Jewish or a non-Jewish (i.e. Gentile) background.

19–20 *Thus* links this thought directly with that contained in the previous section. The phrase *aliens in a foreign land* disguises the fact that two different nouns for people (as opposed to one for people and one for a place) is what the Writer gives. The RSV equivalent of the phrase is 'strangers and sojourners'. The term rendered as 'sojourners' becomes an important self-designation in other Christian writings, including I Peter 2.11 and *The Epistle to Diognetus* 5.5 (a passage which clearly is dependent upon Ephesians 2.11–22). There is within verse 19 a direct connection to 2.12 in that the derisory Greek word *xenoi* is here repeated, although the REB misses this by rendering it here as *aliens* (in 2.11 the same term is given as *strangers*). The all-important term *hagioi* is rendered by the REB as *God's people*. In one sense this is unfortunate since it tends to force one particular meaning on what is a very ambiguous word in Greek. To translate it as *God's* people is to associate it too readily with the kind of language we are used to using when we mean the Jewish covenant people. Thus, when the Writer declares that '(you are) *fellow-citizens with God's people*' it is all too easy to take this to mean 'you (Gentiles) have now been given the same citizenship that they (Jews) already enjoy'. This is to fail to recognize that the argument being put forward here is that both groups, Jewish-Christians and Gentile-Christians alike, have had to take up new citizenship in Christ. In this respect we would do better to translate *hagioi* as 'fellow Christians'. One enters this new citizenship and becomes part of the new corporate humanity not on the basis of being a Gentile, or on the basis of being a Jew, but on the grounds of being a Christian, a member of what Adolf Harnack described in an influential phrase as 'the third race'.[47] Taking up citizenship in the new country means one has to surrender one's old passport.[48] Dual nationality is not allowed in the new nation of Christ. Acceptance as a new citizen implies the abandonment of old ties.

And yet, we may not have grasped the whole meaning of the Writer's words here for we still need to determine the social context of his declaration 'you are fellow-citizens with the saints'. Who does the Writer have in mind when he speaks of 'fellow-citizens'? And who are 'the saints'? As we suggested above (in the discussion on Provenance above on pp. 39–47) it is likely that the Writer's use of two different categories of people is a reflection of the relationship between the 'daughter-church' at Hierapolis and the 'mother-church' in Colossae. On this reading of the epistle the 'fellow-citizens' means the members of the church at Hierapolis and 'the saints' means the members of the church at Colossae. In short, the Writer is stating that the Christians of Hierapolis are on an equal footing with the Christians of Colossae who helped establish their congregation; women and men of both churches, whether they be Jewish-Christians or Gentile-Christians, are now joined together as *members of God's household*.

With the phrase *members of God's household* we are introduced to the first of a number of allusions to what we might describe as a metaphor of a building under construction (the image reappears in each of the succeeding three verses). The whole of the pericope presents the people of God as akin to an ecclesiastical building site (the same basic idea reappears in 4.11–16). Yet the familial nature of this phrase must not be lost – this is a family business, so to speak. The point here is that the believer is a member of God's family, with all of the attendant rights and privileges such membership carries. We may catch something of the intimacy which is involved if we translate the phrase as 'flatmates in God'. The Writer proves his ability to mix his metaphors with the best of us, combining pictures of 'a household of God' with pictures of 'a temple of God' willy-nilly. The idea of a community being described as a heavenly temple is not unknown within the first-century world; there are plenty of texts from the Dead Sea Scrolls of Qumran which do exactly the same thing.

The words *are built* translate an aorist participle, the sense of which could be sharpened up by rendering it as 'having been built'. The point here is that the initial phase of the building project has already been completed. The Writer goes on to confirm this by saying that the building proceeds *on the foundation of the apostles and prophets* as if that foundation has already been laid. Just what does the Writer have in mind by mentioning the *apostles* and *prophets*? The precise grammatical relationship between the genitive *tōn apostolōn kai prophētōn* and the dative phrase *epi tō themeliō* is open to question. Does the Writer intend us to understand that the foundation *consists of* the apostles and prophets, or that it is *based upon* the work of the apostles and prophets? Both possibilities have been argued by competent interpreters and it is difficult to choose between them. How we resolve the matter depends largely on how we conceive I Corinthians 3.9–17 to have influenced the Writer's perspective on the issue. In that passage Paul presents himself as the master architect laying the foundation of Christ upon which others, notably Apollos, built. In contrast, it appears that in Ephesians 2.20 it is that apostolic substructure itself which is now the basis upon which further construction proceeds. This is the way the *New Testament in Basic English* understands the verse, translating the relevant portion as 'resting on the base of the Apostles and prophets, Christ Jesus himself being the chief keystone'. *The apostles and prophets* are mentioned again in 3.5 and 4.11.

Moreover, this *foundation* is further defined in verse 20 in terms of it having *Christ Jesus himself as the corner-stone*, and perhaps that offers some resolution to the debate. In short, the verse is shot through with images of building and architecture, but it is imagery which has as its focus the person of Christ. At the same time, the building metaphor implies that the believers are the various bricks which are used in the construction of this new building. But there is an all-important feature of this image which needs to be recognized. Far from viewing themselves as 'just another brick in the wall' of despair and self-isolation (to allude to a line from Pink Floyd's influential song from 1979 entitled 'The Wall'), they are here encouraged to realize their invaluable place within the erection of a new temple of God.

The 'brick' image here is remarkably similar to what is said in I Peter 2.5 and there may be some connection between the two in the form of the provocative images contained in Psalms 118.22 and Isaiah 28.16. Both OT texts speak of the rejection of a valued stone and both are applied to Jesus of Nazareth as the rejected Messiah of

God whose worth is only later recognized. It is beyond doubt that
this idea of Jesus as a rejected building-stone was widely understood, and readily appreciated, by early Christians as a confirmation
of his messianic status.

The precise architectural meaning of the word *corner-stone* has
been the subject of a long-standing debate among NT scholars. The
question is whether *akrogōniaion*, probably taken from the LXX of
Isaiah 28.16, refers to a foundation stone (at the base of a building)
or to a capstone (set within the central point of an archway at the
entrance to a building). Generally discussion of verse 20 has
concentrated on Isaiah 28.16 and the way in which it is used by the
various NT writers who quote it or allude to it. Even the Qumran
community was influenced by this passage, as 1QS 8.7 indicates,
talking of the community as 'the precious cornerstone' of God's
people. However, the overall temple-building image may in fact be
drawn from Zechariah 4, a suggestion given added weight by the
fact that the historical setting of Zechariah 1–8 is one in which the
people of God had newly returned from exile having been strangers
and aliens in a foreign land (see verse 19 above!). In 4.6–9 the leader
Zerubbabel is instructed by God to rebuild the temple and solidify
the peoples' hopes. In the course of this reconstruction Zerubbabel is
said in 4.7 to bring forth the 'top stone' (RSV). This has been taken by
some to support the suggestion that the *akrogōniaion* was a capstone
as opposed to the foundation stone. However, many OT scholars
have argued that the context of the passage is that of a foundation
ritual, stressing the first part of the declaration made in 4.9, 'The
hands of Zerubbabel have laid the foundation of this house; his
hands shall also complete it' (RSV). The truth of the matter is that the
temple-building imagery of Zechariah 4.6–9 is as ambiguous as that
contained in Ephesians 2.20; it can be employed to support either
interpretation. However, one other detail arising out of Zechariah
4.6–9 and its possible influence upon Ephesians 2.20 is worth
mentioning. It has to do with the messianic understanding of the
akrogōniaion in Ephesians 2.20 which is implied by the REB phrase
Christ Jesus himself as the corner-stone. Interestingly the LXX is much
more messianic than the MT in how it presents Zechariah 4.6,
stressing that it is God himself who brings forth the stone of *inheritance*. If we assume that the Writer of Ephesians was familiar with
the LXX of Zechariah, then we have a nice textual bridge between
the post-exilic vision of rebuilding a physical temple and the
Christian realization of that hope in the spiritual temple which is

built on Christ himself. Moreover, there is much to be said for the suggestion that, at least as far as the building metaphor's significance for the theology of Ephesians is concerned, another way of understanding the *corner-stone* must be considered. Assuming that the foundation stone image is the one which the Writer had in mind here, we could view the image in a slightly different way and concentrate on the stone as the place at which two walls meet and from which they extend outwards. The two walls represent Jewish-Christians and Gentile-Christians within the church, both of whom find their bearing and discover their point of union in Christ.

Whether we choose to focus on the beginning of the temple's construction (Christ as the *foundation stone*), or upon its completion (Christ as the *capstone*) or upon its cornerstone as being the place of union (Christ as the *joining stone*), is largely irrelevant. The fact is that he is all three, not only the temple's foundation and its completion, its beginning and its end, its Alpha and its Omega, but also its centre, its mid-point, its pivot. To analyse the *corner-stone* image with all the vigour of a building inspector, seeking to apply all of the latest governmental regulations and restrictions, is to miss the essential point. To adapt the metaphor slightly, we could say that Christ is the point from which all other points are measured, much in the same way that distances from Rome were plotted from the golden milestone in the Forum and distances from London are technically plotted from a brass plaque in Trafalgar Square which marks the original site of Queen Eleanor's cross, a monument erected by King Edward I as part of his Queen's funeral procession in 1290 (a commemorative monument was later moved to nearby Charing Cross station). Indeed, this geographical fixed-point holds the key to the mystery of London's street numbering system, with house number 1 being assigned to the point in each street nearest to the monument. To return to the architectural image of Ephesians 2.20, we could say that the Writer wishes to make a similar point. *Everything* finds its place in relation to Christ.

Regardless of the architectural image we think the Writer primarily had in mind when he described Christ's role in the building of his church, there can be no doubt that Ephesians 2.20 has captured the imagination of Christians ever since. Nowhere is this more evident than in the hymnody of the church. For example, the classic hymn 'The Church's one foundation' by S. J. Stone (1839–1900) makes explicit reference to the biblical verse, as

well as picking up imagery drawn from Ephesians 5.25–30, in
the opening stanza of the hymn.

> The Church's one foundation
>   is Jesus Christ her Lord;
> she is his new creation
>   by water and the word:
> from heaven he came and sought her
>   to be his holy bride;
> with his own blood he bought her,
>   and for her life he died.[49]

Another good example is 'Christ is made the sure foundation' by
J. M. Neale (1818–1866). What is interesting about this particular
hymn is that it combines the two most common interpretations of
akrogōniaion we have been discussing within its opening stanza. In
effect, this is a good example of someone adopting a composite
approach as he attempts, through his hymn-writing, to give
expression to the truths contained in 2.20. Also worth noting is the
way in which the idea of the believers as living stones of the temple
is brought out in stanza three. The two relevant stanzas are.

> Christ is made the sure foundation,
>   Christ the head and corner-stone,
> chosen of the Lord and precious,
>   binding all the Church in one;
> holy Zion's help for ever,
>   and her confidence alone.

> We as living stones implore you.
>   come among us, Lord, today!
> With your gracious loving kindness
>   hear your children as we pray;
> and the fullness of your blessing
>   in our fellowship display.[50]

21–22   Here the Writer elaborates on his description of the people of
God as a new temple which is in the process of being erected.
Formally the links between the two verses are strong and they can
easily be set out in parallel.

Verse 21	Verse 22
In him (Christ) the whole building is bonded together and grows	In him (Christ) you are also being built with all the others
into a holy temple in the Lord.	into God's dwelling place in the Spirit.

It appears that what the Writer has done is to start with the Pauline image of the people of God as a living body, and then superimpose upon it the idea that they are also a holy temple which is in the process of being constructed. The result is that we get a mixing of metaphors here, particularly in verse 21: we could express this as 'body-building' and 'temple-growing'. This might be likened to the blending of images by an overhead projector which has two transparencies on it, one laid on top of the other. When the machine is turned on and the projection appears on the screen the details of the individual transparencies are very difficult to sort out; they are blended together. So it is with the case of our text here; some of the details of the 'body' metaphor and the 'temple' metaphor have become blended together in a highly creative fashion.

The words *with all the others* in verse 22 are supplied by the REB in an attempt to bring out the force of the prefix *sun* in the main verb of the verse (*sunoikodomeisthe*); this matches its counterpart in verse 21, the compound participle *sunarmologoumenē* which the REB brings out by the word *together* (the idea of growth as a 'bonding together' is used again in 4.16). It is significant that in both instances the present tense is used, stressing that this bonding and building is in process, it is on-going. In this sense Markus Barth is not far wide of the mark when he says that the verse calls us to recognize that the church is, in the words of Martin Luther and others, constantly in need of being reformed: *ecclesia semper reformanda*.[51] In terms of the Writer's own setting, it appears that by using the *sun* compounds here he is suggesting that the church in Hierapolis is being built alongside, and is growing together with, the other churches in the area. Thus, Hierapolis takes her place alongside Laodicea and Colossae as embodying the Christian presence in the Lycus region.

By applying the word *spiritual* adjectivally to *dwelling* the REB has opted for one particular interpretation of the Greek phrase *en pneumati*. This would imply a contrast with a number of modern instances where such temple imagery is applied to a concrete, physical building, such as the Temple of Angor Wat in Thailand, or the Amritsar Temple in the Punjab, India, or the Mormon Temple in Salt Lake City, Utah. The crucial point here is that the Greek word *katoikētērion* designates not so much a place where God is *worshipped* as a place where he *dwells* (the word is perhaps best rendered as 'a dwelling-place'). Hence the focus is more on the people than on the place where they happen to congregate. In this regard the Writer goes one step beyond the declaration of 'in-dwelling' found in Colossians (upon which he is generally reliant). The verb 'to dwell' (*katoikein*) is used twice in Colossians (in 1.19 and 2.9). In both instances it refers to the fullness (*to plērōma*) of God dwelling in the person of Jesus Christ. Here in 2.22, however, the dwelling-place of God is said to be the congregation itself (a statement which is later elaborated upon in the letter in 3.17 where the cognate verb is used). It may well be that we can detect a hint that the Writer is addressing the Jewish-Christians within his audience and graciously acknowledging their former status as members of a Jewish settlement (*katoikoi*) within the larger population of the city of Hierapolis (again, for more on this see the discussion on Provenance above on p. 39).

However, other ways of translating the concluding phrase of 2.22 need to be noted. It is entirely possible to take it to mean 'you are being built into God's dwelling *by the Spirit*'. Such a rendering lends itself to a 'trinitarian' understanding of the passage and was adopted by many of the early Church Fathers. A deliberate contrast between life in the flesh and life in the Spirit may also be in the back of the Writer's mind, particularly if we feel that there is here a conscious harking back to the phrase *en sarki* in 2.11. This allows the whole of 2.11–22 to be seen as a single unit, deliberately structured so as to bring out this juxtaposition of flesh and spirit. Alternatively, it is possible to associate the words *en pneumati* more directly with the 'dwelling-place of God' and take the phrase to be a definition of the means whereby God inhabits his dwelling-place. Thus, we could translate the sense of the phrase as 'the dwelling-place in which God's presence is manifested by his Spirit'.

A Prisoner of Christ Jesus

3.1–7

This pericope, together with the one which follows in 3.8–13, has been the focus of intense debate about Pauline authorship of the letter. Much of the debate concerns the personal details of Paul which are contained in these verses and whether or not the phenomenon of pseudepigraphy can account for them. We need not rehearse these matters here (see the discussion of Authorship above on pp. 21–30). Suffice it to note that pseudepigraphical writings often use the grammatical singular with the pronouns 'I', 'me', and 'mine' and verbs in the first person singular appearing in abundance. This is precisely the case in 3.1–13; the passage contains three first-person singular verbs ('I previously wrote' in verse 3; 'I was made' in verse 7; and 'I ask' in verse 13). In addition, there are six first-person pronouns in the Greek: one emphatic use of 'I' in verse 1, together with three occurrences of 'to me' in verses 3, 7, 8 and two instances of 'my' in verses 4, 13 (although the REB renders *'my* insight' (*tēn senesin mou*) in verse 4 as '*I* understand').

The passage opens with a bold declaration of the Writer's imprisonment for the sake of the Gentiles (3.1), breaks off the thought and then proceeds to expound how he came to be in that position in one long sentence (3.2–7). The REB uses five sentences to translate the passage, including combining verse 2 with verse 1 so as to complete the thought of that initial unfinished sentence. Two key ideas form the substance of the argument in 3.2–7: the Writer stresses that the mystery of God's purposes has been revealed to him and that this revelation unveils tremendous benefits for the Gentiles. There is much which suggests that Colossians 1.23–29 lies behind what is contained here. The list of linguistic parallels between the two passages is impressive, with the overlapping words and ideas appearing in largely the same order in both letters.

1   The Writer here adopts the name of his admired teacher *Paul* and describes himself as *the prisoner of Christ Jesus*. The term *prisoner* is used one other time in the letter, in 4.1, where the Writer describes himself as 'the prisoner in the Lord'; related imagery of imprisonment is also used in 6.20 ('I am an ambassador in chains'). This builds on the tradition that Paul was imprisoned on numerous occasions (II Corinthians 6.5; 11.23; Philippians 1.7, 12–17; Colossians

4.3, 18; Philemon 10, 13) and proudly described himself as 'a prisoner of Christ Jesus' (Philemon 1, 9). Indeed, Clement of Rome, writing in about 96 CE, says that Paul was in chains *seven* times (1 Clement 5.5–7).[52] In Colossians 1.23 (the counterpart to Ephesians 3.1) the word *minister* is used instead of *prisoner* (see below on verse 7). What is striking here is the way in which the Writer describes himself as a prisoner of *Christ Jesus*. Of course it is not Jesus Christ who was responsible for imprisoning Paul (or even the Writer of the letter if he too happened to share his teacher's fate!); we can presume that the Romans were responsible for that, particularly if we see the account of Acts 21.27–28.31 as underlying the tradition of Paul's arrest in Jerusalem and his subsequent imprisonment on the way to Rome. But it is nevertheless true that he remains a prisoner of the Lord in so far as he is there because of his commitment to Christ. To the external eye he is a prisoner of the Roman state, but to the spiritually discerning eye he is a prisoner of the risen Saviour.

Throughout the letter the Writer seems more interested in the *idea* of Paul's imprisonment than in giving us any details about the incarceration itself. Indeed, nothing at all can be learned about his being in prison from the letter, which could be taken to support the view that Paul's imprisonment is a part of the fiction of pseud-epigraphy. In this sense Paul is something of a typological prisoner, not only for the Writer but also for the church to whom the letter is addressed. Nonetheless, imprisonment is something of which the Writer is proud; it functions as a badge of his assumed 'apostle-ship' and authenticates his relationship with the church as their representative. It also serves as a platform from which he can act as an ambassador for Christ (see 6.21–22). One could speculate that the church was suffering similar threats of imprisonment and that the memory of Paul's imprisonment becomes important for them in such an atmosphere. We suggested above (in the discussion on Provenance on pp. 31–48) a scenario for the relationship between the Writer and the church in Hierapolis. On this reading the Writer dons the cloak of pseudonymity in order to emulate the Apostle Paul and address the congregation at Hierapolis in the same way that the church at Colossae was addressed by Paul a generation before. The extensive use of first-person language in 3.1–18 is best viewed in light of this proposed reconstruction of the circumstances surround-ing the writing of the letter.

The REB adds the words *I pray for you* to the verse, no doubt to smooth out the roughness of the passage and to link it to the boast

made in 1.16. In fact there is no verb here at all. By adding the words
there is a danger of overlooking the fact that the thought here is
left unfinished. The Writer begins to say something (we are not
immediately sure what), but having made mention of his imprisonment on behalf of the Gentiles he then wanders off into a rather long-
winded excursus on how he came to be called by God's grace to their
service. We get an indication that this is indeed what has happened in
3.14 where the words with which he here begins 3.1 are repeated,
with this in mind. It is as if he returns to his original thought in 3.14
having enjoyed himself on a long mental stroll. In short, the whole of
3.2–13 is often viewed as something of a rambling digression, an
aside, to which the REB alerts us by ending the verse with a hyphen.
However, appearances can be deceptive and Martin Kitchen has
offered another way of viewing this so-called digression. Far from
seeing it as a diversion along the way, a detour in the Writer's
thought before we get back on the road in 3.14, Kitchen suggests that
3.1–13 be viewed as a conscious device which draws attention to the
person of Paul, and especially his status as an apostle to the
Gentiles'.[53]

The role that the readers have in the Writer's imprisonment is
made clear when he says that he was made a prisoner *for the sake of
you Gentiles*. He is thereby stressing his willingness to undergo
imprisonment on their behalf. Part of what it means for him to be a
minister (verse 7) is to be a *prisoner*; he is a minister to them and is
'imprisoned' because of them in imitation of Paul who was a
prisoner for the sake of the church at Colossae. It may well be that
the Writer is motivated to adopt this position because he is a
member of the church at Colossae who has a special interest for the
'daughter-church' in Hierapolis.

2–4   The Writer builds upon traditions about Paul's life which
would have been known by his readers. Chief among these is the
God's gift of grace to me which serves almost as a definition of Paul's
understanding of his ministry, his calling as 'an apostle to the
Gentiles' (Romans 11.13). A virtually equivalent line appears in
verse 7 which shows just how much the Writer sees his ministry as
being a gift from God. Unfortunately the similitude is lost completely in the REB translation. Note the similarity between the two
lines, as well as the vast difference in the way the REB renders them.

2: *tēn oikonomian **tēs charitos tou theou tēs dotheisēs moi*** (*eis humas*)
   God's gift of grace to me was designed (for your benefit)

7: *(egenēthēn diakonos kata) tēn dōrean* **tēs charitos tou theou tēs dotheisēs moi**
> *(I was made a minister by) God's unmerited gift*

The term *oikonomia* is used here to refer to the Writer's 'steward-ship' (RSV) of the gospel message. The same word is used in 1.10 and in 3.9 to refer to God's plan of action in achieving the salvation of humankind. Clarence Jordan translates the term here in 3.2 as 'my assignment', which conjures up, to my mind at least, those memorable lines from the old *Mission: Impossible* television series: 'Your mission, Mr Phelps, should you decide to accept it . . .'.

The Writer describes how he has been brought to know the *secret purpose* of God, which he says came *by a revelation (kata apokalupsin)*. The term *apokalupsis* as a description of Paul's conversion/call is explicitly given in Galatians 1.12 and may be in the back of the Writer's mind here. The communication of the substance of this revelation to the church was obviously important to our Writer for he declares that he has *already written you a brief account of this*. It is difficult to know how one should take this. Is he alluding to another letter altogether, one which has not survived (such as that to the Laodiceans mentioned in Colossians 4.16)? Or perhaps he has in mind one of the other letters of Paul in which the mystery of the inclusion of the Gentiles within God's purposes is discussed (Romans being the likely candidate given the discussion contained in 9–11). Indeed, to take this last idea one step further and apply E. J. Goodspeed's theory about Ephesians as a covering letter to the Pauline corpus to the matter, could he be meaning all of the Pauline letters as the *brief account* which he has written? Or could it be that he is referring to what he has just written to them in *this letter*, effectively calling attention to what was said in 1.9? Most commentators opt for this last possibility.

By reading it would probably be better rendered by 'as you read it (this letter)'. It assumes that the letter would be given a public reading in the church. *I understand the secret purpose of Christ* sounds rather boastful and should be viewed as part of the device of pseudepigraphical writing. The Writer's understanding of *the secret purpose of Christ* (i.e. that both Jewish-Christians and Gentile-Christians have been united in Christ so as to form a new race) is slightly different, at least in accent, from Paul's understanding of the matter. However, such authorized extrapolation is the genius of pseudepigraphy.

103

5–6 These verses are virtually a restatement of what was said earlier in 2.11–12. *Mankind* wisely avoids the difficulties of 'the sons of men' (RSV). The mystery of God's grace *has been revealed to his holy apostles and prophets*, not to the saints at large as is stated in Colossians 1.26. We may detect yet another hint of the importance of the 'mother-church' in Colossae to the life of the congregation in Hierapolis by the way in which the word 'saints' (*hagioi*) is used in the letter. In our reconstruction of the situation 'saints' is used in 1.1 to refer to the members of the church in Hierapolis, in 1.15, 18; 2.19; 3.8, 18 to refer to the members of the church in Colossae, and in 4.12 and 5.3 to refer to the members of all of the churches in the Lycus region; it seems that there is a logical progression of thought here.

Although the Writer has retained the word *holy* from Colossians he applies it adjectivally to the focus of his concern, the *apostles and prophets*. Thus, it is almost certainly the case that the Writer's emphasis on the apostolic foundations of the church is a development of the thought contained in Colossians. Certainly our Writer is more interested in the *apostles and prophets* than is Paul in Colossians, using the phrase three times (here and in 2.20 and 4.11) as opposed to Colossians which never mentions the *prophets* and only uses *apostle* as a title for Paul in its opening greeting.

How has this revelation come to the apostles and prophets? The answer is given as *by inspiration* (*en pneumati*) a phrase which is perhaps better translated as 'by the Spirit'. There is something of what we might call 'a progression of revelation' here. In 3.3 the secret plan of God was revealed to the Writer; here it is revealed to the apostles and prophets; in 3.9–10 it is revealed to the whole of the created order as represented by *the rulers and authorities in the heavenly realms.*

The essence of the gospel message is that *the Gentiles are joint heirs with the Jews*, a theme which runs like Ariadne's thread through the maze of the letter and enables us to find our way home. The word *joint heirs* is the first of three successive compound nouns which are used to explain the benefits of the promise of Jesus Christ. These are akin to the trio of *sun* verbs which we noted in 2.5–6, and we could render them similarly: *co-heirs, joint members of the body*, and *co-sharers*. The REB adds the words *with the Jews* in an effort to fill out the meaning of *joint heirs*. However, as was the case with the translation of *hagioi* as *God's people* in 2.19, the danger here is that the misleading idea of Gentiles *being added to* the Jews is introduced. Again, the point needs to be stressed that for the Writer of the epistle both Jewish-Christians and Gentile-Christians share the promise on equal footing and both approach new ground, albeit from different directions.

7   The Writer here describes himself as a *minister* of the gospel; the only other occurrence of the term in the letter is in 6.21 where it is used of Tychicus (although there it is inexplicably rendered as *helper*). The same term is used twice in Colossians, with Paul describing himself as having been made both a minister of the gospel (1.23) and of the church (1.25). The Greek word is often translated as 'servant' and is generally acknowledged to be less 'official' than other terms in use within the church, notably 'apostle', 'prophet' and 'bishop'. It is, of course, the word that is used in the Pastoral Epistles (I Timothy 3.8, 12–13; 4.6)[54] in a more formal sense and figured prominently in the setting up of church offices in the church at the beginning of the second century. However, there is little to suggest that such ideas are necessarily in mind here.

The Writer's calling is said to be *by God's unmerited gift*. This recalls not only the declaration made in 2.8 that salvation was a divine gift, but also re-emphasizes grace (the word rendered as *unmerited* here) as the basis for all of God's dealings with us. We get an indication of how important the gift of grace is within the epistle when we note that the word *charis* is used a dozen times (1.2, 6, 7; 2.5, 7, 8; 3.2, 7, 8; 4.7, 29; 6.24). Given the richness of the meaning of the term it is understandable that the REB is not consistent in its rendering of it (what translation could be?). Generally the REB uses either *grace* or *gracious*, but in 3.8 *charis* is translated as *privilege*, while in 4.7 it is translated as *special gift*, and in 4.29 it becomes *blessing*.

The words *so powerfully at work* render a phrase which is very odd in Greek. Literally it might be translated as 'according to the energizing of his power'. The REB adds *in me*, no doubt reasoning that if the Writer is the one who has been made a minister, he is also the one who is being empowered. It seems a pity that this translation results in our losing clear-cut mention of the one who is doing the empowering, namely God himself. The final word in the Greek makes this more explicit, stressing that it is power 'of (or from) Him'.

God's Hidden Purpose for the Gentiles
3.8–13

This section continues the thought begun in 3.2–7. It falls into two parts, consisting of two sentences in Greek, which the REB breaks into four. In 3.8–12 the Writer elaborates on the calling he has received to continue the Apostle's work in proclaiming the gospel to the Gentiles and explains again the nature of God's secret plan for them. Many of the ideas mentioned in 3.1–7 find fresh expression here and the theme of Gentile-Christian participation in the church predominates. In the concluding sentence of 3.13 he harks back to the statement which initiated the long excursus of 3.2–12, picking up the thread of his thought once again.

8 *To me, who am less than the least of all God's people* shows considerable rhetorical flourish and grates on the ears of those who appreciate that the declaration conceals a deliberate violation of Greek grammar. It concerns the Greek word *elachistoteros*, technically a superlative adjective to which has been added a comparative ending. E. K. Simpson likens the idea to Shakespeare's 'the most unkindest cut of all'.[55] We might capture the sense of the word by rendering it as 'the lowest of the low', or 'less than the least' (Moffatt, Weymouth, Wuest), 'the least likely of all the Christians' (Jordan), or 'the most despicablest of all'. I once heard a preacher proclaim, 'Paul was so snake-down low that he had to look up to see the bottom', which just about captures the gist of the matter. The point here is that grammatical rules are broken for rhetorical effect. It is probable that I Corinthians 15.9 lies behind the statement, although there it is the straightforward superlative that is used and only the apostles that Paul compares himself with (as opposed to the Writer's comparison with the whole of God's people, 'the saints'). As suggested above in connection with our discussion of the Provenance of the letter (p. 48), it may be that the declaration in 3.8 is both an indication of the Writer's sense of unworthiness in following in the tradition of Paul, as well as a hint of the relationship between the church in Hierapolis and the 'mother-church' in Colossae the membership of which the Writer describes as 'the saints'. Occasionally it is suggested that both I Corinthians 15.9 and 3.8 contain a deliberate play on words

focussing on the Latin name of Paul (*paulus* meaning 'little' or 'small').

The privilege is a translation of the key word *charis* and, as we noted in connection with our comment on verse 3.7 above, demonstrates the variety of meanings that the word can bear.

A second example of language being used to communicate superlatives occurs when the Writer alludes to the *unfathomable riches of Christ*. Once again the point is that Christ offers us more than we could ever reasonably hope or expect to be true; his bounty exceeds our wildest dreams. We will never be able to 'break the bank' of God's grace in Christ.

9–11   In these verses we find many of the key phrases and ideas so important to the thought of the letter: *secret or hidden purpose, the church, rulers and authorities,* and *in the heavenly realms,* are all mentioned. They are all mixed together in the rush of thought like flecks of precious ores carried along by a fast-flowing mountain stream. Now that we can examine the letter with hindsight, now that these deposits have settled, as it were, we can better appreciate the richness that is contained here. This does not mean, however, that we can follow the precise progression of thought here any more easily. The Writer is again giving expression to his guiding theme, namely that God's purposes are no longer hidden, that they have now been revealed, and that they have been embodied in Jesus Christ who has created and is creating a new Humanity as part of his cosmic purposes (the link to 1.9–10 should not be missed). Two items of special note have been added to this particular restatement of the Writer's main theme.

The first concerns the revelation of *the wisdom of God in its infinite variety. Wisdom* was mentioned earlier in 1.8 in connection with human insight which comes to us through the grace of God. It was also mentioned in 1.17 where it is described as a spiritual gift and is linked with vision or perception. Here, however, we have *the wisdom of God* mentioned (the only time in the letter that it is). The phrase *in its infinite variety* translates a single word in Greek (*polupoikilos*) which is used only here in the whole of the NT. It is a splendidly evocative word to describe God's wisdom and something of its flavour can be seen in the various ways translators have chosen to express it: 'the manifold wisdom of God' (RSV); 'the wisdom of God in all its varied forms' (NEB); 'comprehensive wisdom of God' (JB); 'his (God's) wisdom in all its varied forms' (GNB); 'the complex wisdom of God' (Phillips); 'the innumerable aspects of God's wisdom' (Weymouth); 'the full sweep of divine wisdom' (Moffatt); 'the many-splendoured wisdom of God' (Bruce); 'the extraordinary plan of God' (Petersen); and 'God's richly colored wisdom' (Jordan). The word *polupoikilos* has at is heart the idea of iridescence and hence a translation like 'multi-coloured' or 'variously shaded' is appropriate, in much the same way that Desmond Tutu describes the various tribes and groups that make up the nation of South Africa collectively as 'the *rainbow* people of God'.

The second point worth noting here is the astonishing declaration that *the church* is said to be the agent of transmission of God's wisdom. Her task is to make God's plan known to *the rulers and authorities in the heavenly realms,* a task which later in 6.11 is described as spiritual warfare. The little word *now* is significant for it stands in contrast to the hiding of God's plans which happened 'then', or as the Writer puts it, these plans *lay concealed for long ages.* The point is that a contrast between 'then' and 'now', between 'hidden' and 'revealed', underlies the whole of the passage. Yet this is seen to be part of the very intention of God who is described as the *Creator of the universe,* the only time that God's role in the initial creation is explicitly mentioned in the letter; language of 'creation' and 'making new' is generally reserved for what is being accomplished *now* (i.e. the new creation in Christ Jesus).

The word *church* was used once earlier (in 1.22), but that was primarily a definition about *who she is* – the body of Christ; this is a declaration about *what she does* as the body of Christ. Perhaps such a 'mission statement' can only be made once it is clear how the church was brought into being, which the Writer has done by detailing Christ's actions on the cross (2.11–18). Precisely how the church is to accomplish her task, and what exactly it is about the wisdom of God that she is to make known are never spelled out in detail within the letter. Neither is it wholly clear how the church on earth can address something as ethereal as *the rulers and authorities in the heavenly realms.* What is certain is that the church is not to proclaim herself for she is not the subject of verse 10 – the wisdom of God is. The church merely serves as an illustration for, and indeed, an embodiment of, divine wisdom. At the same time the primacy of the church within the thought of the letter cannot be denied. As Rudolf Schnackenburg, commenting on this verse, notes.

the Church herself becomes the Mystery of Salvation, and this

ecclesiological outlook is what is special and unique in Ephesians,
. . . Now the Church comes to the forefront as God's great concept,
the divine instrument of salvation through which the Mystery of
Christ becomes a historical reality.[56]

In so far as she exhibits her very nature as a new Humanity, she
makes known the wisdom of God and the mystery of Christ. In that
sense the difference between *who she is* and *what she does* are not as
great as we might think. In just the same way that it is in one sense
misleading for a person to say that he or she has a body but more
correct to say that she or he *is* a body, so too is it proper to say that
the church does not have a mission; she *is* mission.

For more on *the rulers and authorities in the heavenly realms* see the
discussion on 6.10–20 below.

12   It is in Christ that we are said to have *freedom of access to God*. A
similar statement about freedom is found in 6.19 where the
Writer asks his reader to pray that he might be able to proclaim
the gospel *boldly and freely*. The REB here adds the words *to God*
which do not appear in the Greek, although they are perhaps
understandable given the earlier mention of access to the Father in
2.18. The phrase *with the confidence born of trust in him* is potentially
misleading and loses the ambiguity contained in the Greek. Literally
it means 'through the faith of him' or even 'through his faith'. If we
accept the last option, as many commentators do, then the point is
that it is by means of the faith of Jesus Christ himself that true
confidence comes. In this sense *his* faith can be said not only to serve
as a model for *our* faith, but the very means of its realization. It is not
so much *our faith in him* as *his faith in us* that produces confidence
before God.

I beg you could just as easily be translated as 'I pray' or 'I ask' and
recalls 3.1. It supplies the missing verb to the unfinished thought
contained there. However, to whom is this prayer directed? The REB
supplies *you* but it is equally possible that God is the object and that
the Writer is asking God that the readers not lose heart, or even that
he himself might not lose heart and become discouraged. On balance
the REB translation makes the most sense given the fact that the rest
of the sentence clearly has the readers foremost in mind with stress
being made to 'sufferings *for you*' and '*your glory*'.

The Writer mentions his *sufferings for you*, recalling the statement
made in 3.1 that he was 'in prison' on behalf of them (his pre-

dominantly Gentile-Christian readership). This echoes an important idea contained in II Corinthians 4.7–12 where Paul declares that through the various trials and tribulations of his life he is actually manifesting the sufferings of Christ. Indeed, what that entails in terms of Paul's *physical* suffering is made even more explicit in II Corinthians 12.7–10 and Galatians 6.17. Even more striking is the bold and paradoxical statement in Colossians 1.24 where Paul declares that his 'sufferings on their behalf' actually complete the sufferings of Christ. It is likely that 3.13 reflects the claim made in Colossians 1.24, although the staggering idea of filling up something lacking in Christ's passion is not carried through here (although see the discussion on 1.22–23 for an equivalent idea). In any event, the readers are encouraged here by the Writer to view *his* sufferings as *their* glory.

Throughout this passage the Writer is astonished that he has been given the privilege of participating in the proclamation of God's purposes as revealed in Christ. For him the message, rather than the messenger, is what is important. William Barclay, in his discussion of this passage, relates a story which helps bring this out.

> Toscanini was one of the greatest orchestral conductors in the world. Once when he was talking to an orchestra when he was preparing to play one of Beethoven's symphonies with them he said: 'Gentlemen, I am nothing; you are nothing; Beethoven is everything.' He knew well that his duty was not to draw attention to himself or to his orchestra but to obliterate himself and his orchestra and let Beethoven flow through.[57]

There is undoubtedly a truth in this, but perhaps we get a little closer to the thought of the Writer of the letter here if we adapt the image and push the point one step further. The focus should not even be on Beethoven but on his music, or even better, on the *Source* of the inspiration for the music. As Beethoven himself once wrote to his publisher about his music.

> What is all this compared with the great Tonemaster above! above! above! and righteously the Most High, whereas here below all is mockery, – dwarfs, – and yet Most High![58]

A Prayer for Further Understanding
3.14–19

In terms of the overall structure of the letter this short paragraph functions as the complement to 3.1, thus completing the opening greetings and prayers. Here it seems, the Writer finally gets around to finishing the thought that was begun in that verse. It contains an intercessory prayer offered to God by the Writer on behalf of the readers. The prayer can be divided into two parts: an introduction (verses 14–16) followed by three major petitions (verses 16–19). The paragraph is one continuous sentence in Greek which the REB breaks into three. The influence of Colossians 2.2–9 is evident within the passage and at least a half a dozen or so linguistic and conceptual borrowings from it can be identified.

14–15 *With this in mind* repeats what was said in 3.1 and confirms this paragraph as the conclusion of the thought started there. *I kneel in prayer* is probably better rendered as 'I fall to my knees', but since such prostration is clearly with a view to prayer the REB rendering is understandable. It matches the interjection of *I pray* by the REB in 1.17, 18; 3.1 which we noted above. Praying on one's knees is somewhat unusual given what we know of other examples of Jewish practice in which standing was the norm (as in the parable of the Pharisee and the tax collector recorded in Luke 18.11–13). Nevertheless, there are a number of passages from the OT which do describe prayer conducted in this way, and the mention of 'every knee shall bow' in Philippians 2.10 confirms the image as one readily connected with homage to Christ.

There is a word play in Greek between the words *Father* (*patera*) and *family* (*patria*) which is difficult to reproduce in English. Essentially the idea is that the family derives its being from the father of the household, and in this sense the phrase *from whom every family in heaven and on earth takes its name* proclaims God as the Father of all of the families of the world. The extent of God's paternity is emphasized by the use of *heaven* and *earth*, which may be a coded way of referring to the various churches of the Lycus valley which was instantly recognizable to the people of the locality but is rather lost on us today. On this reading the inhabitants of Hierapolis live in the hills above ('in the heaven') and inhabitants of

Laodicea and Colossae reside 'below' in the valley (see the discussion on Provenance above on p. 36 for more on this).

16–19   John R. W. Stott likens the substance of the Writer's prayer contained in these verses to a prayer-staircase of four steps 'by which he climbs higher and higher in his aspiration for his readers'.[59] He identifies the four steps with key ideas within the prayer, namely 'strength', 'love', 'knowledge' and 'fullness'. While Stott's analysis will not quite stand up to the scrutiny of a formal analysis of the passage, he has rightly fastened on the key ideas contained within it. There are in fact only three petitions within these verses, each of which is introduced by the Greek word *hina* (usually translated as 'in order that'). The REB attempts to convey the force of this by a four-fold use of *may*: *that he may grant*. . . (verse 16); *may dwell*. . . (verse 17); *may you*. . . (verse 18); and *so may you* . . .' (verse 19). The basic structure of the Greek, which is quite untidy, can be set out thus:

> *in order that:*
> (God) may grant you inward strength and power through his Spirit that through faith Christ may dwell in your hearts in love.
> *in order that:*
> you may be strong to grasp (the dimensions) of Christ's love and to know it, though it is beyond knowledge.
> *in order that:*
> you may be filled with the very fullness of God.

Each of the three petitions echoes statements made earlier in the letter, notably within the prayer of thanksgiving in 1.15–24. Thus, in verse 16 the phrase *the treasures of his glory* recalls the idea of a *rich and glorious . . . share* in 1.18 (the Greek phrasing of the two verses being closer than the REB suggests). Likewise, the idea of one receiving *inward strength and power through his Spirit* is similar to the prayer for *spiritual gifts of wisdom and insight* found in 1.17. Such language of spiritual strengthening and empowering is quite wide-spread in the ancient world. There are many parallels to this kind of expression contained in the writings from the Qumran community. We can safely assume it was an idea common to the Writer's time and would have been readily understood by his readers.

Nevertheless there are one or two special features of this prayer which are worthy of brief note. One of the most interesting is in verse 16 where the REB renders the Greek phrase *eis ton eso anthrōpon* with the single word *inward*. The RSV translation of this is a bit more literal, 'in the inner man'. Although this is an unusual expression in the Pauline writings (but see Romans 7.22 and II Corinthians 4.6), it matches up with the frequent use of anthropological language within our epistle.

The inner dimension of life is also the focus of the succeeding clause where the Writer's prayer is that *Christ may dwell in your hearts in love*. This is reminiscent of the remarkable statement made in Galatians 2.20, although here the image is of 'Christ living in the heart'. This particular expression has passed into the coinage of common pietism, despite the fact that it is really only here in the whole of the NT that the actual phrase occurs. Nevertheless, it has, in some circles, become one of the most prevalent ways in which people define their conversion experience: one regularly hears 'I accepted Jesus into my heart' used in this way. Songs using the idea of Christ 'dwelling (or living) in our hearts' are often sung in revival meetings or old-time gospel halls around the country. Sadly, all too frequently the corporate dimension of the prayer (the *your* in 3.17 is plural!) can be lost as the indwelling becomes a matter of personal, privatized faith. A typical example that springs to mind is Alfred H. Ackley's 'He Lives!' (1933), which has as its first verse and chorus.

> I serve a risen Saviour, He's in the world today;
>> I know that He is living, whatever men may say.
> I see His hand of mercy, I hear His voice of cheer;
>> And just the time I need Him, He's always near.
> He lives, He lives, Christ Jesus lives today!
>> *He walks with me and talks with me along life's narrow way.*
> *He lives, He lives, salvation to impart!*
> *You ask me how I know He lives? He lives within my heart.*[60]

To return to our epistle, it seems that the difference between the 'strengthening of the Spirit' and the presence of 'Christ in our hearts' is a matter of phrasing rather than experience. Both testify to the believers' new found life in Christ.

There may be a subtle play on words being made here by the Writer's use of *dwell* (*katoikēsai*), the only time that the verb occurs in the letter (although the cognate noun 'dwelling-place' is used in 2.22). It is related to the word *paroikoi* used in 2.19 which we noted above carries the sense of 'a resident-alien' or 'stranger'. The point is that *dwell* implies a sense of permanence, a settling down in which the transient life of a wanderer is abandoned. The prayer is that the Spirit of God will take up permanent residence within the life of the congregation. As noted above in the discussion of 2.22, the idea of God's *dwelling-place* may be a deliberate acknowledgment by the Writer of the special status that the Jewish-Christian members of the congregation held within the life of the city of Hierapolis (see the discussion of this in connection with the Provenance of the letter on p. 39 above).

The mixed metaphor *deep roots and firm foundations* in verse 17 draws upon the worlds of agriculture and construction and brings to mind not only OT associations about the cedars of Lebanon, but also the NT parable of Jesus about building wisely upon a rock (Matthew. 7.24–27/Luke. 6.47–49). The two participles (*errizōmenoi* and *tethemeliōmenoi*) are probably taken over from Colossians 2.7 and 1.23 respectively, although Paul does use a similar mixed metaphor in I Corinthians 3.9. There is also a linguistic link between *firm foundations* and the *foundation of the apostles and prophets* mentioned in 2.20 (the two words rendered as *foundation(s)* share a common root). We have already had occasion to mention debate surrounding the word *hagioi* in verse 18 which the REB translates as *God's people* (see the remarks on 1.1).

The phrase in the passage which has attracted the lion's share of attention is *the breadth and length and height and depth of Christ's love*. This is a powerful phrase, all-embracing in its scope and reminiscent of Paul's breath-taking declaration of Romans 8.37–39. All the geometric dimensions of the physical universe are called into court to testify to the vastness of the love of Christ. In the stirring translation of Peterson, the verse proclaims:

> The extravagant dimensions of Christ's love. Reach out and experience the breadth! Test its length! Plumb the depths! Rise to the heights!

The major interpretative issue arising out of the phrase concerns the religious background of such thought, particularly when the Writer prays for his readers *to know it, though it is beyond knowledge*. As one might expect, those wishing to argue a Gnostic setting for the epistle have got a lot of mileage out of 3.18–19. There is no agreed opinion as to the question of the background, however. It can best be seen simply as a rhetorical flourish designed to extol the endlessness of Christ's love in the same way that Job 11.7–9 extols the vastness of the wisdom of God.

11.7   Can you fathom the mystery of God,
             Or attain to the limits of the Almighty?
11.8   They are higher than the heavens. What can you do?
             They are deeper than Sheol. What can you know?
11.9   In extent they are longer than the earth
             and broader than the ocean.

Perhaps similar expressions of such cosmic comprehensiveness for us today would be 'the four corners of the globe', or 'the four points of a compass', or 'the four winds of the earth'.

So may you be filled with the very fullness of God recalls what was said in 1.24 where God (or Christ?) is said to be *filling the universe in all its parts*. Here again the note of comprehensiveness is sounded; there is nothing which stands outside God's power or control and the whole of the universe will be brought to its divinely-intended purpose. Who does the filling, God or Christ? The verse does not say, and as we noted above in connection with 1.24 it is foolhardy to be dogmatic on the matter (also see 4.10 on this matter).

In this prayer of 3.14–19 the idea of the totality of life being brought under the sway of Christ's love is a focal point. The Iona Community's song entitled 'Christ Be Beside Me', based on a traditional Celtic prayer, gives us another way of approaching this truth:[61]

1. Christ be beside me,
      Christ be before me,
      Christ be behind me,
          King of my heart.
      Christ be within me,
      Christ be below me,
      Christ be above me,
          never to part.

2. Christ on my right hand,
      Christ on my left hand,
      Christ all around me,
          Shield in my strife.
      Christ in my sleeping,
      Christ in my sitting,
      Christ in my rising,
          Light of my life.

A (Detachable) Doxology

3.20–21

The doxology here follows on from and completes the intercessory prayer which was begun in 3.1, interrupted by the parenthetical pericope of 3.2–12, and then was picked up again in 3.14–19. It is one sentence in Greek, broken up into two clauses to which the two verses correspond. The REB renders it as a single sentence punctuated by the inclusion of the exclamation 'Amen' at the end. The doxology here may have been modelled on the one found in Romans 16.25–27; there are notable similarities of style and phrasing between the two passages.

20–21 Although God is not mentioned in these verses by name it is clear that he is the focus and that the doxology is offered to him. It is God *who is able . . . to do* and it is God to whom *glory* is ascribed (the verb *be* is supplied by the REB). By *the power which is at work among us* the Writer probably has in mind the abiding presence of the Holy Spirit in the three churches of the Lycus region (see 1.17 and 3.16). Unfortunately, we lose in English translations the linguistic connection between the words *able* and *power* (they share a common root). In 1.19–20 this divine *power* was said not only to be active in the resurrection of Jesus from the dead and in his exaltation to the right hand of God, but also available to those who believe. The nature of the doxology as a prayer offered by the whole church is hinted at in the words *we can ask or conceive*. Both of these Greek verbs are in the plural and suggest that the Writer includes the church at Hierapolis with the churches in Colossae and Laodicea and thereby seeks to give a wider vision of the church universal. Similarly, the use of *Amen* at the conclusion of the doxology suggests the liturgical response of the church in Hierapolis as she recognized her inclusion within the body of Christ worldwide. Whatever it is that we might corporately ask or conceive, the Writer asserts that God is able to do *immeasurably more*. This is the REB's attempt to make sense out of a very rare adverb which is nearly impossible to translate into English without using a whole phrase.

The inclusion of *from generation to generation* is unusual in the Pauline letters, but it is not unknown in other Jewish and Christian doxologies of the period. Literally the phrase means 'throughout all generations'. The expression *for evermore* is also slightly unusual.

Literally it might be more accurately rendered as 'for the age of the ages'. The Writer here brings together both time and eternity and views them from the perspective of the glory of God. Once again the cosmic scale of God's purposes as set out in 1.9–10 is emphasized. Also indicative of the Writer's own interests and concerns is the mention of *in the church* within the doxology. Since he sees the local church as the means whereby Christ's rule in the cosmos is accomplished (see 1.23 and 3.10), then it is understandable that she be the focus of special mention within the doxology. As David E. Garland puts it.

> The church is not to be a curator of the theological wisdom of the ages, nor simply a cheerleader praising God for his splendid salvation scheme; it is to be an essential agent in the accomplishment of God's design.[62]

However, there can be no ascription of praise to God for glory in the church without acknowledgment that her position is dependent on the Lord and the Writer makes this point by following *in the church* by *and in Christ Jesus*.

The words of 3.20–21 have become an exclamation of Christian praise the world over, and they are frequently detached from the surrounding context of the prayer of 3.14–19 and printed separately in worship books and service manuals in a wide number of denominations, sometimes without even acknowledgment of their source. Like the words of 'The Grace' of II Corinthians 13.13, we can easily end up saying these words of 'The Doxology' as a matter of routine and habit, forgetting that they serve a particular purpose in the structure and thought of the letter and are intended move a local congregation (in Hierapolis) to consider afresh her place within the larger purposes of God.

117

Living in Unity with One Another
4.1–6

This pericope begins the second half of the letter. With the introductory greetings and prayers now complete (chapters 1–3) the
Writer can turn his attention to the practical details of Christian living (chapters 4–6). We should not think of the two halves of the letter
as independent units, however. The separation of the first three
chapters from the last three, so symbolically represented by the two-
volume commentary by Markus Barth, is potentially misleading, for
the halves of the epistle are by no means water-tight. There are many
links between what was said in the first three chapters and how
those things work themselves out in practice. In this regard R.P.
Martin usefully likens 4.1–16 to the hinge of a diptych, holding
together the two panels of the artist's work.[63]

In 4.1–6 the Writer issues a strong exhortation to his readers that
they might fulfil their calling, based on the unity that permeates their
faith; in 4.7–16 this will be balanced by an emphasis on the diversity
that characterizes their congregational life together. In short, unity
and diversity are the governing themes for 4.1–6 and 4.7–16
respectively.

There are a number of terms and ideas in the passage which seem
to be borrowed from Colossians, notably the use of Colossians
3.12–15 that is found in 4.2–4. The passage is again a single sentence
in Greek which is effectively broken in two parts by means of a semi-
colon which appears at the end of verse 3. The REB divides the
passage into four sentences, but does manage to keep the second half
as a unit by rendering verses 4–6 as a single sentence punctuated by
two semi-colons.

1   The Writer dons the robe of his teacher once again, here describing himself as *a prisoner for the Lord's sake* and alluding to the earlier
reference in 3.1 to Paul being *the prisoner of Christ Jesus*. A third
reference to the imprisonment will follow in 6.20.

The sentence begins with an exhortation *I implore you*, the object of
which is contained at the end of the verse (having been interrupted
by the personal remarks about imprisonment): *live up to your calling*.
A similar exhortation is given in 4.17 which uses the same key word
'to live' or 'to walk' (*peripatein*) in the sense of ethical conduct or
lifestyle (we discussed this above in connection with 2.10). This

admonition to 'live' a worthy life forms the basis upon which the rest
of the moral teaching in chapters 4–6 is based and is repeated in 4.1,
17; 5.2, 8, 15. The use of an exhortation to introduce an extended
section of advice-giving like this is common within Paul's letters.
Throughout the ethical exhortation we may detect the pastoral heart
of one who is concerned about the life of a congregation for which he
has a particular affinity. Our reconstruction of the historical setting
which lies behind this concern is that the Writer is a member of
the 'mother-church' in Colossae which planted the congregation in
Hierapolis. We may even speculate that the Writer has been given
special responsibilities by the church in Colossae to oversee the
project, perhaps because of his close connection with the Pauline
school and the mission of Epaphras a generation before.

2–3 Three qualities are singled out in the beginning of verse 2 as
necessary for the readers to demonstrate the reality of their calling.
In Greek they are all abstract nouns but the REB uses an expression
in keeping with the nature of the passage as an exhortation: *be
humble always and gentle, and patient too.* All three of these qualities
(*humility, gentleness* and *patience*, to use their noun forms) are mentioned at other places in the Pauline letters: Jesus Christ is said to
have exhibited *humility* in Philippians 2.6 (part of the great christological hymn of 2.6–11); he is described by Paul in II Corinthians 10.1
as exhibiting *gentleness* (as well as *meekness*); and *patience* is described
(together with *meekness*) as one of the qualities of the fruit of the
Spirit in Galatians 5.22–23. Why have these particular qualities been
identified? Part of the reason seems to be the influence of Colossians
3.12 which lists them, together with *compassion* and *kindness*, as
things with which the Christians are to clothe themselves (an
altogether different image of clothing will be used in 6.10–20!). An
example of what *patience* means in practice is given in the next
phrase.

Putting up with one another's failings in the spirit of love is something
of a paraphrase of the Greek with several extra words added by the
REB in an attempt to interpret the meaning of the original. A more
literal rendering might be 'hold one another in love'. The difficulty is
in trying to give a meaningful translation of the participle within the
clause, 'putting up with' (*anechomenoi*). The REB's attempt sounds
rather negative, as if an atmosphere of resignation pervades.
Interestingly the exact same phrase (*anechomenoi allēlōn*) is used in
Colossians 3.13 which the REB renders as *be tolerant with one another.*

This is slightly better in that it at least avoids the harsh and judg-mental word *failings*. It is significant that the Writer here adds the words 'in love' as if to suggest that this is the only way such an attitude can ever be made real.

Spare no effort to make fast is a powerful expression in the Greek and conveys the idea of action that lets nothing get in the way. It assumes that the unity so dearly won in Christ is something that has to be maintained or kept alive, and hence *made fast*. The unity which the Spirit has created can be compromised or curtailed, or even destroyed by our actions, so it must be guarded at all costs. The phrase *with bonds of peace* cleverly alludes to the imprisonment motif (the words for *bond* and *prisoner* being linguistically related). However, the Greek word rendered as *bonds* is much more vivid than the REB translation suggests and needs to be sharpened up in two ways in order for us to appreciate the full impact of what is being said here. The first thing to note is that the noun is singular; *with the bond* would be more accurate. The second thing to note is that it is another one of those *sun* compound words of which, as we noted in connection with 2.5–6 and 3.6, the Writer is so fond; with the *co-bond* or *joint-bond* would capture the idea better. Once this is appreciated we can perhaps understand why the REB transforms the singular idea into the plural; it is the 'mutual bond', the 'common bond' of peace binding one person or group to the other which is in mind here and that readily becomes, in sense at least, a plural expression. In any case, it is likely that the use of 'mutual bond' (*sundesmos*) comes from Colossians 3.14 where love is said to be, in the words of the RSV, that 'which binds everything together in perfect harmony' (*ho estin sundesmos tēs teleiotētos*). The REB gives this as 'to bind everything together and complete the whole'.

It is not difficult to see that 2.14–16 lies behind the reference to *peace* here. That passage asserted that peace was bought by the death of Christ and consisted of the two (Jews and Gentiles) being made one, and it is this which is referred to when the Writer mentions *the unity which the Spirit gives*. In fact there is no verb attached to *Spirit* here; the REB adds *gives*. The RSV uses the more literal 'in the unity of the Spirit'. *Unity* is a term found only here and in 4.13 in the whole of the NT and there is something to be said for taking both occur-rences to be genitives of apposition (see below on 4.13).

Does the constant call to unity here betray a fragile peace within the church to whom the letter is addressed? Are the Jewish-Christian and Gentile-Christian components in open conflict with one another? How we answer this depends in part on what we take to be the historical circumstances and setting in which the letter was composed. It is difficult to give a precise answer to this question, although our reconstruction suggests that the tension between 'we' language and 'you' language within the epistle has more to do with the relationship between the 'mother-church' in Colossians and the 'daughter-church' in Hierapolis than it does with Jewish-Christian and Gentile-Christian tensions within his intended audience.

In any event, it is perhaps worth stressing that nowhere does the Writer here try to persuade his readers to *create* unity or to make peace. Both of these have already been achieved through Christ's death, resurrection and exaltation to the heavenlies. What he does strenuously encourage his readers to do, however, is to live together in light of those things which have already taken place. Little wonder then that the letter has proved to be a most important document over the years in providing a scriptural basis for those engaged in healing divisions among Christian denominations and promoting reconciliation between groups who still harbour bitter enmity or detached malice against one another.

4–6 Most commentators agree that these verses contain some traditional credal statements within them, although there is a wide range of opinion as to what those traditions might have been and to what extent they are incorporated within the passage. The reference to *baptism* in verse 5 is frequently pointed to as providing the most likely liturgical setting for such credal material as there might be concealed here. In this sense, the placement of *one faith*, sandwiched between *one Lord* and *one baptism*, becomes significant in that it is taken to mean the common act of faith in Jesus Christ the Lord which has been (or is being?) demonstrated in baptism. Indeed, in light of this explicit mention of *baptism*, the only one contained in the letter, it has even been suggested that the letter was designed to be read at a Christian baptismal service. Baptism is seen as a corporate act by means of which those who are baptised witness in faith to the claim of the Lord Jesus Christ upon their lives. They accept thereby his Lordship over their lives and take his name upon themselves (see Matthew 28.19; Acts 2.38; 8.16; 10.48; 19.5; 22.16; I Corinthians 1.11–16 and 6.11), pledging to live as one of his subjects, to 'sail under his banner', so to speak.

There is is not found in the Greek and is supplied by the REB in order to set up the thought that follows. It is helpful to view verses

4–6 as a unit if for no other reason than it forces us to see how the theme of unity pervades the passage as a whole. Seven different things are described as *one*: *body, Spirit, hope, Lord, faith, baptism,* and *God*.[64] We should probably not attempt to impose a sequence upon them, or try and detect a theological progression lying behind the Writer's use of the terms. Trinitarian ideas can be found in the verses but only by the dubious virtue of an anachronistic reading of them. However, the phrase *one hope held out in God's call to you* is slightly unusual in that it is the only one of the seven components which has an expansion attached to it (notwithstanding the inclusion of *Father of all, who is over all and through all and in all* which follows the reference to *one God* and thereby concludes the sentence in a typical liturgical fashion not unlike that which is seen in I Corinthians 8.6). The *one hope* may be deliberately designed to recall what was said about the Gentile-Christians (a cipher for the whole of the people of God) formerly being people *without hope* (2.12). Now, however, *hope* has been found in Christ the *Lord* and the sequence of nouns which concentrate on the word *one* is again taken up. How far the Writer intended us to see the *one hope* in eschatological terms is difficult to know for sure. Suffice it to say that he has not altogether abandoned a futuristic hope (as is sometimes argued), but rather has subdued his futuristic eschatology in favour of one which stresses its realized dimensions.

One Lord, one faith, one baptism loses something in the translation, namely the stylized form of expression used to convey unity. In fact three related Greek words are translated as *one* here, and just to complete the hat-trick and make the point, they are grammatically different in gender (masculine, feminine and neuter respectively). An English expression which is similar to this might be found in such a statement as, 'I did not have one single, solitary thing to do with it.' Applying this to the verse we could catch the sense of the expression if we translated it as 'one Lord, a single faith, a solitary baptism'. The order of the three parallels that found in I Corinthians 12.4–6 and is probably dependent upon it.

This highly rhythmic phrase has been the focus of attention throughout the history of the church, largely because it stands as something of a summary declaration of the Christian faith. The verse has served as an artistic inspiration for countless hymn-writers and musicians who have incorporated it within their work. Frequently the reference to baptism as a symbol of entry to the life that is found within the Church is brought out. For example the much-loved hymn 'The Church's one foundation', which we already had occasion to refer to above in connection with 2.20, makes explicit reference to the biblical verse in the second stanza of the hymn.

> Elect from every nation,
>   yet one o'er all the earth,
> her charter of salvation
>   *One Lord, one faith, one birth;*[65]

Similarly, E. H. Plumptre (1821–1891) picks up on the theme in his hymn entitled 'Thy hand, O God, has guided'. The third stanza of the hymn might well be described as a summary of much that is contained in Ephesians and includes these lines.

> Their gospel of redemption,
>   Sin pardoned, man restored,
> Was all in this enfolded,
>   *One Church, one Faith, one Lord.*[66]

The Gifting of God's People
4.7–16

This passage continues the thought of 4.1–6 and serves together with it as an introduction to the practical advice for Christian living which is carried through to the end of the epistle. If *unity* in Christ was what characterized 4.1–6, then *diversity* (as opposed to uniformity) within the church's life is what characterizes these verses.

The paragraph can be divided into four parts: an introductory statement about the individual gifting of God's people (verse 7); a quotation from Psalms 68.18 concerning God's granting of gifts (verse 8); an explanation of the meaning of the OT quotation (verses 9–10); and a discussion of the nature and purpose of such gifting in the life of the church of God (verses 11–16). The second half of the paragraph is long and unwieldy with verses 11–16 constituting a single sentence in Greek, one of the most difficult in the epistle, if not in the whole of the NT. The REB uses five sentences to convey this complicated thought.

Again, the influence of Colossians can be seen in the passage, particularly in verse 13 which picks up an idea from Colossians 1.28, in verse 14 which alludes to a phrase contained in Colossians 2.22, and most notably in verses 15–16 which is an extensive reworking of Colossians 2.19.

7 The Writer has been talking in 4.1–6 about the church as a corporate whole. Here, however, the focus is shifted to the individual members of the congregation as the singular *to each* indicates; the Writer identifies with them by adding *of us*. The value of each person is affirmed by the granting to them of a *special gift*; we presume that God is the one ultimately responsible for the granting although it is done in Christ (in Romans 12.3 God is said to distribute his largess while in I Corinthians 12.11 the Spirit is responsible for the distribution of the various *charismata*). The word used here is the all-important Greek term *charis* which, as we noted in our comments on 3.7, is widely used in the letter, and the REB chooses to render it in a variety of ways. Having spoken of the *special gift* the REB adopts another word for a very similar term giving us the *bounty* of Christ. The two words appeared together in 3.7 in connection with the Writer's calling as a minister which is said to be *God's unmerited gift*. Perhaps the deliberate echo of 3.7 is intentional, setting up the

discussion of the gifts which are given to each person in the church based on the Writer's certain knowledge that God had already given such a gift to him. In short, an argument of *a minore ad maius* (from the lesser to the greater) may be in play here.

8–10   The word *scripture* is supplied by the REB, no doubt under the influence of the quotation from Psalms 68.18 (LXX 67.19) which follows. The relevant portion of RSV translation of the OT text declares.

> Thou didst ascend the high mount,
> leading captives in thy train,
> and receiving gifts among men.

Why is the controversial quotation used here? No doubt because it was a convenient OT proof-text which mentioned the giving of gifts. The context of the passage is Yahweh's ascension to Mount Zion after having destroyed his enemies; from there he receives the spoils of his victory from the hands of men. The Writer understandably has to alter the verse to fit his own needs and this he does in several ways. First, in the initial line of the quotation he substitutes a non-specific participle 'when he had ascended' (*anabas*) for the second person singular verb 'Thou didst ascend' (*anebēs*); this has the effect of making Christ the implied subject of the ascension. Meanwhile, in the third line of the quotation he substitutes a different verb as well as altering it from second person to the third person. Thus, instead of 'you received', we get 'he gave'; this again is to make Christ the focus of the action while at the same time reversing the direction of the gift-giving. It is the gift-giving itself which has attracted the Writer's attention and he uses the image from the Psalm to support what was said in verse 7 about Christ giving gifts to each member of the church (note the same verb 'gave' is used in 4.11). It is sometimes suggested that the Writer either knew of or used a Syriac version of the passage which makes similar changes to the text. Other interpreters argue that he was inspired by the Aramaic Targum on Psalm 68, a passage set as a lectionary reading for the festival of Pentecost in synagogue worship, in which Moses ascends Mount Sinai and then descends to give the gift of the Torah to the people of Israel. Both suggestions, although intriguing, are impossible to prove.

Most agree that verses 8–10 break up the flow of thought in the passage; one can run straight from verse 7 to verse 11 quite easily without the interruption. Given this fact there is little wonder that the use of Psalms 68.18 in verses 8–10 has led to theories of them being an interpolation into the letter. Two other brief points are worth considering when trying to interpret the meaning of this cryptic passage. First, it is interesting that the Writer does not choose to follow up the idea contained in the second line of the quotation ('leading captives in thy train') in the way that Paul did within Colossians 2.15. One is tempted to ask what this might indicate in terms of the setting and date of the epistle, given the fact that the Roman triumph of Vespasian and his son Titus in June of 71 CE, following the destruction of Jerusalem, would have been a perfect illustration of leading of captives in a train of triumph. Dare we posit our dating of the epistle against this historical event? Should we assume that the Writer's lack of reference to the Flavian triumph in Rome means that he is historically distanced from it? Is it so far in the past as to be of no contemporary significance, either to him or his readership? If so, how far should we date the epistle from the events surrounding the traumas of 70 CE?

Second, we have to reckon with the possibility of the association of this idea of God's gifting of his church with Pentecost. To put the essential point in the form of a question: Is the Pentecost episode (recorded in Acts 2) the point at which God has poured out his blessings upon the church and bestowed upon it the various gifts mentioned in 4.11? Many, most notably G. B. Caird in his *Paul's Letter's from Prison* (1976), have seen this as the most satisfactory way of interpreting what is a very mysterious passage within the letter.[67]

Having chosen to quote Psalms 68.18 to make his point, something of a red herring was introduced by the Writer in the first two lines of the verse in that they mention ascension to the heights and the pardoning of captives. This leads to verses 9–10 being included as an explanation of the meaning of those images. In other words, we should take verses 9–10 to be a parenthetical clause which is connected to verse 8. The REB does not separate them in any way although other translations do (including the NIV, the NASB, Knox, and Weymouth). Technically verse 9 is put in the form of a question ('now what is "ascension" except . . .'), in fact, the only question within the letter. The REB has turned this into a statement and linked it to verse 10 in terms of sense. The descent is said to be *to the lowest level, down to the very earth*. But what precisely does this mean? Are we to understand it in terms of credal declarations like the

Apostles's Creed which declares that Christ 'descended to hell' (*descendit ad inferna*)? Or are we to take it as a reference to the incarnation, the descent from heaven to earth? Or should we perhaps even view it as the descent of the Spirit in which Christ addresses the believing community by means of his Spirit who pours upon them the gifts of grace (as G. B. Caird suggests)? The decision we make on this matter has implications for our interpretation of Ephesians as a whole, yet these are difficult questions to answer with any certainty. It is probably fair to say that the majority opinion is that Christ's descent refers to his incarnation, although as we suggested above (see the discussion on pp. 33–37), it is possible that the somewhat awkward interjection of the ascent/descent motif in verses 9–10 was designed to communicate on more than one level and may in fact be an indication that the letter was originally intended for the city of Hierapolis.[68]

Whatever one's opinion on the matter, it is certainly true that stories of a descent into the regions of hell, or the underworld, were common in the ancient world. Perhaps the three most famous examples from Greek and Roman mythology are Aeneas' descent to the underworld recorded in Book 6 of Virgil's *Aeneid*, Orpheus' descent to recover his beloved Eurydice recorded in Book 10 of Ovid's *Metamorphoses*, and the descent of Hercules to the underworld to fetch the three-headed Cerberus, dreaded guard-dog of Hades, told (among other places) in Book 2 of Apollodorus' *Bibliothetica*. In this sense the reference to Christ's descent to the underworld comes as no surprise, especially given the testimony of I Peter 3.18–21. The earliest exploration of this comes in the second half of the *Gospel of Nicodemus* (written perhaps as early as the second century). Here we find an extensive discussion of Christ's 'descent into hell' including an almost humorous dialogue between Satan and the personification of Hades about what his arrival might mean in terms of them losing their inhabitants.

The topic of the underworld has continued to fascinate writers and artists ever since, with the most illustrious example being Dante's 'Inferno', the first section of his classic *The Divine Comedy*. Indeed, in the Middle Ages many works were produced which explored the idea of Christ's descent into Hades, or the 'harrowing of hell' (as it came to be known). One of the most famous was Langland's *Piers the Ploughman* which describes Christ's triumphal entry into Lucifer's domain in Book 18 of the story. More recently, the theme is the subject of Charles Williams' *Descent into Hell* (1947) which explores the double-entendre contained in the title nicely through the two main characters of the novel, one who has descended into a sort of psychological hell of his own creation and the other who comes in the name of Christ to effect rescue. An unusual twist was given to the idea by C. S. Lewis in *The Great Divorce* (1946), a modern fantasy in which a load of bus passengers in hell reverse the direction and take a day excursion in a bus to the outskirts of heaven.

The words *so that he might fill the universe* clearly recall what was said in 3.19, although there it was the church which was said to be filled with the fullness of God. Once again we are confronted with the question of who does the filling? Sense would dictate that it is Christ since he has been the subject of verses 8–9, although the Greek is ambiguous and the REB rightly keeps this intact by using the non-specific *he* (see the discussion above on 1.24 and 3.19).

11–13   The *he* in verse 11 is emphatic and probably means Christ as opposed to God, although again it is ambiguous in Greek. Five particular giftings (or 'ministries' or 'offices' as they are often described) are identified in verse 11: *apostles, prophets, evangelists, pastors* and *teachers* (the last does not carry an article with it which is why the REB does not add the corresponding *some*). The list should be compared to those found in I Corinthians 12.27–28 and Romans 12.4–8. When this is done we see that verse 11 is by no means a definitive listing, but is rather a representative sample of the kinds of giftings that God provides for his church. There are some overlaps between the three passages, notably the priority of place given to *apostles* and *prophets*, but none of them is exactly the same. The Writer has already had occasion to associate *apostles* with *prophets* twice within the letter (2.20 and 3.5), so it is evident that these are particularly important to him. Other groups mentioned elsewhere in the Pauline epistles are not included here, notably 'bishops' and 'deacons' (Philippians 1.1). The mention of *evangelists* in verse 11 is somewhat unusual given the fact that it does not appear in either I Corinthians 12.27–28 or Romans 12.4–8, the two passages upon which the Writer seems to be dependent. The term is used only here in Ephesians and does not occur in the undisputed Pauline letters (and only in Acts 21.8 and 2 Timothy 4.5 within the rest of the NT). It is possible that the Writer deliberately adds *evangelists* to the list in order to provide a gentle reminder to the church in Hierapolis of how they came to Christian faith through the agency of the church in Colossae, probably under the leadership of Epaphras in 52–55 CE.

On this reading of the phrase, the church at Colossae sent out evangelists to the city of Hierapolis and helped to establish a new church there. In addressing the 'daughter-church' in Hierapolis it would only be natural for the Writer to allude to the fact that God had provided evangelists among his gifts since the church there was a direct result of their missionary activity. The work of the evangelists in Hierapolis also appears to be alluded to in 4.20–21 with the mention of 'learning Christ' and 'being taught the truth' (see below).

It is unwise to view the five categories of people here listed as evidence of the prevailing ecclesiastical structures of the time, or to take them as an indication of the situation of the church to which the Writer directs his letter. Likewise, it is not at all clear that what is intended here is a hard and fast distinction between the clergy and the laity, as the insertion of a comma between the phrases 'to equip the saints' and 'for work in his service' in some translations of verse 12 suggests (the REB avoids this by running the two phrases together). One must look elsewhere, such as the Pastoral Epistles, to substantiate a theology of the two-fold office of Christian ministers, since ecclesiastical legitimization of the forms of an ordained ministry is not the Writer's focus here. It is surely not without significance that *neither* of the two ordained ministries described in I Timothy 3.1–13 and Titus 1.7, those of bishop and 'deacon', is mentioned here at all. Neither does the related ministry of 'elders', mentioned in I Timothy 5.17, 19 and Titus 1.5, appear anywhere on our list. Rather our Writer is concerned with explaining the gifting of God's people as a means of bringing about the growth and development of the body (hence the quotation from Psalms 68.18 in verse 8). It is difficult to establish what precisely the differences between the five groups mentioned were in practice. Did pastors teach? Did teachers ever shepherd a congregation? How wide-spread were the evangelists and what was their task? Were there a fixed number of apostles and prophets or were new ones being given to the church in order to meet new needs and situations? Who determined if someone was to be considered a prophet or a pastor? The NT texts, including Ephesians 4.11, can never answer these sorts of questions to our satisfaction and, if the truth be known, one inevitably tends to read them in light of one's own ecclesiastical and denominational tradition. We do often speak today of new apostles and of modern prophets, of television evangelists and of teaching ministries, and perhaps this is in keeping with the original meaning of the passage. Through Christ the head of the body, God equips and enables the

129

church as needed in order that she might meet the tasks to which she has been called.

Popular attempts to compose a comprehensive list of 'spiritual gifts' by harmonizing the three scriptural passages (I Corinthians 12; Romans 12; Ephesians 4) and then encouraging interested Christians to discover their particular gift are misguided and potentially destructive to life within the church. I remember some years back running across a popular book entitled *19 Gifts of the Spirit and How to Find Which One is Yours* which seemed to turn the whole exercise into a gigantic spiritual Easter-egg hunt. This is far from the spirit of the passage which focusses on the graciousness of God and the bounty of his provision *for the life of the church*. This is brought forcibly home in verses 12–16 where a series of interlocking 'purpose clauses' are given and the intended results of God's gifting are expounded.

The Greek of verses 12–13 is exceedingly difficult to unravel and appears to switch back upon itself several times. Precisely how the various phrases and sub-clauses fit together is anyone's guess. Nevertheless, as an opening gambit it might be helpful to look at verses 12–13 together, focussing on the nouns that appear within these verses. Grammatically the accusative case nouns of verses 12–13 function as the objects of the *has given* mentioned in verse 11 and they may provide some way of seeing the overall point of the two verses. Unfortunately it is not always easy to translate them as nouns, and gerund forms have been the norm in many translations. We shall avoid this temptation to try and illustrate the way in which there is a cohesion to the verses, even though it is not immediately visible. We could say God's giving of gifts to his people is intended to:

> provide for the *preparation* of the saints (12a)
> produce a *work* of service (12b)
> assist in the *construction* of the body of Christ (12c)
> enable us all to attain the *unity* of faith (13a)
> allow us to explore our *knowledge* of the Son of God (13b)
> attain the *maturity* of adulthood (13c)
> show in us a *measurement* of Christ's own fullness (13d)

All of these are positive things, noble and worthy pursuits to be sought after. They stand in opposition to the kind of Christian living within the church which is described in verse 14 (see below).

By rendering *tōn hagiōn* in verse 12 as *God's people* the REB may be misleading the reader into assuming that Christ must be (by virtue of contrast) the *he* of verse 11. We have already had occasion to note the difficulties of the phrase *God's people* within the interpretation of the epistle as a whole (see the discussion on 1.1; 2.19 and 3.5, 18 above).

In verse 13 *unity inherent in our faith* recalls 4.3, the only other mention of *unity* within the epistle. What is meant by this? It is probably best to view both references as genitives of apposition wherein the noun in the genitive case serves to define the noun to which it is related. This is what the REB attempts to do by adding the words *inherent in* to the phrase. Alternatively we could express the main point of the two phrases, together with the ones which immediately follow them, like this.

4.3   *the unity* (which consists of life) *in the Spirit*
       (is at the same time manifested) *with bonds of peace.*

4.13   *the unity* (which constitutes the basis of and purpose) *of our faith*
       (is at the same time demonstrated as) *our knowledge of the Son of God.*

The REB adds the word *our* in verse 13; literally the phrase is simply 'the unity of faith'. However, the addition seems justified since the Writer does use plural language in the verse ('when *we all* . . .'). This suggests that the Writer identifies himself with the congregation to which he addresses the letter and sees *unity* as a common goal, the desired destination of the journey of faith. As we suggested above (see the discussion on Provenance on pp. 31–48) this may well be an indication of the Writer's desire to create within the church of Hierapolis a sense of common purpose and encourage them to identify with the other churches in the Lycus region.

The reference to *Son of God* is the only time that this particular christological title appears in the epistle. On the other hand *the full stature of Christ* is a phrase which we encountered above in connection with 1.23. It is another example of the 'fullness/completion' language so characteristic of the epistle as a whole (see 3.19 for another important instance of it). The phrase *to mature manhood* is probably an echo of Colossians 1.28 in which Paul speaks of his aim to present 'every man mature in Christ'. The verse from Colossians speaks of individual people being mature, painting a mental picture of a person being a Christian version of a 'Renaissance man', so to speak. In contrast, here in our passage the Writer is speaking of the whole church, collectively conceived, as a mature person (comparable to the 'new man' of 2.15). This is generally taken to be another indication of the way in which he reworks Colossians to suit his own aims; it also serves as another indication of his heightened ecclesiology. At the same time this challenges the modern mindset which views Christian maturity and personal development in individualistic terms. The force of the Writer's argument is to suggest that such a pursuit is potentially dangerous and illusory. Personal fulfilment is not the answer here; corporate service is.

The sentiment of 4.7–13 and its emphasis on the purposeful gifting of God's people by his Spirit is captured in John Bell's hymn 'One is the body and one is the head' (1993):[69]

1.
One is the body and one is
    the head,
One is the Spirit by whom
    we are led;
One God and Father,
    one faith and one call
        for all

2.
Christ who ascended to
    heaven above
Is the same Jesus whose
    nature is love
Who once descended
    To bring to this earth new
        birth.

3.
Gifts have been given well-suited
    to each,
Some to be prophets, to pastor or
    preach,
Some through the Gospel
    To challenge, convert and
        teach.

4.
Called to his service are women
    and men
So that his body might ever again,
    Witness through worship,
    Through deed and through
        word
        to Christ our Lord.

14   The major point of discussion arising from verse 14 concerns what it might tell us about difficulties in the church to which the Writer is addressing his letter. Were there some *cunning rogues* who, with dice-like dreams of winning the lottery, were promoting their *deceitful schemes* within the fellowship? Who were the *dupes* that fell for these *devilish schemes* (note the parallel in 6.11!) and showed themselves susceptible to the latest idea to come along? Too much weight can be placed upon this one verse in this regard. It cannot be used to reconstruct the circumstances of the congregation; it is simply too vague and non-specific to do anything more than tease our imaginations and provide a generalized picture of Christian life, be it in Ephesius, Hierapolis, or anywhere else.

The imaginative power of the verse is carried by two memorable phrases, one drawn from the image of a sea-storm and one from the image of a violent wind-storm, perhaps even a tornado. The REB renders these as *tossed about by the waves* and *whirled around by every fresh gust*. This is quite a common pairing, as James 1.6 testifies, applying them to someone who doubts. Assuming for the moment that the letter is addressed to the church in Hierapolis, it may at first glance seem a bit strange that the Writer uses sea-storm metaphors and directs them to inhabitants of a city which lies nearly 125 miles inland from the port of Ephesus. One wonders if the images of being *tossed about* and *whirled around* were extended to refer to earthquakes, in much the same way that we today talk about the 'shock waves' of an earthquake. The Lycus region was well-known as an area prone to such seismic disturbance and we know that the city of Laodicea had been destroyed by an earthquake in 60 CE (see Tacitus *Annals* 14.27.1; Strabo *Geography* 12.8.16; and *Sibylline Oracles* 3.471; 4.106–107; 5.290–291; 7.22–23; 12.279–281 (which also mentions Hierapolis); cf. Suetonius *Tiberius* 8.1). In any event, the Writer's use of such sea metaphors on a land-locked people should not worry us too much. Clearly they were proverbial images and were widely understood, even by those who had never seen a sea or set foot in a boat.

Somewhat strangely the Writer here associates these two storm images with living as *children*, as if to suggest that mature people are not frightened by such things. Clearly the reference to *mature manhood* at the end of verse 13 prompts such a juxtaposition; the Writer is wanting to contrast *maturity* with *childishness* and thereby encourage the church to live as a mature adult, to 'come of age' as we might say now. The images of being tossed about and whirled around are paralleled in verse 16 by two others which are more positive as descriptions of life as the body of Christ (see below).

15–16   The co-ordinating metaphor in these two verses is a somatic one in which the church is presented as the body of Christ and Christ himself is its head. The assumption is that a living and healthy body is in the process of growth. In the REB the word *grows* appears twice, once as a verb with an understood subject *we* (verse 15) and once in what technically is a noun construction which the RSV renders as 'bodily growth' (verse 16). The phrase *so shall we fully grow up into Christ* in verse 15 is fraught with difficulties. The REB brings the word *Christ* forward from its position at the end of the verse which means that the Greek order is broken ('all things grow up into him, he who is the head, Christ' would be a more literal translation). A new short sentence is then created out of 15c and 16a which brings together the key nouns: *He is the head and on him the whole body depends.* The REB translates the phrase *ta panta* as the adverb *fully* which is sensible although many commentators keep it as a noun and interpret it to mean 'all things (grow up into him)'. Those who follow this line of thought argue that the cosmic sense of ta panta is what is in mind here since that is how the phrase is used elsewhere in the letter (see 1.10, 22–23 and 4.10 in particular). The question really depends on whether we feel the somatic image of verses 15–16 should determine the meaning of *ta panta* or not.

There are two interlocking images which give expression to this somatic metaphor in verse 16, one which we could render as 'being fitted together' and the other as 'being bonded together'; both terms seem to derive from the terminology of Greek medicine. Together they represent yet another example of the Writer's fondness for *sun* compounds which serves to illustrate his ideas about the unity and oneness in Christ (see the comments on 2.5 and 3.6 above). In one sense these two serve as the counterpart to the images of being *tossed about* and *whirled around* associated with life as children mentioned in verse 14 (see above). The Writer borrows from Colossians 2.19 here and thoroughly reworks the verse to suit his purposes. His main point is to stress that *every part* of the body contributes to this process of growth and development, with *every constituent joint* making its contribution and *the proper functioning of each part* adding to the overall building up of the body (see 2.21 above). All of this is specifically said to be accomplished through the agency of *love*, the word with which this long sentence concludes. In fact the thought contained in verses 15–16 is framed by two references to love. Just as 'maintaining the truth' (not merely 'speaking the truth' as the RSV would have us believe) is done in love, so too is 'growing into wholeness' done in love. We could even say that maintaining the truth in love is the means whereby the church grows and develops and is built up. The 'maintaining' and the 'growing' are one and the same; they constitute life in the body of Christ.

Pagan Decay and Christian Renewal
4.17–24

Having completed his two-fold description of the nature of the church as embodying both unity in its calling by Christ (4.1–6) and diversity in its gifting by him (4.17–24), the Writer now proceeds with his practical teaching on Christian living. He begins with an exhortation not to live as the pagans do (verses 17–19), and then opposes this with a longer section on living in the light of what has been taught by Christ (verses 20–23). In short, this paragraph contrasts a life characterized by deceit with a life characterized by truth, the old with the new, what was past with what is now. It also serves notice for further ethical teaching which is to follow, and leads comfortably on to the advice given in 4.25–32.

As we have mentioned several times already, it appears that the Writer is reliant upon Colossians for many of his key terms and ideas. The same holds true here in that the passage as a whole contains many points of contact with Colossians 2.6–7 and 3.5–10. There are also close similarities between 4.17–19 and Romans 1.21–24. The paragraph contains two sentences in Greek which correspond to the two contrasting exhortations. These the REB divides up into six, three for each of the two parts.

17–19 The seriousness of the Writer's feelings on the matter of lifestyle is indicated by the opening declarations of the verse, *I urge it upon you in the Lord's name*. The sense of the verb *urge* can carry with it the idea of testifying before a court, or of making a solemn declaration in a public setting. His exhortation is that his readers are no longer to live as pagans live, an exhortation which contains two particular points worth noting briefly. The first concerns the words *give up living*, or as the RSV puts it 'no longer live…'. The verb here, which literally means 'to walk', is one that we have already had occasion to note within our discussion, namely in connection with 2.10; 4.1. This ethical sense of one's 'way of walking' as an indication of their 'way of living' is very common in the NT and is picked up again later by our Writer in 5.2–15.

The second point concerns the word *pagans* (*ta ethnē*). Elsewhere in the letter this term is used in an ethnic or racial sense to denote 'the Gentile-Christians' (as opposed to 'the Jewish-Christians'), and the REB consistently renders it as *Gentiles* in 2.11; 3.1, 6, 8 (as we noted above the REB also uses it to fill out the meaning of 'both' in 2.14). However, most commentators agree that the Writer uses the term in a slightly different sense here. The context is no longer the question of Jewish-Gentile relationships within the life of the church (as it was in chapters 2–3), but of humanity at large. In this sense the REB catches the nuance of the Writer's shift in meaning by using *pagans* here. The shift in meaning is also indicative of the Writer's perspective of the new Humanity in Christ as transcending the earlier categories of Jews and Gentiles; here in 4.17–23 life in Christ is being contrasted with life outside of Christ, and the old term is drafted into new service. It may also serve as another veiled hint that the Writer of the epistle was himself a Jewish-Christian.

With their futile notions, or 'in the futility of their minds', is later contrasted with the 'renewing of minds' in verse 23. In Romans 1.21 such 'futility' is ascribed to people who do not acknowledge the creative purposes of God.

In verses 18–19 a number of negative descriptive phrases are applied to the pagans. They are summarized as being 'closed-minded', 'ignorant, 'hard-hearted', 'depraved', 'insensitive', and 'indecent'. None of these is particularly unusual as a description of pagan character and all can be found in other lists of sins and vices which abounded in literature known to those living in the first century (*Wisdom of Solomon* 12–15 being a good case in point). However, one other phrase mentioned is worth examining in more detail.

With the words *they are alienated from the life that is in God* we are presented with something of a riddle. The participle contained within this phrase was used earlier in the letter in 2.12 to describe the uncircumcised Gentiles who were *excluded* (the REB changes its translation here) from the promises of the nation of Israel, who were described as 'the so-called circumcised'. Here, however, the term is used to describe alienation from God. How do we explain this shift in meaning, one which is highlighted by the different renderings of the REB? The most likely solution is that the Writer here borrows the idea of the alienation from God from Colossians 1.21. In other words, the earlier idea of exclusion on the human plane is laid aside for the idea of alienation from God himself. After all, it is difficult to talk of people being *excluded* from God, since he is open to all and such exclusions are invariably human devices; it is much easier to talk of people being *alienated* from him. All of which serves to demonstrate the Writer's reliance upon Colossians 1.21 in this particular verse.

20–21. The pagan behaviour is now contrasted sharply with what was learned about Christ. The paired ideas of 'learning' and 'teaching' are used here and invoke the image of discipleship (the words for 'to teach' and 'disciple' sharing a common root in Greek). What they *learned* was what they *had been taught* when they *heard* the truth about Jesus. And yet, that is not quite all of it because the Writer does not say that it is the truth *about* Jesus which has been learned, but Jesus himself ('Jesus' is the object of the verb). Just as devout Jews 'learned Torah' so here the Writer suggests that dedicated Christians 'learned Christ' (as suggested, this is an odd phrase in Greek and only appears here in the NT).

When did all this take place? We can only presume that it was at some specific point in the past (all three verbs are in the past tense). Our suggestion is that the church at Hierapolis (to whom the letter is directed) was founded as a 'daughter-church' by the church at Colossae, probably under the leadership of Epaphras who was sent into the region as part of the Pauline mission in circa 52–55 CE. It was probably in connection with the mission of Epaphras that the believers in Hierapolis committed themselves to Christ, having *learned Christ* from the church in Colossae. Such a scenario helps explain the Writer's addition of the term *evangelists* to his list of God-given giftings in 4.11; we can assume that these evangelists worked alongside Epaphras and were part of the mission to Hierapolis.

The REB adds the words *as Christians* to verse 21 and turns that part of the declaration into a question. This is in one sense unfortunate since it forces a break between the key verb *you learned* in verse 20 and the three infinitive verbs contained in verses 22–24. The concluding phrase of verse 21 is decidedly unusual and probably means 'the truth is in Jesus!' This is the only unqualified mention of the earthly name of the Lord within the letter; the only other unqualified occurrence in the so-called 'Captivity Epistles' is in Philippians 2.10 within the final stanza of the (pre-Pauline?) christological hymn.

22–24 The central message contained within these three verses is exceptionally important for the Writer's purposes, but it is exceedingly difficult to extract. It might help if we attempt to get an overview of the thought before turning to consider one or two of the individual phrases and ideas contained within the verses. In order to do this we have to pay particular attention to the trio of verbs within the verses, for they are the key to any interpretation of the thought. The words *you must lay aside* (*apothesthai*) in verse 22 and *you must be renewed (ananeousthai)* in verse 23 veil the fact that both verbs are actually infinitives. A third infinitive occurs in verse 24 which the REB renders *(you must) put on (endusasthai)*. All three are grammatically linked to the verb *you were taught* in verse 21, and in effect give substance to what was taught to the believers. Many translations give the infinitives imperatival force; hence the REB's use of *you must*. A translation such as 'you were taught... to lay aside... to be renewed... to put on...' allows us to appreciate the connection between verses 20 and 22–24 more easily.

It is also important to note that each of the three imperatival infinitives has an object attached to it. At the same time two of these objects, those describing *the old human nature* and the *new nature*, have additional descriptive phrases which fill out their meaning. If we set these out in parallel fashion we can begin to unravel the connections between the various phrases contained in the verses and grasp what is being said a bit better:

> You were taught:
>> to lay aside *(apothesthai)*   *the old human nature* (which)
>>> belongs to your former way of life
>>> is deluded by its desires
>>> is in the process of decay
>>
>> to be renewed *(ananeousthai) in mind and spirit*
>>
>> to put on *(endusasthai)*   *the new nature* (which)
>>> is created in God's likeness
>>> shows itself in a truly upright and devout life

One of the advantages of setting the phrases out in this fashion is that the central position of the *renewal in mind and spirit* within these verses is evident. Such renewal is the means whereby the old human nature is laid aside and the new one put on. There is a 'putting off' as well as a 'putting on'; both are intimately bound together with the renewal of the person and signify a change of identity. And yet it is striking that the 'putting off' and the 'putting on' are both actions which are in the past (both verbs are aorists) whereas the 'renewing' is on-going (it is a present tense verb), as if the Writer wished to stress that, having finished 'putting off' the old and 'putting on' the new, one must '*continue* to be renewed'. Language of 'putting on

Christ' occurs elsewhere in the Pauline letters, notably Romans 13.12–14 and, even more significantly, Galatians 3.27 where it is associated with Christian baptism, and these may lie behind the Writer's use of the image here. Certainly the practice later adopted of undressing before baptism and dressing in a new set of clothes appropriate to Christian life following baptism fits the image here. This is brought out particularly well in the translation of J. B. Phillips: 'fling off the dirty clothes of the old way of living, which were rotted through and through with lust's illusions … put on the clean fresh clothes of the new life'. Similarly, the juxtaposition of 'old man' and 'new man' (the REB's *old human nature* and *new nature*) is a familiar one within the Pauline letters, appearing in Romans 6.6 and Colossians 3.9–10. Later in the letter the Writer uses the verb 'to put on' in connection with the 'armour of God' which is needed to conduct spiritual warfare (6.11).

It goes without saying that *you must lay aside* and *(you must) put on* are active commands whereas *you must be renewed* is passive; the first two are things that the members of the congregation were taught to do and the third was something that was done to, or for, them. But how is this *renewing* accomplished? Who does it? A possible clue comes in the next phrase which the REB renders as *in mind and spirit*. The RSV is closer to the Greek when it gives 'in the spirit of your minds', and it has led some to take the meaning of '*in* the spirit' to be '*by* the (Holy) Spirit'. However, this leaves the words 'of your minds' hanging in mid-air and the attempt to turn the statement in 4.23 into an explicit reference to the Holy Spirit is probably therefore to be rejected. It is much more likely that the Writer means that the Christian's spirit is the motivating force in how he or she thinks and lives; the REB translation captures the sense of it well. A similar reference to the renewal of the mind is found in Romans 12.2, while II Corinthians 4.6 speaks of the renewal of the 'inner man' and Colossians 3.10 speaks of the renewal of the 'new man'. Clearly all of these images can be collectively gathered together and filed under 'Renewal', although they each have their own particular ways of expressing what is essentially an image of the new Humanity in Christ which has been created and is in the process of growing to maturity.

Not so fortunate is the REB movement of the phrase *renouncing your former way of life* to the beginning of verse 22. This has the effect of breaking the symmetry of the passage for the reader, although to be fair the phrase does come between the infinitive verb 'to lay aside' and its object 'the old human nature' and one can understand why it was done.

Some Practical Advice on Christian Behaviour
4.25–32

This passage contains some practical words of advice for Christian living. The Writer here builds upon the exhortations given in 4.22–24 which contrasted the 'old' way of living with the 'new' and reminded his readers of the need to be continually renewed. Here we see some of the ways in which that renewal is to be made manifest in their conduct. There are seven or so separate pieces of advice that are offered here; they are loosely connected together and there is no immediately obvious link from one to the other. The eight verses contain seven separate sentences, corresponding in the main with the versification (the exception being verses 26–27 which belong together). The REB has followed this pattern exactly and contains seven sentences; verses 26 and 27 are linked by means of a semi-colon. The influence of Colossians 3.8–13 upon the passage is evident, particularly in terms of the vocabulary used in verses 31–32.

25–29 *Then* connects the advice given here with what preceded in 4.17–24. An additional connection to the previous passage lies buried in the words *have done with falsehood*; the participle used here is from the same verb which appeared in 4.22, which the REB rendered as *you must lay aside*. We might translate the opening phrase of verse 25 more accurately as 'Therefore, laying aside the lie …'. This allows us to see 4.22a and 4.25a as parallel statements in the sense that the earlier exhortation given in 4.22a *you must lay aside the old human nature* now finds its realization in 4.25a, which we could translate as 'therefore we have laid aside the lie, our old human nature'. In other words, the opening phrase of 4.25a looks backwards in the text as well as looking forward to the imperative command ('Speak the truth!') which follows it. This connection to the earlier exhortation is somewhat obscured by the REB translation. Something of this idea is found in the English phrase 'to live a lie', by which we mean to live in such a way that it clashes fundamentally with who we really are. The Writer wants us to understand above all that Christian living proceeds on the basis of it being an altered existence; who we really are has been changed. A transfer of nature has taken place and the resulting transformation is in the process of being worked out.

Having set the agenda, that the lie of our old nature has been safely and securely laid aside, the Writer then in these verses addresses four different ethical topics: truth-telling, anger, stealing and malicious talk. In three of the four instances a positive course of action to be followed is backed up by an explanation of why it is beneficial. Thus:

Speak the truth to your neighbour *because* we belong to each other (verse 24)
When angry do not sin; do not give the devil an opportunity (verse 25–26)
Do not steal but work hard *in order that* you can give something to the needy (verse 27)
Say only what is good and not evil *so that* your listeners might be blessed (verse 28)

The motivations for correct action give force to the imperatives, and it is worth noting that in three of the four the motivations involve the benefits which will accrue for others, presumably other members of the congregation of Hierapolis. This leads us to consider the ecclesiastical setting of such ethical advice.

The opening command 'Speak the truth!' is generally taken to mean 'speak truthfully' to other members of the congregation, largely because of the presence of the phrase 'members of one another' at the end of the verse. In fact, a literal translation of the Greek might be 'let each one speak the truth to his or her neighbour', which leaves us having to decide who is our neighbour (shades of Luke 10.29 !). The phrase is almost certainly an allusion to Zechariah 8.16, where the people of Israel, freshly returned from exile, are given instructions by Yahweh on how to live in their new setting. That the Writer means church-neighbours in the nearby cities of Colossae and Laodicea is probable, particularly since the phrase 'members of one another' is found in Romans 12.5 and there it is speaking of members of the wider body of Christ, the church. The Writer himself makes a similar declaration in 5.30, where the 'body of Christ' metaphor is explicitly used. Here in verse 25 the REB adds the words *of one body*, no doubt under the influence of this somatic metaphor.

We should not miss the fact that in 4.16 the Writer declared that truth was to be maintained within the life of the church by means of love. Senator Hiram Johnson (1866–1945), at the height of the debacle that was the First World War, said in a speech before the US Senate: 'The first casualty when war comes is truth.' The Writer might well echo this by saying that within the life of the church, a church which is itself engaged in a spiritual war (see below on 6.10–20), every effort must be made to ensure that truth is not compromised, that it does not become a casualty in the struggle.

The phrase *do not let sunset find you nursing your anger* in verse 27 is a paraphrase of the well-known 'do not let the sun go down on your anger' (RSV). This was something of a proverb within the ancient world and many parallel examples can be found, most notably Plutarch *Moralia* 488c. Peterson's rendering of it as 'Don't go to bed angry!' is a good modern equivalent. The injunction attempts to offer a guideline about the resolution of anger rather than setting a time limit upon how long one is allowed to have it. The oft-repeated comment by Andrew Fuller is worth mentioning again here for he captures this point well:

> Let us take the Apostle's meaning rather than his words ... not understanding him so literally that we may take leave to be angry till sunset, then might our wrath lengthen with the days; and men in Greenland, where days last above a quarter of a year, have plentiful scope for revenge.[70]

Verse 27 assumes that anger is going to be a fact of life, even for Christians. In this sense the words *if you are angry* at the beginning of verse 26 should be understood as *'when* you are angry' (note the parallel in Psalms 4.4). *Give no foothold to the devil* means 'provide him no place of entry, no opportunity to gain control'. The *devil* is also mentioned in 6.11.

We should not infer that since the Writer discusses theft in verse 28 that the church was composed of kleptomaniacs. The mention of *the thief* serves to illustrate a much more important issue, namely that care and provision for the needs of others is paramount. The focus is not so much on the *stealing* but on the *hard work* which is to take its place. Thus the whole church is to benefit from one who *works hard with his hands to earn an honest living*. The idea of *sharing with the needy* the fruits of our labours is supremely seen in the collection for the saints in Jerusalem, a task which clearly was close to the heart of Paul (as witnessed by his frequent references to it, notably Romans 15.26; I Corinthians 16.1–4; and II Corinthians 8–9; cf. Acts 20.16, 22; 22.17). Sometimes it is suggested that we have here a reflection of the kind of problem which is mentioned in II Thessalonians 3.10 where some members of the congregation appeared to be sponging off others. In that sense *theft* may here be metaphorical. There is a

well-established tradition within the Pauline letters that the Apostle
Paul himself earned his living by hard manual labour and that he
prided himself on this (see I Corinthians 4.12 and I Thessalonians
2.9).

The old adages from the Second World War that 'Loose lips sink
ships!' and 'Careless conversation costs lives!' might allow us to
catch something of the spirit of verse 29. The Writer is concerned
about what effects unsolicitous comments and ill-judged remarks
might have upon the life of the congregation. He exhorts his readers
to avoid these things and effect a *blessing* upon others. The word
used here is *charis*, which as we noted above in connection with 3.7
appears frequently in the epistle but with a wide variety of meanings
(see 1.1; 3.7, 8; 4.7 for other translations of the term). It may be that
Jesus' words about good trees and bad trees and the fruits they
produce (Matthew 12.33/Luke 6.43; cf. Matthew 7.16–20) are in the
back of the Writer's mind. The word for a *'bad* tree' is the same one
that is given here as an *offensive* word (logos *sapros*); it can mean
'putrid', or 'decaying', or 'rotten'. In both gospel accounts the tree
metaphor then gives way to a further discussion of the words that
good and evil people use and how they are a reflection of the
treasure which is in their hearts (Matthew 12.34–37/Luke 6.44–45).
Jesus is in effect saying that what we say is an indication of who we
are, or as my father once explained it to me, 'Whatever you got in the
well will come out in the bucket.' This emphasis on speech as a
revelation of character fits the context of verse 29 quite well. In verse
28 it was what one *did* which was the focus; here in verse 29 it is what
one *says* which is the focus. Both words and deeds must be brought
under control for the sake of the common good.

30   Clearly this verse calls to mind what was said in 1.13–14. Three
of the key ideas which occur here were first brought together there:
sealing, the *Holy Spirit* and *redemption*, or *liberation* as the REB here
renders the key term *apolutrōsis*. Given this richness of terminology it
is hardly surprising that 4.30 becomes a focus of discussion for the
eschatology of the epistle, as well as its pneumatology, and its teaching about the atonement.

This is the third time that the word *apolutrōsis* is used in the letter;
it appeared in 1.7 (where it was translated as 'release'), and it
appeared in 1.14 (where it was used in a verbal expression, 'to
redeem'). The REB (following the NEB) here adds the word *final* to
the verse as a means of bringing out the meaning of *the day* of

liberation, effectively associating it with the day of the Lord. It is clear that the verse expresses the Writer's eschatological perspective and shows that for all the emphasis on 'realized eschatology' in the letter, there also are important indications of a 'future eschatology'. In this sense the *liberation* which is awaited is intimately connected with the liberation which has already taken place through the shedding of Christ's blood (1.7).

As we noted above in connection with 1.13, language describing 'the seal of the Holy Spirit' is interpreted by many to refer to Christian baptism. Assuming that this is correct, some have seen baptismal rites as an important indication of the setting of the epistle as a whole.[71]

The REB's phrase *for that Spirit is the seal with which you were marked* is rather long-winded and attempts to give a definition to the meaning of the verb contained within it. Literally it reads 'in which (or whom) you were sealed'. In 1.13 the exact same verb was translated as *you were stamped with the seal*. Thus the REB is inconsistent in its translation, alternating between 'marking' and 'stamping'. Both are closely tied up with the underlying idea of the Greek noun *sphragis*, however, and at least some attempt is made to keep this connection by adding the word *seal* to both verses. It needs to be stressed that in both cases the verb is in the passive voice and in both instances it is plural. An equivalent translation might be 'You all have been sealed'!

We must not lose sight of the real point of the verse here, however, which is that it is an exhortation not *to grieve the Holy Spirit of God*. In other words, the injunction is another example of how Christian life should be conducted and the verse takes its place alongside the other six of the passage. Nowhere else is the idea of 'grieving the Holy Spirit' ever mentioned, although one cannot help but think of Jesus' words about 'blasphemy against the Holy Spirit' (Matthew 12.31–32/Mark 3.29/Luke 12.10). The fact that verse 29 appears to be reliant upon Matthew 12.33–37/Luke 6.43–45, the pericope immediately preceding the one about blasphemy against the Holy Spirit (see above), makes it seem at least within the realm of possibility that the Writer has these gospel sayings in mind. On the other hand it may be that Isaiah 63.10 lies behind the unusual expression; there the Israelites are said to have rebelled against God and 'grieved his holy spirit'.

31–32 These two verses give us a contrasting list of vices and virtues; six undesirable qualities are set over against three positive ones. Such lists were a common feature of ethical writing in the ancient world and examples can be found from most cultures and from a variety of religious traditions. The influence of Colossians 3.8 upon verse 31 and of Colossians 3.12–13 upon verse 32 is generally acknowledged. Four of the six vices mentioned here are listed in Colossians; only *spite* ('bitterness' in the RSV) and *insults* ('clamour' in the RSV) are original to this letter. Some have seen a progression of wickedness in the catalogue of vices as they move from *spite*, to *bad temper*, to *rage*, on to *insults*, eventually culminating in *slander* (or 'blasphemy'). It is difficult to know if this is intended by the Writer since the words overlap so much in meaning. Collectively, however, they do illustrate the destructiveness of anger and ill-will which is left unchecked; such raw emotions have an impact upon the life of the church of God and affect our relationship with God.

One of the most powerful illustrations of the power of an all-consuming jealousy is the film *Amadeus* (1984), directed by Miloš Forman and based on the play by Peter Schaffer. The film is a highly fictionalized account of the life of the classical composer Wolfgang Amadeus Mozart (1756–1792) and his relationship with the Italian composer Antonio Salieri (1750–1825). The story is told as Salieri sees it, from his own envy-ridden viewpoint. Salieri resents the God-given musical talents of the younger man Mozart who, displaying all the rashness of youth, is rude, ill-disciplined and wanton in his appetites. In Salieri's opinion Mozart is nothing but a 'giggling, dirty-minded youth', 'a conceited brat', an 'absurd instrument'. He admires Mozart, but that admiration soon becomes metamorphosed into something evil and wicked within him. The bitter longing to succeed eventually leads Salieri to plot against Mozart, and in one of the most powerful scenes from the film, this anger becomes directed at God himself. To God Salieri swears: 'From now on you and I are enemies. You chose a smutty boy!'; and 'I will ruin your incarnation.' Anger and bitter spitefulness have set his feet on the path of destruction, and it results in the destruction of the personality of Salieri himself. In the end Salieri's struggle with jealousy and envy was not so much about his relationship with Mozart, but about his relationship with God.

In a similar way, the Writer here challenges his readers to recognize the destructiveness which is resident in such vice-like emotions. In verse 32 he encourages them to cultivate other attitudes which are more in character with the life that has been granted in Christ. The evidence for the influence of Colossians on this verse is even more impressive than it was for verse 31. All three virtues mentioned here have an equivalent in that earlier letter.

The final phrase *as God in Christ forgave you* is an adaptation of Colossians 3.13 which reads *you must forgive as the Lord forgave you*; both give the verbs in the aorist tense suggesting a particular time in the past when the action took place (probably at conversion, or even at baptism?). This attitude of forgiveness is to pervade the whole of the community, or as the Writer puts it *forgiving one another*. This is not the word for forgiveness which is usually used in the NT, such as the line from the Lord's Prayer in which the petition 'Forgive us as we forgive others' is made. The Greek verb here is *charizomai* and is related to the word *charis*, grace.

More Practical Advice on Christian Behaviour

5.1–5

This passage is a continuation of the words of practical advice begun in 4.25–32. It carries on the call for a Christian lifestyle and bases such an exhortation on the example of Christ (verses 1–2). Verses 3–5 address three particular ethical topics, namely sexuality, indecency and greed. The paragraph contains three sentences in Greek (verses 1–2, 3–4 and 5) which the REB divides up into five sentences (with each verse being a separate sentence). One special item of interest in the passage is the exhortation to imitate God (the '*Imitatio Dei*' theme) in verse 1. The three sins mentioned in verses 3 and 5 are taken over directly from Colossians 3.5. The possible influence of Colossians 1.13 upon the phrasing of verse 5 is also to be noted.

1–2   The passage begins with two obvious connections with what had preceded in 4.17–32, neither of which is obvious from the REB translation. The first is the opening phrase *In a word*, which is simply the word 'therefore'; the second is contained in the command *you must be* which appeared at the beginning of 4.32 and was given there as *Be*. In addition, it may be that the mention of *God* in 4.32 sets up the corresponding mention of *God* here in verse 1. Given these links it is understandable why many commentators see 4.24–5.2 as a unit and treat it as a single pericope.

The words *like him* contain within them a Greek word upon which our English words 'mimic' and 'imitate' are based. The command is that *God's dear children* are to be 'imitators of God', to act as he acts. This is an unusual command; nowhere else in the NT are Christians asked to 'imitate God', although the idea is not unknown within other writings from Hellenistic Judaism, most notably Philo of Alexandria where the motif is used many times. In other Pauline letters the call is to imitate Christ (I Thessalonians 1.6), or Paul himself (I Corinthians 4.16; 11.1; Philippians 3.17; I Thessalonians 1.6; II Thessalonians 3.7, 9), or the conduct of other churches (I Thessalonians 2.14). It is possible that the Writer here appeals to his readers to 'imitate God' because he has a sense of his own unworthiness to serve as a role-model in the way that Paul his master did (see the discussion above on p. 47 for more on this idea).

What does the Writer mean here when he asks his readers to imitate *God*? The answer lies in asking a related question: how does God act? What is it about him we are to imitate? The answer comes immediately: God acts in *love* and this, the Writer goes on to declare, is to be the pattern of life for the church. The REB gives us *live in love*; the RSV and others give 'walk in love'. This is another instance where the idea is of the believers' walk as a reflection of their lives (see the discussion above on 2.2, 10; 4.1, 17; 5.2). Having mentioned the love of God the Writer then turns to the supreme expression of this love of God, the person of Christ himself. He switches ethical examples (from God to Christ) and exhorts his readers to a 'walk of love' based on the fact that *Christ loved you and gave himself up on your behalf*. Both verbs here are in the aorist, pointing to his death on the cross. Another statement of this self-sacrificing love of Christ follows in 5.25. Occasionally the verb rendered as *gave himself up* can mean 'to surrender' or 'to hand over' or even 'to betray' (as in Judas's betrayal of Jesus in Luke 22.48). This act of selfless giving is then amplified by sacrificial language, namely *an offering and sacrifice whose fragrance is pleasing to God*. This may come from II Corinthians 2.14–16 where Christ's triumphal procession is mentioned and the Christian believers are described in similar terms (although such sacrifical language is quite common in the OT). Interestingly, the same words are used by Paul in Philippians 4.18 to describe the gifts sent to him from the church via Epaphroditus.

3–5 Here a number of qualities commonly found in the outside world but unsuitable to Christian life are discussed. In verse 3 *fornication*, *indecency* and *ruthless greed* are singled out as being unfit for *the people of God* (or 'the saints'; the word *God* is added by the REB in accordance with its rendering of the term elsewhere in the letter). Many feel that all three terms are primarily sexual in meaning, but this is by no mean certain. The word rendered as *ruthless greed* (*pleonexia*), for example, can have money or power or possessions as much at its heart as it can sexual desire; insatiability can contaminate many appetites and destroy human relationships, as John Huston's Oscar-winning film *The Treasure of the Sierre Madre* (1948) so graphically illustrates.

That the three vices are uppermost in the Writer's thought is borne out by the fact that they reappear in verse 5, although the REB translation does not always allow the connection between the words to be seen. The point is that *fornication*, *indecency* and *ruthless greed*, which are mentioned in verse 3, are again condemned in verse 5, where those ensnared in *fornication, vice,* and the *greed which makes an idol of gain* are said to have forfeited *any share in the kingdom.* There may be an echo here from Galatians 5.19–21 or I Corinthians 6.9–10 where lists of similar undesirable traits are given and people exhibiting these things in their lives are prohibited from inheriting the kingdom of God.

The use of the word *share* in this passage is highly ironical, given the fact that it has come to be associated in the minds of people living in Britain in the 1990s with the privatization of public utilities such as water, gas and transport. To 'have a share' in one of these privatization schemes means to invest financially in them and doing so is often hailed as a sign of vision, as a demonstration of a progressive attitude in the drive to build a strong market-based economy. Whether such schemes will prove to be beneficial in the long run is a matter of tremendous political debate. One sometimes wonders if the national obsession with buying shares is actually another indication of the *ruthless greed* (verse 3), a Scrooge-like existence in which greed is *an idol of gain* (verse 5). Ours is a world in which scandals over 'insider-trading' and 'corporate take-overs', over 'executive pay-rises' and 'incentive bonuses', are everyday items on the news. The (in)famous line uttered by the character Gordon Gecko in Michael Stone's *Wall Street* (1987), that 'Greed is good!' has become the personal motto for perhaps many more than we would care to admit. We are so surrounded by examples of greedy selfishness and the desire for more that these things do not even faze us any longer; we have become used to them.

There are many indications that such problems continue to plague us, both inside the church and outside it. It is clear that in most Western societies national lotteries have become an obsession. Real questions remain, in my mind at least, about whether such 'get rich quick' programmes are actually the hidden face of *ruthless greed* against which the Writer warns his readers. In Britain our national lottery is slickly and professionally presented, backed up, no doubt, by the latest research into psychological techniques which are designed to have the maximum effect on the most people. Little wonder then that, according to the latest statistics, approximately nine out of ten adults 'have a flutter' on the lottery. It is truly a marketing dream, or a nightmare of greed, depending on how one looks at it. Similar manifestations of the evils of *fornication* (or 'sexual misconduct' as it might be translated since the term has a wide range of meanings) and *indecency* (or 'public corruption' as we might now term it) are easily found in life. It is a sad, but true, fact that these things are to be found in the church as well as outside it.

Sandwiched between the two tirades against sexual misconduct, indecency and financial impropriety in verses 3 and 5 is the prohibition in verse 4 against *coarse, stupid,* or *flippant talk*. Again the Writer insists that these things are inappropriate for Christian life and are to be replaced by 'thankfulness' (the REB adds *God* and reworks the whole phrase). The verse is similar in import to 4.25, 29 (see above). There may be a deliberate play on words here within verse 4: the nouns *eutrapelia* ('flippant talk' or, as the NASB gives it, 'coarse jesting') and *eucharistia* ('thanksgiving') are very similar sounding. We could try and reproduce the play on sound by translating the sense of it as: 'not smutty squawk but thankful talk'.

The reference to having a *share* in the kingdom recalls both 1.14 and 1.18. The same term is rendered as *inheritance* by the REB in both places. The description of the kingdom as being both *of Christ and of God* is very unusual. It appears nowhere else in the Pauline letters, nor indeed anywhere else in the NT (although 'the kingdom of the Lord and of Christ' in Revelation 11.15 is close). Why the double qualification? Could it be that we have here the vestiges of an earlier Jewish understanding of eschatology, one in which a temporary Messianic kingdom eventually gave way to the kingdom of God? It is certainly clear that this was an important strand of thinking in Jewish and early Christian apocalyptic literature, as I Enoch 93.1–10 and 91.12–17, IV Ezra 7.26–30 and 12.31–34, and II Baruch 27–30 and 36–40, Revelation 20–22 and I Corinthians 15.23–28(?) all testify. That 5.5 reflects this tradition has sometimes been suggested, but the difficulty with such a theory is the singular noun *kingdom* (its only occurrence in the letter). The verse does not speak of *two* kingdoms (the Messianic kingdom *and* the kingdom of God) but of one. It is likely that the mention of *the kingdom of Christ and of God* here owes much to Colossians 1.13 which declares that 'He (God) rescued us from the domain of darkness and brought us into the kingdom of his dear Son'. In short, it is the mention of God's action in Christ which is responsible for bringing together the words *of Christ* and *of God* in our verse.

Living in the Light
5.6–14

The passage is easily divided into three sections. First, there is a general statement in which the readers are exhorted to guard against those who might try and deceive them (verse 6), followed by a discussion about living in the light as opposed to living in the darkness (verses 7–11), which leads to a statement about light as an image of the resurrection of Christ (verses 12–14). The Greek contains four sentences, including one long sentence running from verses 7–11 which contains a number of sub-clauses. The REB uses seven sentences to convey the same material.

6   The practical advice continues with the exhortation not to permit anyone to *deceive you with shallow arguments*. Presumably the threat is perceived to come from outside the church community; in this sense the exhortations all serve to remind the believers of their previous life before Christ. It is not clear precisely who these outsiders were nor what their teachings might have been, but regardless, such ideas were considered dangerous and led to *divine retribution*. The idea of 'the wrath of God' (a more traditional translation of the words used here) is much discussed and need not detain us. The phrase occurs elsewhere in Paul's letters in Romans 1.18; 5.6; Colossians 3.6. Given the heavy reliance upon Colossians 3.5–10 throughout chapter 4, it is probable that the Writer picks up the idea from Colossians 3.6. *God's rebel subjects* is a repeat of the phrase which we encountered before in 2.2 (see above for a comment on this).

7–11   Presumably the exhortation in verse 7 that the readers are to *have nothing to do with them* refers to those from outside the church who would try to deceive (verse 7). The Writer goes on immediately to clarify what this means in verse 8 by using the powerful image of light and darkness to hammer the point home: *you once were darkness, now as Christians you are light*. By painting a picture of the church as light the Writer is encouraging them not to fall back into pagan ways of darkness. The REB uses *as Christians* to translate 'in the Lord'; mention of 'the Lord' occurs again in verse 10 and we can presume that in both instances it is Christ and not God that is meant. *Prove yourselves at home in the light* is slightly misleading since it implies a settled state as opposed to an on-going action. The verb at the centre of the phrase is 'to walk' or 'to live', a frequently appearing idea within the epistle (see the comments above in connection with 2.2, 8, 10; 4.1, 17; 5.2). Living in the light produces *goodness, righteousness,* and *truth,* a trio of positive qualities which contrast with the negative trio described in 5.3. The readers are exhorted to cultivate a discriminating eye with regard to their behaviour, to be discerning and not afraid to expose *the barren deeds of darkness.* The phrase *take no part* conceals another example of the familiar *sun* language for which the Writer has such an affinity. In fact, there are two such words in the passage, the first (a noun which also is used in 3.6) in 5.7 and the second (a verb) in 5.11. Both are used to a negative purpose (they are both prohibitions) and we could render them as we have with similar instances of this kind of expression (see 2.5–6; 4.3 above):

5.7   Do not be *co-sharers* with them
5.11   Do not *jointly commune* with the barren works of darkness

What is most interesting about verses 7–11, from the standpoint of what they can tell us about the background and historical circumstances surrounding the writing of the letter, are the remarkable parallels that exist to some of the sectarian documents from Qumran. The use of light/darkness imagery to convey ethical dualism is a widespread phenomenon, stretching back to the beginnings of religious thought. Perhaps the most familiar use of it in the NT occurs within the Johannine writings (including John 8.12; 12.35–36 and I John 2.9), although it is used occasionally by Paul (I Thessalonians 5.5; Philippians 2.15). Our Writer himself has already alluded to it twice before (in 1.18 and 4.18). Nevertheless, the similarities between what is said here and what is found in the Dead Sea materials is such that direct influence upon the epistle has often been claimed. The best example is perhaps from *The War Scroll* (1QM) which gives details of the eschatological battle between 'the sons of light' and 'the sons of darkness'. Note, for instance, these words:

[The seasons of righteous]ness shall shine over all the ends of the earth; they shall go on shining until all the seasons of darkness are consumed and, at the season appointed by God, His exalted greatness shall shine eternally to the peace, blessing, glory, joy and long life of all the sons of light (1.8–9).[72]

Similar descriptions of 'the sons of light' are found scattered through the Qumran materials. We quote one further example, this time taken from *The Rule of the Community* (1QS), which contrasts 'the children of light' with 'the children of darkness':

> All the children of righteousness are ruled by the Prince of Light and walk in the ways of light, but all the children of falsehood are ruled by the Angel of Darkness and walk in the ways of darkness (3.20–21).[73]

This is not the only place that epistles in the Pauline corpus are said to have included, or at least been influenced by, the writings of the Qumran sect. It is felt by many that II Corinthians 6.14–7.1 also derives from the Qumran community, especially since it appears to be an interpolation into the letter.

12–14   What is meant by *It would be shameful even to mention what is done in secret*? What are the *secret* things? It may be that this again refers back to the sexual improprieties hinted at in 5.3–5. In any event, the lifestyle which the pagans have is not to be pursued by the believers; as the Writer has already reminded them in 1.18, *their inward eyes have been enlightened*. Darkness, in contrast, is to be exposed and illuminated by the light, for as the Writer stresses *whatever is exposed to the light itself becomes light*. The exact meaning of this phrase is very uncertain and its interpretation contentious. Two complementary verbs are used in these verses, one meaning 'to expose' and one meaning 'to illuminate'. The order of them is significant: exposure *precedes* illumination, but once exposure has occurred then illumination begins and it is not complete until transformation into light is achieved. This seems to be what the Writer means by this highly compressed verse.

In verse 14 we have the second explicit quotation formula of the epistle (the first was in 4.8): *That is why it is said*. This may tell us something of how much the Writer valued the saying, since it is given the same introduction as an authoritative quotation from scripture. What prompts the insertion of the quotation? Most probably it is the idea of illumination, for the verb that the REB renders as *will shine* is linguistically related to the verb 'to enlighten' used in verse 13. The Writer here inserts three lines, words which are filled with resurrection imagery:

> Awake, sleeper,
> rise from the dead,
> and Christ will shine upon you.

We may even have here a short section from one of the hymns which the Writer in 5.19 says were an important part of the church's worship. The inclusion of these words in the letter is taken by some to prove that the epistle as a whole was written to be used within a baptismal ceremony. Those who see a baptismal liturgy behind 5.14 argue that rising from baptismal waters stands as a metaphor of spiritual resurrection. The connection between the idea of resurrection, and the act of Christian baptism as a visual representation of it, was quickly made within the life of the church. Sleep was often used as a metaphor for physical death in the ancient world and we may see that being reflected here. Earlier interpretations of 5.14 which concentrated on the world of Gnosticism as a backdrop for the verse have now been largely rejected in favour of an interpretation which takes the verse to be an allusion to Christian baptism and not the spiritual enlightenment of an initiate who is being called upon to recover his 'divine spark'.

Interestingly, all of the language here, verbs, participles and pronouns, is in the singular. An *individual* sleeper is commanded to *awake* (or 'get up') and *rise from the dead*, and it is upon an *individual* that Christ is to shine; the *you* is singular.

Too much can be read into the future tense of *will shine*. It does not simply mean that in the future parousia Christ will grant the resurrection body, although there is of course a sense in which this is true. Here it means that from the standpoint of the baptismal ceremony, the believer, who has not yet entered the baptismal waters, is exhorted to rise from the water in order to experience the subsequent illumination which Christ grants. The baptismal context suggests that the verb should be taken as a logical rather than a temporal future.

The hymn 'Awake, Awake! Fling off the night!' by John Raphael Peacey (1896–1971) is based, in part, upon the baptismal imagery contained in 5.14. It also brings together nicely the clarion call to an ethical lifestyle which is at the heart of the Writer's words in 5.1–20. The first two stanzas of the hymn serve to illustrate the point:

1.
Awake, awake: Fling off the night!
For God has sent his glorious light;
and we who live in Christ's new day
must works of darkness put away

2.
Awake and rise, by God renewed
and with the Spirit's power endued,
the light of life in us must glow,
The fruits of truth and goodness show.[74]

Seize the Day!
5.15–20

This short passage continues the theme of Christian lifestyle, drawing out some of the implications of the lines from the baptismal hymn cited in 5.14. Now that the believers have been awakened, have been raised from the dead, and have the light of Christ shining on them, they are to behave accordingly. The pericope divides into two complementary parts: one which stresses the need to live wisely (verses 15–17), and one which stresses the need to be Spirit-filled in worship (verses 18–20). The second section is particularly interesting because it gives us a rare, behind-the-scenes glimpse of what went on in a Christian service (perhaps equalled only by I Corinthians 14.26–40 within the Pauline corpus). Understandably it has been the focus of much attention by specialists in liturgy and hymnody.

The Greek text of this pericope contains three sentences (verses 15–16, 17 and 18–20) which the REB gives as four, managing in the process to keep verses 18-20 intact as a single sentence punctuated by several semi-colons. The influence of Colossians 3.16–17 and 4.5 upon the passage is evident.

15–17   The passage begins with a stern caution of watchfulness, 'Be very careful then …'. The word *behave* correctly conveys the idea of lifestyle or practice of life which the Greek word carries with it although the REB shows itself inconsistent (or flexible, depending on one's point of view) with the previous ways that the term was translated. This is the final occurrence of the verb 'to walk' (*peripatein*) in the epistle and we have already had occasion to note its importance above (see the comments on 2.2, 10; 4.1, 17; 5.2, 8). With *act sensibly, not like simpletons* the REB loses the play on words that the Greek contains; a translation such as 'act sensibly, not senselessly' would retain it. Both words are built on the Greek word *sophos* meaning 'wisdom', and the point is that one can walk 'wisely' or 'unwisely', in accordance with wisdom or in defiance of it.

The opening phrase of verse 16 is somewhat awkward, perhaps because of a scribal confusion between two similar verbs (*exagorazesthai* and *ergazomai*). Literally the Greek phrase might be translated as 'working the moment', or 'make the best use of your time' (Phillips). How might we express it today? The Academy-

Award winning film *Dead Poet's Society* (1989), directed by Peter Weir and starring the versatile actor Robin Williams, may be able to assist us in grasping the point that the Writer of Ephesians makes here. As the REB renders it, the Writer encourages his readers to *use the present opportunity to the full*, an exhortation which is well within the bounds of *Dead Poet's Society's* all-important hook-line 'Seize the Day!' In the film Williams plays an idealistic English teacher who is desperate to inspire a group of boys in a 1950's prep school to realize their potential, and to grasp with both hands the opportunities that life presents to them. The allusion is, of course, to the famous line from Horace *Odes* 1.11, *Carpe diem!* (literally 'Pluck the day!').

The times are *evil*, the Writer warns (perhaps echoing Galatians 1.4), so Christians must 'Seize the day!', not prove themselves to be a foolish people. Rather they are to proceed onwards, confident of who they are and how they must live, because they have been given the great gift of knowing *what the will of the Lord is*.

18–20   Verse 18 contains two commands, one negative and one positive. The Writer warns his audience against one form of intoxication and exhorts them to pursue another; they are not to be filled with wine, but to be filled with the Holy Spirit. At first glance this seems to be an odd contrast (but see Acts 2.4–15 for another contrast between being drunk and being Spirit-filled). What do *drunkenness* and Spirit-filling have in common (besides the pun that the English word 'spirits' offers)? Is the church experiencing problems with some of its members drinking too much, as appears to have been the case in Corinth (I Corinthians 11.21)? Other prohibitions against excessive drinking are known within Jewish writings, including Proverbs 23.30b LXX (which interestingly contrasts the injunction *Be not drunk with wine* with *but converse with just men and converse with them openly*) and *Testament of Judah* 16.1.

It is possible that the Writer is reacting to a situation in which drinking was linked to festive celebrations, such as those associated with the cult of Dionysus. Christians are not to live like pagans who get drunk to induce a religious experience; rather they are to enjoy the ecstasy provided by the Spirit of God. We should perhaps enlarge the scope of the passage to make it more relevant to our contemporary setting and say that what is true for alcohol is also true for other forms of drug-taking and substance abuse. Intoxication is to be through the Spirit of God and not by any artificial means which counterfeit that which is right and proper and true.

It is interesting that both verbs in verse 18 are put in the passive voice, suggesting that wine does the controlling, or the Holy Spirit does the filling. The REB handles the key point of this nicely following the lead of the NEB with its translation *let the Holy Spirit fill you*; literally the phrase is 'Be filled with (or 'in') the Spirit'. We could stress the present tense of the verb and render it as *'continue* to be filled by the Holy Spirit'. The phrase 'in the Spirit' is used three times elsewhere in the letter (2.22; 3.5; 6.5), and similar descriptions of a filling by either God or Christ are mentioned three times (1.23; 3.19; 4.3). Here being filled with the Spirit has four specific results which are expressed in the Greek in the form of four present tense participles. Each of these participles is in the plural as if to emphasize that this is a community event, not just an isolated, personal experience. Such filling by the Spirit produces four things: 'speaking', 'singing', 'music-making', and 'thanksgiving' (although see the comment on 5.21 below). The 'speaking' is further defined as *speaking to one another in psalms, hymns, and songs*, whereas the 'music-making' is said to be *from the heart to the Lord*, and the 'thanksgiving' is made *to our God and Father* and is offered *in the name of our Lord Jesus Christ*. The full title *the Lord Jesus Christ* used here is one of only five times that it appears in the letter (see 1.3, 17; 3.11 and 6.24 for the other instances). Thanksgiving is to be made *daily* and is said to be *for everything*. The suggestion that thanksgiving should be offered *for everything* has raised the eyebrows of some commentators, although it is clearly based on the parallel passage in Colossians 3.17 which reads: 'Let every word and action, *everything* you do …'.

The statement in 18–20 nicely balances the horizontal and vertical dimensions of worship; it is offered *to God* and at the same time involves members *speaking to one another*. For some inexplicable reason the REB fails to include the word 'spiritual' which follows *songs* in the Greek (the word is missing in some important manuscripts but most scholars accept it as part of the original text). This is unfortunate for it means that a second reference to the source of these various forms of worship, namely the Holy Spirit, is lost. Perhaps the command *let the Holy Spirit fill you* in verse 18 was thought to be so dominating for the thought of what follows that the second reference to the Spirit was deemed redundant. The Writer's point is that *songs* are 'inspired by the Spirit' and arise from the people of God as they are filled by that same Spirit. It is unwise to try and distinguish rigidly the difference between a *psalm*, a *hymn* and a *song*, although modern equivalents might be a scripture song, a traditional hymn and a contemporary chorus.

The transition to the next section of the letter is rather awkward. It is not immediately clear what the teaching about Christian marriage, and about the relationships between husband and wives, has to do with singing in public worship! One common way of handling this is to regard the whole of 5.15–6.9, (or even 5.15–6.20) as of one piece. That is to say, that the various ethical teachings and practical advice that follow to the end of the letter are all dependent on the Spirit-filling mentioned in 5.18.

Advice to Those Who Are Married

5.21–33

These verses introduce what is frequently known as *Haustafeln*, a term first used by Martin Luther to describe a collection of house-hold codes or rules. We might liken them to the 'Rules of the House' which are often found prominently displayed at the entrance of English pubs. The various 'do's and don'ts' of the pub are set out and patrons are thereby notified about what is expected of them in terms of conduct when they frequent the establishment.

The *Haustafeln* here run from 5.21–6.9 and are divided into three parts. The rights and responsibilities of married men and women are set out in 5.21–33; of children and parents in 6.1–4; and of slaves and masters in 6.5–9. Such 'codes of conduct' were not uncommon in the first century world, particularly in the circles of Hellenistic Judaism as represented by Philo of Alexandria. No doubt they were designed to give guidance to people of the larger Graeco-Roman world about how they might live their lives in accordance with divine plans and purposes, how they might conduct their lives to fit into the cosmic order of things. Notable parallels from the writings of Plato, Aristotle, Plutarch and Stoic philosophers, many of which follow the basic three-part pattern noted above, are also well-known. The *Haustafeln* have attracted the interest of a number of specialists, particularly in the last thirty years or so, and many new important insights have been discovered as to the place and purpose of such codes within the life of a community. The advice given in such codes is quite specific, designed to meet the needs of a particular time and a particular setting. It is also culturally and sociologically condi-tioned and is predicated on the assumption that the man is the head of his household (the three-fold division mentioned above thus reflects the man's various roles as husband, father, and master). That is both the strength and the weakness of *Haustafeln*, for it means that they can sometimes appear to us to be dated and out of touch, ethical 'dinosaurs' of a by-gone era.

Such 'Household Codes' as we find in the NT, notably Colossians 3.6–4.1; Ephesians 5.2–6.9; I Timothy 2.8–3.13; 6.1–2; Titus 2.1–10; and I Peter 2.18–3.7; 5.1–5, are by no means exclusively Christian creations. They are examples of a much wider religious and socio-logical phenomenon and Christians held no monopoly on such matters. However, the 'Household Codes' of the NT are distinctive in the way that they frequently set their ethical teaching against a christological backdrop. This is seen most clearly in Ephesians 5.21–33 where the advice offered on the topic of marriage is based on the relationship between Christ and the church.

Here in 5.21–33 the Writer gives some practical advice to those who are married, basing the instructions on his understanding of the relationship which exists between Christ (the bridegroom) and the church (his bride). The thought goes to and fro, between human marriage on the one hand and the relationship between Christ and the church on the other. The interconnections between the various statements are complex and difficult at times to follow. Yet the flow of the analogy is always in one direction: from the heavenly pattern to its earthly counterpart. That is to say, lessons from the great truth of Christ's union with the church are applied to the human men and women joined together in marriage (and not vice versa). In the end, the fact that the union of Christ and the church is used as an analogy for earthly marriage results in the transformation of the idea of marriage itself. Marriage thereby moves speedily along the road to becoming a sacrament in so far as it reflect this heavenly union. This is perhaps the most important contribution that 5.21–33 has made in terms of Christian theology over the centuries.

The pericope can be divided into five parts: an introductory exhortation for mutual surrender (verse 21); some instructions to wives to surrender to their husbands based on the model of the church's submission to Christ (verses 22–24); some instructions to husbands to love their wives based on the example of Christ loving the church and giving himself for her (verses 25–30); a short declaration about the mystical union between Christ and the church which is based upon a midrash of Genesis 2.24 (verses 31–32); and a concluding statement about the responsibilities of husbands and wives (verse 33). The Greek of verses 22–33 consists of eight sentences. The REB renders this by nine sentences, in addition to making the floating participial clause in verse 21 (see below) a sentence on its own. The passage as a whole is reliant upon Colossians 3.18–19, although it expands the borrowed section very considerably.

21–24   The opening words of verse 21 present us with a complicated grammatical problem. The difficulty lies in the fact that the opening phrase consists of a participial phrase and one has to decide whether or not to associate it with the other four participles found in 5.19–20 above. In terms of syntax, there is no difference between the earlier participles and this one in verse 21, which means that the opening phrase here can be viewed as another item listed under the heading of 'Be filled with the Holy Spirit'. Filling by the Spirit then includes 'mutual submission to one another'. The REB renders the critical phrase as if it were an imperative verb followed by its object: *Be subject to one another*. But in which direction does the command for mutual submission point? Should we see verse 21 with 5.18–20 and view it as the culminating idea of the Spirit-filled life (as the AV does)? Or should we see verse 21 as the introduction to 5.22–32 and view it as establishing the basis of submission upon which a Spirit-led marriage is to develop? Is it a principle for the church's life in general, or is it a principle for husbands and wives in particular? These are exceedingly difficult questions to answer and much depends on what role one assigns to verse 21; the decisions that are made about it determine, in no small measure, what is meant by verses 22–32, and indeed 6.1–9, which follow. Not surprisingly, two major lines of interpretation have arisen which correspond to these observations about the ambiguity of verse 21. Here, as perhaps nowhere else in the NT, attention should be paid to the way in which various translations choose to paragraph the passage. Does verse 22 start a new paragraph or not? (Note the differences between the NIV, the NASB and the RSV as a case in point!)

But if it is the case that verse 21 can, in terms of syntax at least, be connected to what goes before rather than to what follows, why is it that the majority of translations opt for the the latter possibility and show this by beginning a new paragraph with the verse? And why do virtually all commentators follow this example and discuss verse 21 in their commentaries as if it is part of 5.22–33? Part of the answer to this has to do with verse 22, *wives, be subject to your husbands as though to the Lord*. In fact, there is no verb in the Greek of this verse and what tends to happen in practice is that the verb from verse 21 is imported to finish the thought of verse 22 (the verb 'be subject' does occur in the parallel passage in Colossians 3.18). The REB does this by adding *be subject* to the verse, and then completes the thought with *as though to the Lord* as a counterpart to *out of reverence for Christ* which is found in verse 21.

Much hinges on the translation of the participle *hypotassomenoi*. Does it mean 'to subject', or 'to submit', or perhaps even 'to surrender'? All three are valid translations and each gives a slightly different nuance to the action implied. Some have felt that the idea of subjection or submission to another, particularly when it is women who are commanded to do so to men, is offensive and degrading. It proceeds, so many would say, from the basis of an inferior acceding to a superior, and there is no doubt that the text has been abused along those lines far too frequently in the church's history. However, it is important not to lose sight of the words which follow the participle itself, *to one another*. This lays the stress of the action upon both parties; it is to be *mutual submission*, or *mutual subjection*, or *mutually agreed surrender*. It is not that the women are called upon to submit (but never love) and the men are called upon to love (but never submit), but that both are called upon to surrender themselves *to each other* for Christ's sake (it is worth pointing out that *hypotassomenoi* is a masculine participle and thus strictly speaking cannot have only women in mind). This principle of mutuality governs the whole of the passage, and is the unspoken assumption that must be kept in mind as one wrestles with everything else that is said. The importance attached to this idea of mutual submission can be readily seen by comparing our passage with Colossians 3.18–19. There is no comparable exhortation in the earlier epistle for such mutuality; only wives are required to submit themselves (to their husbands). In this way verse 21 can be seen as a bridge between what has been said before as well as an introduction for what follows. The grammatical difficulty is resolved when we recognize that the verse is Janus-like in its function: it looks backwards (to 5.18) and forwards (to 5.22–6.9) at the same time. Thus, we might illustrate the governing role that 5.21 has with regard to the various exhortations which follow in 5.22–6.9 like this:

> Surrendering to each other *means that* (5.21)
>> Wives surrender to their husbands (5.22)
>> Husbands love their wives (5.25)
>> Children obey their parents (6.1)
>> Fathers discipline their children (6.4)
>> Slaves serve their masters (6.5)
>> Masters care for their slaves (6.9).

To return to 5.22–32, we must not play the egalitarian card too strongly and assume that 'mutual submission' here means 'equal rights' for men and women. The whole idea of a 'Household Code' is that it lists rights and responsibilities, duties and privileges, of

members of a *household*, and for the overwhelming majority of
people that would have meant life in a very patriarchal setting. Men
were at the top of the ladder of society and we can see this inevitably
coming through in the passage under discussion. And yet, there is
something extraordinary in the midst of this (admittedly) male-
centred advice in that the traditional ideas of patriarchical rule *over*
women are challenged by the call to exhibit a partriarchial love *for*
them.

In verse 23 the idea of headship is introduced to explain the
relationship between man and woman (read *husband* and *wife*!). Man
is said to be *the head of the woman*, in the same way that *Christ is the
head of the church* (a point made earlier in 1.22–23 and 4.15–16). We
can detect the influence of I Corinthians 11.1–3 where a similar statement about the relationships between men and women is set within
a hierarchical structure. Here in verse 23 the Writer goes on to say
that Christ is more than just the head of the church; he is in fact *the
saviour of that body*, a claim made nowhere else in the NT (although in
Philippians 3.20 Christ is called 'the Saviour'). The final clause of
verse 23 does not in fact contain a verb and most translations add *is*,
as the REB does here. The declaration is literally, '(Christ), saviour of
the body.' Verse 24 then summarizes the point again by moving
from the church–Christ relationship to the wife–husband relationship: *just as the church is subject to Christ, so must women be subject to
their husbands*. At the end of the phrase, however, the words *in everything* are added. The meaning of *in everything* is never explained, nor
are any examples given to help illustrate what the Writer may have
had in mind. Should it be taken literally? Can it be raised to the level
of a universal truth, held to be applicable to all Christian couples, in
all places and in all circumstances, for all time? Needless to say, such
an understanding of the phrase causes enormous difficulties for us
today.

25–30   These verses deal with the responsibilities laid upon the husbands in the marital relationship. It is the longest of the subsections
in the pericope which indicates something of its importance to the
Writer. Two overlapping reasons are given to support the contention
that *men ought to love their wives* (the central exhortation itself comes
in the middle of the section in verse 28, although it is hinted at in
verse 25 and restated in verse 32). The Writer creatively mixes two
metaphors in the course of the discussion: one which we might call
the 'bride' metaphor and the other the 'body' metaphor (see 4.25).

First, in verses 25–27 Christ's sacrificial giving of himself for his bride, the church, is presented as a model of love within human marriage. Meanwhile, in verses 28–30 the exhortation for husbands to love their wives is given an additional twist. Here the suggestion is that a man cares for his own body, for no one in their right mind ever hates his own body; *on the contrary, he keeps it nourished and warm*. The woman is assumed to be his body and the man is to act accordingly; in the words of our Writer *in loving his wife a man loves himself*. The two metaphors present some problems of interpretation and in some ways are incompatible with one another. E. Elizabeth Johnson describes the tension introduced by verse 25 like this:

> The logic of the analogy collapses because husbands do not die for their wives as Christ died for the church, and Christ did not love his own body, as husbands are urged to do, but rather gave himself up for the church. Men are given an alarmingly self-serving motivation to love their wives (5.28), even though the author says clearly that Christ's love for the church is *self-giving* rather than *self-loving* (5.25).[75]

How might we illustrate this self-giving in love for the modern reader? One of the most moving examples about the love between a husband and wife is that of C. S. Lewis and Joy Davidman. Their story has captured the imagination of many people in recent years, largely through Brian Sibley's book *Shadowlands* and the two film adaptations of the play based on it, one a BBC production from 1985 and the other a Hollywood version from 1993.[76] In many ways the marriage of Lewis and Davidman was unorthodox and unexpected. He was a confirmed bachelor, an academic with a distinguished career at both Oxford and Cambridge, a popular Christian writer; she was a divorced woman with two young sons, an American of Jewish extraction, a former communist. No one would have expected that they would end up getting married, so different were their backgrounds and experiences of life. Tragically Joy contracted cancer and died in July of 1960, only a few short years after their marriage. The story-line in *Shadowlands* concentrates on Lewis' discovery of the true meaning of love so late in life (they married in April of 1956 when he was 57). Through this rather unusual relationship with Joy, Lewis learns what it means to surrender himself to love; he also discovers the cost that such love involves as he has to witness the slow and painful process of her dying. In the opening scenes of the BBC production of *Shadowlands* the voice of Lewis is heard summarizing his feelings for his terminally-ill wife:

> Why am I so afraid? I never knew that love could hurt so much. Yet I love you, and all I want is to love you.

The story illustrates well one example of a husband's love for his wife, a love which finds itself unable to hold back, unable to protect itself from risk, unable to avoid paying the price. In this sense, it reminds us of the Writer's declaration that *Christ loved the church and gave himself up for her*. True love always involves risk, the taking of a step into the fearful unknown. By its very nature love like this demands a surrender to the one loved, and this frequently means that pain and loss are involved.

This powerful statement in verse 25b that *Christ loved the church and gave himself up for her* is reminiscent of Paul's declaration in Galatians 2.20, 'the Son of God who loved me and gave himself for me'. Christ's giving of himself for the life of the church is further explained in verses 26–27. Here the scope of that love and self-giving is widened to include the whole church, which is Christ's bride. It seems likely that the Writer at this point builds upon II Corinthians 11.1–2 in which Paul the Apostle presents himself as a divinely appointed marital matchmaker whose task is to present the Corinthian church as a pure bride for Christ his Lord to wed. In verses 26–27 three phrases drawing from the language of sacrifical purity are brought into service to make the point. Christ gave himself for the church

> *in order to* consecrate and cleanse her by water and word (verse 26)
> *in order to* present her to himself all glorious, without stain, wrinkle or such like (verse 27a)
> *in order to* make her holy and without blemish (verse 27b).

Not unexpectedly, these verses have been taken to be yet another example of baptismal imagery within the epistle (see I Corinthians 6.11 for a parallel). It may be that Ezekiel 16.8–14 lies behind the unusual description here. This passage relates how Yahweh washes the blood (of birth? of battle?) from his beloved bride-to-be, Jerusalem, and claims her as his own in marriage. This image seems to underlie Moffatt's translation which speaks of Christ 'cleansing her in the bath of baptism as she utters her confession'. When is this consecration, this presentation, this sanctification to take place? The Writer does not say, but it can safely be assumed that while there is a sense in which these things are on-going in the life of the church as it is being filled by the Spirit (5.18), there is at the same time a future point of consummation in mind as well, as all three of the clauses outlined above suggest. Thus, the fine balance which the Writer maintains between present realization and future fulfilment is here also expressed.

31–33   The REB adds the parenthetical clause *in the words of scripture* to verse 31 acknowledging that a quotation from Genesis 2.24 (LXX) is being cited. It is a well-known passage, cited by Jesus in Matthew 19.5–6/Mark 10.7–8 in the debate over divorce, and by Paul in I Corinthians 6.16 in the discussion about Christians having sexual intercourse with cultic prostitutes. Clearly the idea of sexual union between a husband and wife is at the heart of the verse as *the two shall become one flesh* indicates. But how does the OT text further the argument; what is its purpose? It is really an extension of the idea that the body of the wife is actually the husband's own body and therefore he should cherish it (verse 28b). Since the two become *one flesh*, whatever is true for the one holds for the other. The logic of this means that the husband's body also belongs to the wife, although this is never explicitly brought out in the passage. This union the Writer describes as *a great truth*. The REB slightly conceals the full impact of these words because it has chosen to translate the key term 'mystery' (*to mustērion*) as *truth* here instead of *secret purpose* or *hidden purpose* as it did the five other times the word is used in the epistle (see 1.9; 3.3, 4, 9; 6.19). The key point here is that the 'mystery' is not the earthly union of husband and wife, but the heavenly union of Christ and the church to which that earthly union points. Although there are many parallels in Gnostic writings to this kind of description of the relationship between Christ and the church, it is improbable that they are responsible for the interpretation of Genesis 2.24 offered here. Such Gnostic interpretations follow on from, rather than form, the *great truth* contained in verse 32.

There is a nice line from the musical *Les Misérables*, the adaptation of Victor Hugo's novel set during the French Revolution by Alain Boubil and Claude-Michel Schönberg, which helps to illustrate the point. It runs, 'To love another person is to see the face of God.' The great truth of which the Writer speaks is that Christ and the church are united in love. Earthly marriage, in as much as it involves loving another person, allows us to see the face of God.

Verse 33 stands as a summary of what has preceded in 5.22–32, although it does reverse the order in which husbands and wives are addressed (husbands come first here). The mention of *reverence* recalls verse 21 and forms something of an *inclusio* of the passage as a whole. The word here, as in verse 21, is 'fear' (*phobos*) and suggests religious awe at the wonder of what God has done in Christ.

There are many questions about human beings and the marriage relationship that the passage does not answer. We are given here an ideal picture of how marriage operates, with mutual submission the key and a common commitment to Christ as an operating assumption for the man and woman concerned. But what if these things are not present? What if a marriage is not characterized by love and a shared vision of life together, but by increasing distance between the partners, which may have even have spilled over into hatred of each other? What happens when love has died and it all breaks down? What does Ephesians 5.21–33 tell us about separation, and divorce, and how to live with them? How is a husband or wife to handle sexual abuse within the marital relationship? The answer is, that the passage tells us nothing about such matters! Neither does it tell us anything about how humans are to handle singleness, or same-sex unions, or living with the death of one's partner. The danger is that we press too far the ideal of marriage as a union of husband and wife and define personal wholeness in these terms. Human identity and value cannot be simply equated with the role that one has in marriage, for life is infinitely more complex than that. Marriage is not the union of two *incomplete* persons, but the union of two *whole* persons. It does not mean the *loss* of human individuality, but the *discovery* of new dimensions of personhood by means of an intimate relationship with another person. At the same time, it must also be said that personal fulfilment cannot ever be limited to those who are married. To suggest otherwise would be to abuse the passage, to miss the essential point of its lessons about Christian living, and to restrict the teachings about Christ's relationship with his church. Great care, and tremendous pastoral sensitivity, must be exercised when interpreting these verses.

Advice to Children and Parents
6.1–4

This pericope forms the second part of the so-called *Haustafeln*, or household rules, which run from 5.21–6.9 (see above pp. 161–162 for a discussion of these moral codes of conduct). Here the duties and responsibilities of parents and children are set out. The short passage is divided into three parts: a command for children to obey parents (verse 1); the interjection of an OT proof-text to encourage such obedience (verses 2–3); and a command for fathers concerning the proper way to raise children (verse 4). There are three sentences in the Greek corresponding to these divisions, and these the REB faithfully reproduces. The passage is clearly reliant upon Colossians 3.20–21.

1 The pattern of the household codes continues here with specific instructions being given to particular groups. In this case, *Children, obey your parents*. The reason for such behaviour is given: *for it is only right that you should*. The RSV of this last phrase is closer to the Greek, rendering it as 'for this is right'. The fact that children are even made the focus of an exhortation can be viewed as something of a breakthrough. In many settings, then as now, children are the forgotten segment of family life, the ones who should be 'seen but not heard'.

Some important early manuscripts include the words 'in the Lord' after *parents*. This is sometimes thought to be an attempt to make the exhortation to the children conform to those given to wives in 5.22 and to slaves in 6.5, with each introductory exhortation then ending on a christological note. The parallel passage in Colossians 3.20 does contain a similar phrase, exhorting children to obey parents in all things 'for this pleases the Lord'. The REB follows the lead of the NEB in not including it, although most other translations retain it, including the AV, the RSV, the NRSV, the NIV, the NASB, the JB and Moffatt. Occasionally translations offer what is in effect an interpretation of what 'in the Lord' meant for the Writer. Note the following examples:

'Children, it is your Christian duty to obey your parents' (GNB).
'Children … obey your parents as those whom the Lord has set over you' (Phillips).
'Children be obedient to your parents as a Christian duty' (Weymouth).

'Children you must obey your parents. This is your Christian duty' (Barclay).

It is unlikely, as sometimes argued, that the inclusion of the controversial phrase should be taken as an indication that Christian children of non-Christian parents are relieved of their responsibility of obedience (i.e. because their parents are not 'in the Lord'). The assumption here is that the advice offered is for a Christian family in which parents who are endeavouring to raise their children in the faith and the children themselves are exhorted to respect the God-given family structure of which they are a part.

2–3   In the preceding pericope on the responsibilities of those who are married (5.21–33) the ethical advice was supported by an OT proof-text, namely Genesis 2.24. Here the command to children is backed up by a modified quotation of Exodus 20.12 (LXX): *'Honour your father and your mother, that it may be well with you and that you may live long on the earth.'* Effectively this is to lay another obligation upon the children: they are not only to *obey* their parents, but they are also to *honour* their parents. The REB divides the OT quotation into two parts and separates them by inserting an interpretative comment on the second half. The command to 'Honour your father and your mother' is said to be *the first commandment to carry a promise with it.* The OT also contains some passages which mention what happened if a child dishonoured his or her parents. Leviticus 20.9 mentions the death penalty for someone who curses his or her parents and Deuteronomy 21.18–21 specifies stoning for a stubborn or rebellious son.

The commandment about honouring one's parents appears frequently in the Gospels (Matthew 5.4; 19.19; Mark 7.10; 10.19; Luke 18.10).

4   The prohibition *do not goad* is directed to the *fathers* and matches the call to obedience which is laid upon the children in verse 1. The REB follows the NEB in adding the words *to resentment* to complete the thought. The NIV gives, 'do not exasperate your children', while Jordan says 'don't aggravate your kids', both of which may capture more of the essence of the underlying Greek verb. In any case, the negative statement is followed by a positive one about what the fathers are to do with their children. Fathers are to *bring them up in the discipline and instruction of the Lord*, quite a positive statement

which has no counterpart in the passage from Colossians 3.21 upon which this verse is reliant.

The discipline and instruction of children is a common theme in Jewish wisdom literature; usually sons (as opposed to daughters) are the focus of such teaching. The well-known passage from Proverbs 22.6 is a case in point: 'Train up a child in the way he should go, and even when he is old he will not depart from it.' Or similarly, Proverbs 13.24 brings together discipline and love: 'He who spares his rod hates his son, but he who loves him disciplines him diligently.' It is possible that the Writer was drawing upon this rich tradition in wisdom literature when he issued this instruction to fathers. At the same time, the value for the larger society of a good educational system of children was well recognized and had been accepted as axiomatic for centuries. In the words of the Cynic philosopher Diogenes (circa 412–323 BCE): 'The foundation of every state is the education of its youth.'

There is no explicit mention of mothers goading their children to resentment, or of mothers taking a role in the education and upbringing of the children. This is slightly unusual given the fact that *parents* are specified in verse 1 and the passage from Exodus 20.12 in verse 2 is a call to honour both father *and mother*. This is but another small indication of the patriarchal nature of Household Codes, the fact that they reflect the male-dominated societies which produced them. The power of the father of a household in much of the Graeco-Roman world was absolute. He could order his children to do as and when he liked. However, the Writer stresses that for the Christian father tyrannical rule over children is not the way to honour Christ. In effect, the authority of parenthood is to be subsumed under the greater commandment of mutual love and submission (remembering that the injunction of 5.21 governs the whole of 5.22–6.9).

Advice to Slaves and Masters
6.5–9

This pericope forms the third part of the so-called *Haustafeln*, or household rules, which run from 5.21–6.9 (see above pp. 161–162 for a discussion of these moral codes of conduct). Here the duties and responsibilities of slaves and masters are set out. The short passage is divided into two parts of rather unequal length: a command for slaves to obey their earthly masters together with some thoughts about slavery and proper motivations for service from a Christian perspective (verses 5–8), and a command for masters to treat slaves knowing that they themselves serve a heavenly Master (verse 9). We can assume that the congregation to which the letter is addressed had Christian slaves and Christian slave owners within it, although it is impossible to determine how large either group was.

The Greek consists of two sentences corresponding to the two parties who are being addressed ('slaves' in verses 5–8 and 'masters' in verse 9). The REB makes each verse of the passage a sentence. The passage has a parallel in Colossians 3.22–4.1 and is heavily dependent upon it.

5–8 In keeping with the ethical advice given in Colossians 3.22, the key command for slaves is given in verse 5 as 'obey'. Such *obedience* is to be *single-minded* (literally 'with unity of heart') and with an eye to it as being actually offered *to Christ*. The masters are described as *earthly* (literally 'according to the flesh'), which carries with it an implicit contrast to the heavenly Master, that is Christ himself. Indeed, in verse 6 the heavenly dimension of existence is brought into play when it is declared that they are actually *slaves of Christ* (verse 6) and *slaves of the Lord* (verse 7), and as such are to act accordingly.[77] A slave's service is to come 'from the soul', or as the REB puts it, *wholeheartedly*. Thus service designed to *curry favour* with the earthly masters or *catch their eye* is out of the question. Verse 8 brings the idea of reward into the discussion, making it clear that both slaves and masters are under heavenly scrutiny, reminding them that *whatever good anyone may do, slave or free, will be repaid by the Lord*. When such reward is to be rendered, and by whom (God himself? Christ?), are not clarified. We can presume that here *the Lord* means Christ, just as in II Corinthians 5.10 where Paul declares that all must

173

appear before 'the judgment seat of Christ' (although in Romans 14.10 it is 'the judgment seat of God' which all must stand before). The juxtaposition of *slave* and *free* in verse 8 recalls Galatians 3.28 where Paul declares that in Christ there is 'neither Jew nor Greek, there is neither slave nor free, there is neither male nor female'. Another instance of this contrast is found in I Corinthians 7.22 where Paul emphasizes that both slave and free find their place in Jesus Christ, even to the point that their roles are reversed: 'For he who was called in the Lord as a slave is a freedman of the Lord. Likewise he who was free when called is a slave of Christ.'

To what extent the Writer is dependent upon Paul for his ideas about slavery as an economic system is difficult to know for certain. The answer to this depends in large measure on how one interprets Colossians 3.22–4.1 and the advice that is given there in relation to the letter to Philemon. Does Paul's exhortation to slaves and masters in Colossians arise directly out of the situation with Onesimus and Philemon? Is he counselling the runaway slave Onesimus to return to his master? Is Paul trying to persuade Philemon to accept Onesimus back, or hinting that he would like Philemon to release him from his slavery so that he can assist him in his ministry? And precisely how does the Onesimus and Philemon episode fit together with the emancipation set out in Galatians 3.27–28 and (depending on how one interprets the controversial phrase at the end of verse 21) I Corinthians 7.20–24? These are matters which need not detain us here, although they do bear directly on the interpretation of 6.5–9 in one important respect.

Some have suggested that the Writer has failed to follow through with the idealized vision of equality which Paul gives in Galatians 3.27–28. On this basis it seems that both Colossians and Ephesians have lapsed back into a casual acceptance of slavery as an institution. In so doing they have defused the theological time-bomb of emancipation which Paul set ticking in Galatians 3.27–28 (and I Corinthians 7.20–24?) and call for a social conservatism which corrects the potentially dangerous teaching of the revolutionary Paul.[78] Paul the apostle of liberation, so the argument goes, would never have condoned the institution of slavery in this way, certainly not within the church, and the advice given to slaves in Colossians and Ephesians is thus seen as a betrayal of his thought. Needless to say such an interpretation has implications for the debate about Pauline authorship of both Colossians and Ephesians.

9   Masters are here addressed and told of their responsibilities to their slaves. The positive exhortation given to them is rather vague and non-specific, *treat your slaves in the same spirit*. Somewhat ironically the fact that masters are not told to 'lead' or to 'command' (as we might expect the counterpart of 'obey' to be), means that a certain degree of equality creeps into the passage. By putting the exhortation as he does the Writer places both masters and slaves on an equal footing; both groups are in the same boat, so to speak. Masters are also commanded to *give up using threats* as the means of motivating their slaves to behave. In one sense such advice is to maintain the status quo, and does not challenge the institution of slavery itself as something incompatible with Christian faith. However, we could say that the seeds of such an idea are sown with the admonition to *remember that you both have the same Master in heaven*. The mention of a *Master in heaven* stands in contrast with the masters on earth mentioned at the beginning of the verse and in verse 5. The Greek word here translated as *Master* (*ho kurios*) is elsewhere given as 'Lord' but the variation helps to bring out the contrast between the earthly and the heavenly.

The word translated as *favouritism* is an interesting one; the RSV renders it as 'partiality'. At its root the Greek word (*prosōpolēmpsia*) has the idea of acceptance based on the recognition of someone's face. The term was a popular one with Christian writers in the early church (Acts 10.34; Romans 2.11; Colossians 3.25; I Peter 1.17; James 2.1, 9).

Interestingly, the phrase *there is no favouritism with him* occupies a different place in the Colossians parallel to this passage. Here it is part of the admonition given to masters; in Colossians it is part of the admonition given to slaves (3.22–25). Thus, in Colossians 3.25 we read, 'For the wrongdoer will be paid back for the wrong he has done, and there is no partiality.' There is no equivalent to the statement about a slave's wrongdoing here in 6.5–9 and this has led to various speculations about why it is included in Colossians. Could it be because Onesimus stole money from his master Philemon, ran away, and was now seeking special consideration since he had become a Christian? Was he asking to be 'let off' because he had found Christ? Could that be the 'wrongdoing' which is in mind here? If so then the mention of *favouritism*, or partiality, could be taken as Paul's assurance to Philemon that he will countenance no such special pleading on the part of Onesimus. Certainly the placement of the declaration about favouritism makes better sense in

Ephesians than it does in Colossians. It is more natural for masters, rather than slaves, to expect privileges due to their higher social position and this the Writer warns against.

There are many good studies of the place of slavery within the ancient world, most of them written by classical historians. In fact, the subject has been something of a growth industry in recent years. These studies have enabled us to have a much more positive view of the social and economic advantages of slavery than was generally held before. This is not to belittle the fact that some slaves were treated abominably, even tortured and killed; that was certainly true. But such instances were the exception rather than the rule. Our task is to use these investigations in order to gain a balanced picture of the situation so that we can understand what the Writer has to say on the subject.

It is quite difficult for us who live in the late twentieth century to appreciate fully the complexities of the institution of slavery which the Writer addresses here. We live in a world in which the enslavement of one group of people by another has largely been abolished, in theory if not in practice. Our perceptions of slavery are inevitably shaped by the way in which it has manifested itself in our own history, namely the subjugation of African blacks by European and American whites. We are influenced by the portrayal of slavery as seen in William Wilberforce's speeches and writings, Harriet Beecher Stowe's *Uncle Tom's Cabin* (1851–52) and Alex Haley's epic novel *Roots* (1976). For us it is all too easy to see every slave master as a Simon Legree who dehumanizes the ones he owns, beating and whipping and raping as he wishes. For the Writer, however, slavery was an accepted fact of life, a way of ordering society which had stood the test of time and had much to say for itself. Approximately one third of the population of the Roman Empire, some sixty million people, were slaves and the majority of these were, as far as we are able to determine, well-treated and happy. Slavery is an economic system which the Writer seeks neither to overthrow or repudiate; he is not calling for a revolt in the spirit of Spartacus, nor for the throwing off of chains in a precursor to the Marxist class-struggle. Rather his purpose was to regulate the relationships within the institution, to make sure that Christian slaves and Christian owners of slaves behaved in such a manner that honoured Christ.

It is important to view the advice given to slaves and masters as part of the *Haustafeln*; these are instructions for the running of a household and they must be set against that backdrop. In this sense our modern preoccupation with the so-called 'nuclear family' is a hindrance for us. It may blind us to the way in which slaves were an accepted part of the household, or as we might describe it, they were part of the 'extended family'. It is also important to remember that slaves were accepted within the church from the beginning and took a full part in the life of the church. There are even examples of Christian slaves holding ecclesiastical office in the second and third centuries, although the mind boggles thinking about how a bishop might handle a dispute in a church which involved his master.

It is quite easy to point the finger at the injustices of the past, such as slavery, and with glorified hindsight pontificate about what should have been done to correct them. It is much more difficult to know what to do about the modern versions of slavery, such as working on a factory assembly line in a job that is despised simply because there are no other opportunities, or eighty-hour weeks for junior doctors who slave away in NHS hospitals at derisory salaries. On an international scale, many of the poorer countries of the world are effectively 'slaves' of richer countries with virtually the whole of their gross national income being swallowed up in paying the interest on the loans that have been taken out.

There certainly are important lessons to be learned from Ephesians 6.5–9, despite the fact that the abolition of slavery means that the language of slaves and masters does not communicate to us what it did to the original readers. Thus, Clarence Jordan's translation of the passage tries to overcome the cultural gap that exists between the first century world and ours by using language of 'employees and employers' instead of 'slaves and masters'.

Arming for Spiritual Warfare
6.10–20

This passage contains the Writer's final instructions to the church. He uses military imagery to describe the spiritual struggle of Christian life, creatively adapting passages from Isaiah 11.1; 52.7 and 59.17 and *Wisdom of Solomon* 5.17–20 in the process. The pericope may be divided into three sections: a call for the church to clothe itself with the armour of God in order to conduct the battle which must be waged against spiritual forces (verses 10–12); a description of the various pieces of military equipment which are to be put on (verses 13–17); and a short discussion on prayer which stresses the need for constant vigilance and asks for intercession that the Writer himself might be able to discharge his duties of proclaiming the gospel message with boldness (verses 18–20).

The Greek uses four sentences here (verses 10, 11–12, 13–17 and 18–20), including one rather long sentence in which the various elements of battle-dress are given. The REB uses eleven sentences to cover the same ground. The material on prayer (verses 18–20) is reliant upon Colossians 4.2–4.

10–12   The Writer now moves toward the conclusion of his work, beginning the passage with *Finally*. The exhortation in verse 10 to *find your strength in the Lord* transforms what is a passive declaration in Greek into an active one. The key verb might be better rendered as 'Be strengthened …' thereby suggesting that God, or Christ, is the one responsible for the strengthening.

In verse 11 one of the images for which this passage is most famous, the 'full armour of God', is introduced. This will be taken up and expanded and elaborated upon more fully in verses 13–17, but here the exhortation is given as: *Put on* the full armour provided by God. Jordan has a nice turn of phrase for this, giving it as 'put on God's uniform'. This armour is provided so that the saints *may be able to stand firm against the stratagems of the devil*. Where does this idea of 'the armour of God' come from? Romantic notions about Paul the Apostle composing the passage while gazing at the equipment worn by one of the Roman legionaries assigned to guard him are not uncommon. Roman military equipment is detailed in both Polybius *Histories* 6.23 and Josephus *The Jewish War* 3.93–97. In addition, there certainly are a number of instances where military imagery is used in the Pauline letters, most importantly in I Thessalonians 5.8: 'Put on the breastplate of faith and love, and for a helmet the hope of salvation', and Romans 13.12, 'put on the armour of light' (also see Romans 6.13, 23; II Corinthians 6.7; 10.3–5). It could be that these are sufficient in themselves to have fired the Writer's imagination to construct his picture of 'the armour of God'. However, we perhaps need to push the question one stage further and ask where Paul may have acquired his inspiration in this matter, particularly for I Thessalonians 5.8. The answer seems obvious when one recalls the long-standing OT picture of Yahweh as the Divine Warrior coming to the rescue of his people. Nowhere is this more clearly presented than in Isaiah 11.4–5; 52.7 and 59.17 and *Wisdom of Solomon* 5.17–20, and it is probably on these passages that both I Thessalonians 5.8 and Ephesians 6.11–17 depend. The texts from Isaiah and *Wisdom of Solomon* are worth citing in full (the REB translation of the Isaiah texts and the RSV of the *Wisdom of Solomon* is used here):

11.4   But with justice he will judge the poor
and defend the humble in the land with equity;
like a rod his verdict will strike the ruthless,
and with his word he will slay the wicked.

11.5   He will wear the belt of justice,
and truth will be his girdle.

52.7   How beautiful on the mountains are the feet of the herald,
the bringer of good news, announcing deliverance,
proclaiming to Zion, 'Your God has become king.'

59.17   He put on righteousness as a breastplate
and salvation as a helmet on his head;
he put on the garments of vengeance
and wrapped zeal about him like a cloak.

5.17   The Lord will take his zeal as his whole armour,
and will arm all creation to repel his enemies;

5.18   he will put on righteousness as a breastplate,
and wear impartial justice as a helmet;

5.19   he will take holiness as an invincible shield,

5.20   and sharpen stern wrath for a sword,
and creation will join with him to fight against the
madmen

The intriguing thing about the Writer's use of the Divine Warrior motif is that the various pieces of equipment which Yahweh is said to wear are now given to the church. In this sense the church truly wears 'the armour *of God*'. It is armour that has been divinely fashioned, as the armour worn by Achilles was made by the god Hephaestus (*Iliad* Book 18).

Such accoutrements are needed to withstand the various wiles of *the devil*, who was mentioned in 4.27, where believers were exhorted not to let anger provide an opportunity for the devil to gain control over them. That devilish *stratagems* may be deployed by earthly agents was suggested in 4.14 where the same Greek word used here was rendered by the REB as *schemes*. The language of *burning arrows of the evil one* is quite dazzling and may remind us of Shakespeare's Hamlet who has to decide

> Whether 'tis nobler in the mind to suffer
> The slings and arrows of outrageous fortune,
> or to take arms against a sea of troubles,
> And by opposing end them?
>
> (*Hamlet* III, i)

For Hamlet, as for our Writer, the question is one concerning the nature of human existence in the face of the hosts of evil which surround. For Hamlet, as for the Christians our Writer addresses, the idea of taking up arms in an act of opposition is entertained. But to what purpose? What does it mean for Hamlet 'to take arms against a sea of troubles'? Does he intend to fight against the sea of troubles and end their power over him? Or does he intend to take up arms against himself, to commit suicide, and thereby end the suffering of his life? Shakespeare's play has been interpreted in both ways; the ambiguity of the passage is celebrated. For our Writer, however, there is no such uncertainty about taking up arms in spiritual warfare, nor are there any doubts as to its outcome. While individual skirmishes must still be fought out on earth, the church can be confident that the war has already been won in the heavenly field of conflict.

It is clear that within these verses the author of Ephesians is using a military metaphor as a means of presenting the struggle against evil which is a part of the church's life. Some commentators take this to be something of a novelty, as if to suggest that Ephesians 6.10–20 is presenting this struggle of Christianity in a way never before understood. In fact, however, the idea of the spiritual life as a battle against forces of evil is widespread within the ancient world, as we noted above in connection with the light/darkness contrast contained in 5.7–11. In addition, the image of the soldier donning armaments so as to engage in spiritual battle is one which has found expression throughout history.[79]

One final comment on verse 11: it is worth noting that the verb rendered as *Put on* was used earlier in 4.24 where the church was exhorted to 'put on the new Humanity'. In effect, this suggests that to 'put on the new Humanity' is to 'don the armour of God'.

Verse 12 is one of the most controversial in the epistle, setting out the image of spiritual warfare which is conducted on a cosmic, as opposed to an earthly, battlefield. The mental picture is quite a striking one, vaguely reminiscent of the wrestling match that Jacob has with an angelic being in Genesis 32.24–30, an image which has fired the imagination of artists over the years. In Jacob's case, however, the struggle was with an angelic being, a 'man', who serves as an agent of God himself; here the image is more malevolent. As the Writer puts it: *our struggle is not against human foes, but against cosmic powers*. These *cosmic powers* are then further explained as *the authorities and potentates of this dark age* and *the superhuman forces of evil in the heavenly realms*. The translation of J. B. Phillips is imaginative and captures the point well; he gives verse 12b as: 'We are up against the unseen power that controls this dark world, and spiritual agents from the very headquarters of evil.' A new term is even coined here by our Writer; the word describing the *potentates* which inhabit *this dark age* is literally 'cosmocrats' (*kosmokratoras*), an astrological term which is picked up and extensively used by later Gnostic writers.

Precisely how these various components fit together, what ranking order they have, and what the hierarchy of the Satanic forces is, are matters which are never set out in the letter. It is unwise to try and determine the rank structure of these forces of evil, as Milton recognized in his *Paradise Lost* where the various levels of Satanic forces ('Thrones, Dominations, Princedoms, Virtues, and Powers', Book 5, line 772) are similarly fluid and often interchanged one with the other. The Writer simply strings together a number of related terms and ideas, piling phrase upon phrase in his own inimitable way. The language owes much to Jewish apocalyptic literature in which battle in heaven between godly and satanic forces was frequently described (as in Revelation 12.7–8 for example).

Yet one thing does stand out as rather odd within the verse. So unusual is the description of *Christians* as engaged in battle against spiritual forces of evil that occasionally verse 12 is regarded as an interpolation into the letter, perhaps coming from the circles of Valentinian Gnosticism. However, there are really no grounds for such a suggestion, beyond the fact that the whole idea of Christians conducting spiritual warfare is explicitly stated nowhere else in the Pauline letters.

The word *struggle* can mean an athletic contest or a wrestling-match; hence the AV translation 'For we *wrestle* not against flesh and blood'. *In the heavenly realms* is a phrase which occurs four times elsewhere in the letter (1.3, 20; 2.6; 3.10), as we have already noted in previous discussion. For some strange reason it is missing from P[46] although there is little doubt that it is original and should be included in the text. The verse is frequently cited in later Gnostic literature, no doubt because it was thought to lend support to their dualistic worldview. What does the Writer mean by describing the spiritual *struggle* as something which takes place *in the heavenly realms*? And more importantly, what does he intend his readers to understand their role to be in this battle? What is the 'battle station' of the church within this spiritual war? An illustration might help us to make progress in understanding the main point at issue, as well as provide an entry-point for discussing what is meant by 'principalities and powers'.

Some years ago a Chinese Christian known by the name Watchman Nee published a small book on Ephesians entitled *Sit, Walk, Stand*.[80] Nee took the three words of his book's title to be a succinct summary of the theological message of the letter. As he puts it, the epistle defines our position in Christ (*sitting* with him in the heavenlies), our life in the world (*walking* as befits a believer), and our attitude to the enemy (*standing* as a soldier of Christ). Nee stressed that the order of these three actions is very important if we are to capture the full meaning of the truth contained in the letter. Christians must learn to sit before they can walk, and be able to walk before they can stand in spiritual battle. This is a simple, but thought-provoking, digest of the theology of Ephesians and there is much to commend it. However, there are further questions which must be put to it. We might ask: *where* does the church fight it out? *Where* does she make her stand? Is it on earth? 'No!', the answer comes back; she makes it *in the heavenly realms*, since that is where she is positioned (seated!) in Christ.

This is why, so it seems, the Writer says in verse 12 that *our struggle is not against human foes, but against cosmic powers*. But does this way of reading the verse do justice to the agonies, the struggles and conflicts, of Christian existence in the real world? Does it not tend to over-spiritualize the issue, to trivialize what are genuine concerns in the life of the church on earth? When the 'powers' of which the passage speaks are identified exclusively, or even primarily, as 'spiritual' or 'heavenly' forces, is there not something lost in the process? Is there a danger that we lose the ability to see that there is also a sense in which the powers are still real and operating in the earthly realm?

Clearly the 'principalities and powers' are somehow related to the social and political structures of the world; they are the invisible spiritual forces which lie behind those structures. The question we desperately need to ask is: what is the *nature* of that relationship? An illustration from a film about the American war in Vietnam may help us to grasp an essential truth here.

Oliver Stone's award-winning film *Platoon* (1986) provides us with a graphic account of the horrors of modern warfare, sparing no details as to the brutality which went on in Vietnam. The story is narrated through the eyes of one young American soldier named Chris Taylor who is assigned to the Twenty-Fifth Infantry Division, serving near the Cambodian border in 1967. We follow him as he first arrives in Saigon aboard a troop transport plane, walking down the exit ramp where he is confronted by scenes of black body-bags which are loaded on to the plane for the return flight to the USA. This is a portent of what is to follow; death is everywhere and survival is a matter of chance. We follow Chris as he learns how to survive the madness of the war, as he learns to kill and to avoid being killed. We watch as the final fire-fight of the film shows us Chris's platoon overrun by hundreds of enemy soldiers; there is killing and slaughter and butchery all around. After the battle is over we hear the radio operator of the platoon report back to head-quarters that hundreds of enemy soldiers had been killed, together with many American troops. Chris has managed to survive, although he is wounded. A helicopter arrives to take him and other wounded soldiers away to safety, and Chris is loaded aboard. The final scenes of the film have him looking out of the open door of the helicopter, viewing the chaos below as the chopper takes off. We see the agony on his face, and we hear his thoughts in the form of a voice-over:

I think now, looking back, we did not fight the enemy. We fought ourselves, and the enemy was in us ...

What does he mean by this? There is, of course, a sense in which Chris is perfectly correct. The 'war' in which he had been engaged was an internal one; it was a spiritual struggle, if you will. The film brings this out very well and captures our imaginations as this theme is explored. Chris is having to learn to live with himself, to identify those competing feelings which reside within his heart and confront them, to fight the demon which oppresses him. We can understand what he means when he says that 'We fought ourselves, and the enemy was in us.' But one wonders at the end of the day what the Vietnamese people would have said about the matter. Was it simply Chris's 'internal war' for them? Do the innumerable dead bodies, on both sides of the conflict, testify to this as essentially a 'spiritual struggle'? Surely we would have to say that such an assessment is an offence; it belittles the conflict and the tremendous human costs involved (let us never forget that nearly *one million* Vietnamese people perished in the conflict). To say that 'we fought ourselves, and the enemy was in us' is not the same as saying 'we did not fight the enemy'. In this sense Chris's final words are right in what they affirm, but they are wrong in what they deny. They are true in so far as they point to the heavenly dimension of spiritual warfare, but they are wrong in suggesting that spiritual warfare is unconnected to the human dimension of such battle.

To apply the idea to our text: we could say that while the Writer stresses *our struggle is against cosmic powers*, we cannot assume therefore that it has nothing whatsoever to do with *human foes*. His contrast between *cosmic powers* and *human foes* is deliberate hyperbole. It is a statement made for effect, and is not to be absolutized. To return to the phrasing of Watchman Nee for a moment, the temptation is to equate 'sitting in the heavenly realms' with 'standing in spiritual battle', and to overlook the 'walking in the world'. This is a grave mistake, for 'walking in the world' is the point at which spiritual battle against cosmic powers *is* battle against human foes.

We have already had several occasions above to note how important the idea of 'walking' as an ethical way of life is within the letter (see the comments on 2.6; 4.1, 17; 5.2, 8, 15). 'Walking in the world' invariably means that evil and wickedness are encountered on the plane of human life, in the real world. This leads us to consider one of the key interpretative debates on 6.12.

Are the 'principalities and powers' impersonal forces or are they evil spiritual beings who exist in their own right and operate through human agents? How far do we need to guard against the tendency to attribute personality to the devil and his minions?[81] The reason why these questions are so important is because they have direct implications for the church's role in opposing human institutions and structures of society. If 'principalities and powers' is theological shorthand for such things as 'the abomination of apartheid' or 'the iniquity of child abuse', then spiritual battle must be waged on earth and our struggle then does become one against *human foes* and human institutions. On the other hand, if 'principalities and powers' means spiritual beings (the devil and his cronies) who populate the air above the earth (see 2.2), then the focus of the battle is on these personified evil entities. Only secondarily do we look at the way in which these evil beings influence human beings and control them, and thereby move to the battle against human foes.

Our task is to sail between the Scylla, which sees the battle as one against social and political institutions and effectively denies that spiritual forces of evil underlie these human structures, and the Charybdis, which views the battle as one against evil spiritual beings and effectively denies that these malevolent forces manifest themselves in very human constructs.

Perhaps there is a way to sail the straits and bring these two different perspectives together, one which involves the simple addition of a clarifying clause to 6.12 so as to get to the Writer's main point and avoid a false dichotomy. If we were to translate the verse as: 'For our struggle is not *in the first instance* against human foes, but against cosmic powers, against the authorities and potentates of this dark age, against the superhuman forces of evil in the heavenly realms', then a proper balance between the earthly and the cosmic dimensions of the spiritual war can be maintained.

Given the importance of such matters for the life of the church it is understandable that the interpretation of 6.12 has been the subject of intense scholarly interest. We have space to mention the work of three different authors who have devoted their attentions to the subject. Together these studies provide much food for thought on this most complicated of issues.

First, we note the work of Walter Wink, who offers one of the most thorough investigations into the issue of spiritual warfare. His 'The Powers Trilogy', *Naming the Powers* (1984); *Unmasking the Powers* (1986) and *Engaging the Powers* (1992), sets a standard against which other studies of the subject are to be measured. Rightfully dismissing any interpretation of 'principalities and powers' which denies that they ever meant personalized demonic forces, Wink attempts to offer an interpretation which is both sensitive to the NT materials and yet intelligible and relevant for the modern person.

Second, there is Clinton E. Arnold's monograph entitled *Ephesians: Power and Magic* (1989).[82] This is an extremely interesting book which attempts to interpret the 'spiritual battle' of Ephesians 6.12 against the setting of first century Asia Minor in which fear of the demonic world prevailed and the use of magic was seen as a means of protection against hostile forces. The great strength of Arnold's study is the way in which he uses other materials from the first century world of Ephesus, capital city of Asia Minor and the site of the all-important Temple of Artemis/Diana, to assist in interpreting the Ephesus setting to which the letter is addressed. Included among these materials are magical papyri, amulets and incantations and the *Ephesia Grammata*, a set of symbols or letters which were worn by people like a lucky charm in an attempt to ward off evil spirits. This interpretation does presume that the influence of the cult of Artemis was widespread, which it would have to be if, as we suggested earlier, the letter was originally directed to the church at Hierapolis (see above pp. 31–48). However, this is not beyond the realm of possibility given the nature of the cult and the fact that it was readily adapted into Roman religion as worship of Diana, goddess of the hunt.

Third, we note Neil Elliott's *Liberating Paul: The Justice of God and the Politics of the Apostle* (1995). Elliott's book is not one dedicated to a study of the 'powers and principalities' *per se*, but he does offer an important challenge to Walter Wink's influential interpretation of the topic. The main point of critique involves Wink's suggestion that the cross represents the *defeat* of the powers of evil, an idea which is based in large measure on his interpretation of Colossians 2.15. Elliott disputes this and says that the cross, far from representing *victory* over the powers of evil, simply reveals the power of *violence* in the world. The defeat of the power of evil is something which is to be awaited in the future resurrection, as hinted at in I Corinthians 15.24. Thus, any reading of Ephesians 6.12 which assumes that the victory over evil has already taken place, or that the focus of the spiritual war is against the cosmic forces in the heavenlies, actually threatens to undermine the real struggle which still continues on earth. In this sense, so Elliott argues, Ephesians can actually become a liability to a church which is seeking to remain true to Paul the Apostle's vision of liberation by spiritualizing the conflict (he assumes that Ephesians is written by a later writer who contributes to 'the canonical betrayal of the apostle').[83] Elliott's book is filled with examples drawn from history and the world of international politics (as is Wink's *Engaging the Powers*) and this makes it particularly interesting to read.

13–17   The metaphor of spiritual armour, 'the panoply of God', first mentioned in verse 11, is taken up and expounded here. Six articles of the spiritual armoury are specified, each of which symbolizes a key aspect of Christian truth. Obviously these truths have an important place in the thought of the Writer, and several of them, such as *peace* and *salvation*, hold special places within the argument of the letter.

Equipment	*Symbol*
a *belt*	of *truth* (verse 14a)
a *breastplate*	of *integrity* (verse 14b)
a pair of *shoes*	of *preparedness* for proclaiming the *gospel of peace* (verse 15)
a *shield*	of *faith* (verse 16)
a *helmet*	of *salvation* (verse 17a)
a *sword*	of the *Spirit, the word of God* (verse 17b)

The image of a soldier properly dressed for battle is a provocative one; what is perhaps most striking about it is that the soldier assumes a *defensive* posture. He is told that he must stand his ground in battle, after having dressed himself appropriately. The four participles in verses 14–16 and the verb in verse 17 are all in the aorist tense, suggesting action that precedes the command to *stand fast* which comes at the beginning of verse 14. The logical sense of these verses is the reverse of what the REB at first glance suggests. We could bring out the order of action with a translation such as: ''Having fastened on the belt of truth around your waist, and having put on the breastplate of integrity, and having shod your feet with the gospel of peace, and having taken up the shield of faith, and having donned the helmet of salvation and the sword of the Spirit, *then* stand fast.'

The REB renders the various participles and verbs in these verses as imperatives, which is possible as long as it does not detract from the initial command to *stand fast* which really governs the action of verses 14–17. In fact the idea of the Christian soldier holding his position, of standing his ground, is found three times in as many verses. He is exhorted: *stand your ground* (verse 13); *stand fast* (verse 14); and to allow the shoes on his feet *to give firm footing* (verse 15). The picture here presented is thus not of a soldier on the march, nor of a soldier advancing or attacking a new enemy, but of a soldier defending, or reclaiming, territory that has already been won. The unspoken suggestion is that Christ himself has already won the spiritual victory over the powers of darkness, that he has already conquered the prince of the powers of the air (2.2). The Christian is thus to face his opponent confident in the victory of Christ and not retreat or turn around and flee in fear. John Bunyan makes great use of this imagery in *The Pilgrim's Progress* (1678) when he describes Christian encountering Apollyon, the figure of Satan, in the Valley of Humiliation:

> Then did Christian begin to be afraid, and to cast in his mind whether to go back, or to stand his ground. But he considered again that he had no Armour for his back, and therefore thought that to turn the back to him might give him greater advantage with ease to pierce him with his darts; therefore he resolved to venture, and stand his ground.[84]

The Christian's job is to stand firm in light of the reality of Christ's victory, and to serve as an occupying force in the land which the Lord has already conquered. Such an interpretation is supported by the fact that the spiritual weaponry catalogued in verses 14–17 is primarily, but not exclusively, defensive in nature. We could say that Christians wage warfare against the principalities and powers not *for* victory, but *from* a position of victory. Thus, the Writer's eschatological perspective shapes the description of this military action; victory is both *now* and *not yet*.

A hint of the realized eschatology, the present reality of victory, is seen in the phrase 'helmet of salvation' in verse 17. In I Thessalonians 5.8 the helmet is described only as '*the hope* of salvation'. For our Writer the focus has shifted; what was hoped for is now realized within the life of the church, at least in part.

Similarly, the phrase *on the evil day* can also be seen to illustrate the Writer's eschatological perspective. The phrase is one that appears frequently in apocalyptic literature and is often associated with the

OT idea of the Day of the Lord when God comes to set right the wickedness of the world. The tradition that human wickedness must reach mammoth proportions, that *the evil day* must come before Christ can return at the parousia is also well known (see II Thessalonians 2.3–12). Probably the Writer has this future day of final judgment in mind here, although the present struggle of the church against wickedness can also be described as *the evil day*. Again, the present and the future are held in dynamic tension within the thought of the Writer of the epistle.

The military imagery of 6.10–27 has been taken up by countless hymn writers over the years. Two examples will serve to illustrate. The first is Charles Wesley's hymn, 'Soldiers of Christ, arise'. Two stanzas will suffice to demonstrate the influence of these verses from Ephesians upon it:

1.
Soldiers of Christ, arise,
and put your armour on,
Strong in the strength which
    God supplies
Through his eternal Son;
Strong in the Lord of hosts,
And in his mighty power,
Who in the strength of Jesus
    trusts
Is more than conqueror.

2.
Stand then in his great might,
With all his strength endued;
But take, to arm you for the
    fight,
The panoply of God;
That, having all things done,
And all your conflicts passed,
Ye may o'ercome through Christ
    alone,
And stand entire at last.[85]

The second example is the traditional Irish hymn 'Be thou my vision', translated by Mary Elizabeth Byrne (1880–1931) and versified by Eleanor Hull (1861–1935). The third stanza reads:

> Be thou my breastplate, my sword for the fight;
> Be thou my whole armour, be thou my true might;
> Be thou my soul's shelter, be thou my strong tower:
> O raise thou me heavenward, great Power of my power.[86]

18–20   The focus now shifts from the military imagery of a soldier, decked out for battle against the powers of evil, to the language of prayer. This is to say, the spiritual battle that the soldier must enter into is one of prayer. Prayer is not another part of the soldier's spiritual equipment, as is sometimes suggested, but is the battle itself. Thus, the command *Constantly ask God's help in prayer* in verse 18 is syntactically dependent upon the command to *Stand fast* at the beginning of verse 14.

Is it not somewhat odd to describe prayer in this manner? In II Corinthians 10.4 Paul declares that 'The weapons we wield are not merely human; they are strong enough with God's help to demolish strongholds' (REB). To force an illustrative point here, the movement from *foothold* to *stronghold* is ominous and warns against the *stranglehold* of Satan which the believer must ever resist. What kind of weapons are in mind here? Mahatma Gandhi once said:

> To recognize evil and not oppose it is to surrender your humanity. To recognize evil and oppose it with the weapons of the evil-doer is to enter into your humanity. To recognize evil and to oppose it with the weapons of God is to enter into your divinity.[87]

Praying and *constantly asking for God's help* are given as the primary ways that the soldier stands his ground; these are the means whereby the weapons of God are brought to bear on the conflict against the powers of darkness. This is again to be reliant upon *the power of the Spirit*. The readers are exhorted in verse 18 to *keep watch and persevere*, and to *intercede for all God's people*. The call for vigilance is reminiscent of Jesus' plea in the garden of Gethsemane for his disciples to stand with him, to stay awake and pray with him in the hour of his greatest need (Matthew 26.3–44/Mark 14.34–40/Luke 22.40–46).

In verses 19–20 the Writer specifically asks for his readers to intercede on his behalf so that he may *boldly and freely make known the hidden purpose of the gospel*. Boldness in speech is also mentioned in both Philippians 1.20 and Philemon 8; clearly it is part of the apostolic response to imprisonment (see Acts 28.31 for another example). This is reflected in our passage where it occurs both as a noun form (verse 19) and a verb form (verse 20). The Writer describes such bold proclamation as his God-given *duty*, tying together his calling and the responsibility of revealing the gospel's *hidden purpose* (see the comments above on 1.9; 3.3, 4, 9; 5.32 for further discussion of this idea of *to musterion* which is so central to the epistle).

Prayer has been a theme within the epistle, as is most evident in the Writer's own prayers on behalf of his readers (1.15–23 and

3.14–21). It is only fitting that he here asks them to return the favour. The appeal for prayer support is based on Colossians 4.3–4 although there the request is that the church might pray for Paul and his fellow-workers; here (under the guise of pseudonymity) it is for the Writer himself, or rather for the Writer to be able to proclaim the message of the gospel openly and freely. The 'mystery of the gospel', the proclamation that God is in the process of bringing everything to its intended purpose, is at the top of the prayer list as far as the Writer is concerned.

In Robert Bolt's award-winning play about the life of Sir Thomas More, *A Man for All Seasons* (1960), we have another story of a man imprisoned, and eventually beheaded, for the sake of his convictions. In this regard the story is not unlike the legends about Paul and his eventual death. The point of controversy was the rightness or wrongness of Henry VIII's marriage to Anne Boleyn; did Sir Thomas approve or disapprove of the marriage? In this case, however, Sir Thomas was imprisoned and killed not because of any open proclamation he had made about the marriage, but because of his silence over the matter. Indeed, Bolt makes much of this theme of silence within the climactic second act of his thought-provoking play when Sir Thomas is on trial before a Cromwellian-led court. On this particular matter the two prisoners (the pseudonymous Writer, presenting himself as 'Paul', and the silent figure of Sir Thomas More) stand in contrast. Our Writer, again donning the mantle of his beloved teacher Paul, asks for the church to pray that he might have the courage to speak openly.

Verse 20 contains the third explicit reference to the imprisonment within the letter (recalling the statements made in 3.1 and 4.1): *I am an ambassador – in chains*. Paul describes himself and his co-workers in similar terms in II Corinthians 5.20 and the verse is reliant upon that tradition. There is something of a deliberate paradox in the description, given that ambassadors in the ancient world would have had diplomatic immunity; an ambassador *in chains* is a self-contradiction. The word translated as *ambassador* is not actually a noun as the REB (and most other translations) suggest. It is actually a verb, but there is no suitable equivalent in English; the nearest we can get is to say 'I *serve* as an ambassador.'

Nelson Mandela stands as the archetypal image of a modern 'ambassador in chains', or rather an ambassador of freedom who has known what it is like to be chained in prison for the sake of one's convictions. He spent over twenty-seven years in various prisons within South Africa, from 5 August 1962 until his much-publicized release on 11 February 1990. Mandela, at the conclusion of his autobiography *Long Walk to Freedom* (1994), writes powerfully of his deep sense of identification with the people of South Africa and of his commitment to help them all learn to live without the restrictions of chains:

> I am no more virtuous or self-sacrificing than the next man, but I found that I could not even enjoy the poor and limited freedoms I was allowed when I knew my people were not free. Freedom is indivisible; the chains on any one of my people were the chains on all of them, the chains on all of my people were the chains on me. It was during those long and lonely years that my hunger for the freedom of my own people became a hunger for the freedom of all people, white and black. I knew as well as I knew anything that the oppressor must be liberated just as surely as the oppressed. A man who takes away another man's freedom is a prisoner of hatred, he is locked behind the bars of prejudice and narrow-mindedness. I am not truly free if I am taking away someone else's freedom, just as surely as I am not free when my freedom is taken away from me. The oppressed and the oppressor alike are robbed of their humanity. When I walked out of prison, that was my mission, to liberate the oppressed and the oppressor alike.[88]

The Promise of a Colleague and Final Blessings
6.21–24

In these concluding words of the letter the Writer promises to send to the church his colleague Tychicus who will keep them informed about his activities and encourage them in their life together. He then offers his final words of blessing to the church (presumably, according to our reckoning, to the church in Hierapolis).

The Greek consists of three sentences (verses 21–22, 23 and 24), which the REB gives as five. The promise to send Tychicus in verses 6.21–22 is a virtual repeat of Colossians 4.7–8.

21–22 These verses contain the longest word for word quotation from Colossians which is to be found in the letter (thirty-two consecutive words at one point). There are only two minor differences between Ephesians 6.21–22 and Colossians 4.7–8. First, in Ephesians 6.21 the phrase *and what I am doing* is added to the statement *You will want to know how I am* (which comes from Colossians 4.7). Second, in addition to describing Tychicus as a *dear brother and trustworthy helper*, Colossians 4.7 also calls him a *fellow-servant*, or 'co-slave', a title which Ephesians drops. This may be due to the Writer wishing to stress himself as the one who is the imprisoned slave for the Lord.

In Colossians 4.9 Tychicus is mentioned along with the runaway slave Onesimus as ones who are being sent by Paul to the church in order to keep them up to date about his activities. However, Onesimus drops out completely from the concluding remarks here and nothing else is heard about him. In fact, Paul mentions the names of a dozen friends and colleagues in Colossians 1.1 and 4.7–17, but only one from that list, Tychicus, reappears here, presumably as the bearer of the letter. Precisely why Tychicus is singled out is a matter of great speculation and is inevitably tied up with debates about Pauline authorship of the epistle. Some even go so far as to suggest that Tychicus was the author of the pseudonymous letter (see the discussion on Authorship above on pp. 26–29).

Technically, the phrase *I am sending him* is in the past tense ('I *sent* him'), but this is an epistolary aorist and the Writer is adopting the perspective of his readers who will receive Tychicus at the same time that they receive the letter he bears. The REB is quite justified in using the present tense here.

23–24   The Writer concludes his letter as he began, wishing that both *peace* (verse 23) and *grace* (verse 24) might be upon the church. Here he reverses the order of the two words from that given in 1.2, effectively starting and ending the letter on a note of *grace*. The final wishes and benediction here are not wildly out of line with what we find elsewhere in the Pauline letters, but they are abbreviated. There is, for example, no promise of a visit from the Writer (as there is in Romans 15.32; I Corinthians 16.5–7; II Corinthians 13.10), nor is there any mention of a personalizing autograph to authenticate the letter (as there is in Galatians 6.1; I Corinthians 16.21; Colossians 4.14 and II Thessalonians 3.17).

In verse 23 the Writer wishes *Peace to the community*. We have already noted how important the idea of *peace* is to our Writer, particularly in 2.14 where Christ himself is described as *our peace*, the one who brings about peace by his death. Interestingly, the word which the REB renders here as *community* is in fact the word 'brothers' and this is the only time it occurs in the plural within the epistle ('brother' is used in 6.21 to describe Tychicus). By translating it as *community* the REB avoids the sexism of 'brothers' and more accurately captures the nature of the community which certainly would have been composed of both men and women. The NRSV similarly uses 'the community' at this point, following through an editorial policy on the part of the translators to avoid sexist language.

The concluding phrase of verse 24 is somewhat unusual, as the variety of translations for the verse indicate; the REB gives it as *with undying love*, the NEB as 'with unfailing love.' Literally, the Greek is 'in immortality' and the word *love* has to be brought in from earlier in the verse to fill out the meaning. Thus, Barclay gives the final phrase as 'with a love that will never die'. However, the Greek word here is *aphtharsia* (only here in Ephesians!) and it is to be distinguished from *aionia*; we are not talking simply of a love which goes on 'forever' on the horizontal plane of history. The point of stress here is not on love that is *unending*, but rather on love that is *incorruptible*, a love that speaks to the vertical plane of relationships and encounter with God, if you will. In short, we could say that the *quality*, rather than the *quantity*, of love directed to the Lord Jesus Christ is what is in mind here (see Romans 2.7 and I Corinthians 15.42, 50, 53–54 for interesting parallels). It is not a question of how long love lasts, but a question of what kind of love it is that occupies our Writer's thoughts. In the end, it is a love which is free from corruption which is praised.

EPHESIANS FOR THE CONTEMPORARY WORLD

No other letter of the Pauline corpus has been so variously assessed as has Ephesians. If it is true that the sign of true art is that it is both loved and loathed, then Ephesians certainly qualifies as an artistic work. At one end of the spectrum we have C. H. Dodd who described it as 'the crown of Paulinism',[89] A. S. Peake who said it was 'the quintessence of Pauline thought',[90] and Samuel Taylor Coleridge who said it was 'the divinest composition of man'.[91] At the other end we have Neil Elliott who describes the letter as part of the 'canonical betrayal of the Apostle',[92] and E. Elizabeth Johnson who feels that the Writer contradicts, rather than merely reinterprets his teacher Paul, particularly in his teaching about marriage. This she says 'must derive from a sense of great peril', and suggests that the author 'operates more from fear than from faith'.[93] This is as if to suggest that Paul's daring dream of equality has been interpreted as a nefarious nightmare whose implementation spells disaster and chaos in society!

Does Ephesians represent the 'Hope diamond' of the Pauline corpus, or is it a mere 'paste', a piece of polished glass which masquerades for the real thing? One of the most important ways of addressing this kind of question is to analyse the impact that Ephesians has had upon the life of the church and to attempt to discover its relevance for the modern world.

Perhaps the most potent image which demonstrates the powerful influence of Ephesians on subsequent generations is from its depiction of spiritual warfare in 6.10–17. In particular, the suggestive picture that Ephesians 6.12 gives of a battle between the forces of good and evil in the heavenly realms has yielded a rich harvest both in literature and art. The image of such a heavenly war is foundational to Milton's *Paradise Lost*, for example. Thus Milton has Satan, admitting that he has been cast from heaven but vowing that the spiritual battle will continue, declare:

195

> We may with more successful hope resolve
> To wage by force or guile eternal War
> Irreconcilable, to our grand Foe,
> Who now triumphs, and in th'excess of joy
> Sole reigning holds the Tyranny of Heav'n.
> (Book I, lines 120–124).

The point here is that from Satan's perspective God's reign in heaven is a reign of tyranny. This sets up the ceaseless battle between the forces of evil and good and leads us back to the struggle against *the cosmic powers*, the *authorities and potentates of this dark age*, the superhuman *forces of evil in the heavenly realms* of which Ephesians 6.12 speaks so powerfully.

Numerous artists give representations of the defeat of Satan and his angelic host by the forces of good and righteousness. Often the archangel Michael is depicted as the field commander of God's army, largely because of the description of the heavenly battle provided in Revelation 12.7–9. Albrecht Dürer's famous woodcut series of 1498 entitled *Die Apokalypse* (see Frontispiece) includes a representation of this scene which might be said to illustrate the imagery of both Ephesians 6.12 and Revelation 12.7–11 admirably. It has Michael and three of his angelic army descending from heaven above, attacking the satanic forces of evil which are depicted as dragon-like beings, complete with wings, horns, claws and forked-tongues. Below them is a scene of peaceful earth, an idyllic portrayal of the countryside surrounding Dürer's native city Nürnberg. The woodcut clearly places the spiritual warfare as taking place 'in the air' (as in Ephesians 2.2), between the earth below (where the saints live) and the heavenlies above (where Christ sits enthroned). The same basic image has been used throughout Christian history, with many other artists choosing to create similar visions of spiritual battle.

We should not think that creative imagination has ceased in the modern era, however. The powerfully evocative image of spiritual warfare which we find introduced in Ephesians 6.12 finds contemporary expression even in the midst of our fast-paced, computer age. As a case in point, we note the release by Wisdom Tree, Inc. in 1992 of a computer game entitled *Spiritual Warfare*. This is a Nintendo-type platform game which is obviously designed to attract the interest of Christians who enjoy computer games but want to avoid the blood-thirsty nature of many 'shoot-em-up' type software programmes on the market. The text of Ephesians 6.13–18 is quoted in full on the opening page of the instruction manual, together with the following two paragraphs which explain the basis of the game itself:

> Experience 'Spiritual Warfare' as you discover firsthand the whole armor of God in preparation to meet the enemies of the Lord. You will also see just how the fruit of the Spirit can impact the lives of others and ultimately win an entire city to God. The shield of faith will be your most important weapon in helping you to remain steadfast. But remember the battle is not yours alone, it is the Lord's.
>
> *Object of the Game*: As a soldier in the army of the Lord, you explore the various sections of the city to collect the six pieces of the Armor of God. During your exciting journey, you will also convert non-believers and destroy the sources of evil. You start with just the basics, but as you progress through the game, you collect more Fruits of the Spirit and Armor of God to become more and more powerful.

We may think the whole idea rather crass and demeaning, particularly in connection with the way in which it uses scripture (the 'fruit of the Spirit' from Galatians 5.22 becomes pears, pomegranates, apples, grapes and bananas). However, it does testify to the abiding power of the imagery of Ephesians 6.10–20 and its ability to speak to the modern world.

The image of Christ breaking down the 'dividing wall of hostility' (to use the RSV translation) remains one of the most memorable images from the letter to the Ephesians. Yet our language is replete with examples of exactly the same kinds of images of separation. Hardly a week goes by without us hearing on the radio or television news of someone crossing a picket line, or breaching security regulations, or imposing a trade barrier, or breaking a quarantine. We may recall Winston Churchill's 'Iron Curtain' separating communist East from capitalist West, or of the 'Bamboo Curtain' separating the West from the Far East, or of the 'North-South Divide' signifying the economic and cultural gulf between the two halves of Britain, or of the 'Green Line' separating the Turkish and Greek halves of the city of Nicosia in Cyprus. More tangible walls, designed either to keep people out or to keep them in, also exist, including Hadrian's Wall in the north of England, or the Great Wall of China. Yet it is difficult to read Ephesians 2.14 without finding our minds transported to what might be the best modern equivalent. One of the most potent symbols of the political and ideological barriers which characterize modern times was the Berlin Wall. For nearly thirty years the Wall symbolized the stark contrast between a capitalist way of life and a socialist way of life. Its dismantling in 1989 stands as one of the key events of our lives, powerfully representing liberation from such a mindset of confrontation and mutual distrust. The 'coming down' of the Wall is a tremendously important step in the reconciliation of a Europe which has been divided since the end of the Second World War. In a very real sense it was not just the people of East Germany who were being liberated but also the people of West Germany who were being set free from a disharmony which had damaged them both.

Eddie Askew, former International Director of the Leprosy Mission, has written a moving meditation and prayer based on Ephesians 2.13–18 and the Berlin Wall. In keeping with the style of his work Askew first relates a meditative story based on the text before going on to offer a prayer for us to consider:

> Two pictures come to my mind from the Berlin Wall. The first is of a young man with a small hammer, enthusiastically chipping away at the concrete. He didn't seem to be getting very far. His hammer just bouncing off the great blocks. People around him were cheering, but I felt he'd finish up with a headache or a sore arm. The second picture was of men driving earthmoving equipment at the wall. With their diggers and cranes, they dislodged great graffiti-covered chunks of it to more cheers. I remember a visit to both sides of Berlin a few years ago. After meeting Christian friends in the East, we stood quietly on the Western side to the wall and looked at three crosses. There were many more, scattered along its length, each marking the death by shooting of someone who'd tried unsuccessfully to get to freedom. 'Unbekannt', it said on the crosses, 'Unknown'.
>
> Why do we put up walls? We surround our lives with them, walls of suspicion and fear. Walls of unfriendliness. We're very careful who we allow into our space. We all have personal checkpoints at which people have to prove themselves to be harmless, to think like we do, to conform, before we let them in. We think the walls are for our own protection, but really they hem us in, limit our freedom. The East German authorities said the Berlin Wall was to protect their people from the West. In reality it

stopped them from leaving.

Jesus came to bring us full life (John 10.10). We enter it by knocking down our personal walls and opening doors, not by installing mental locks and bars and passport checks. Sometimes, God is content to watch us chip away at our own walls slowly with a little hammer, but there are times when he seems to prefer the bulldozer.

> Lord, I need your help today,
> in breaking out.
> The walls I've made,
> and thought were good and comforting,
> now threaten me.
> I've shut my gate on life secure,
> and bolted it.
> All to protect my shopsoiled wisdom,
> bargain priced and cheaply bought.
> Plastic pearls, not worth the keeping.
>
> But when I think about it, Lord,
> it's not security I've found, but prison.
> I'm self-confined within the walls I've built,
> my fear of change the jailor.
> I sit, reluctant,
> trying to retain my grasp
> on the false security
> of life lived timidly.
>
> And when with new found courage
> I start to chip away at the wall,
> my hammer bounces off, with small effect,
> my little efforts useless.
>
> Give me your strength, Lord,
> to face the world afresh.
> To make a move that takes me
> from the sterile shelter of my fears
> into your light outside.
> That's where real life begins.
> And grows.
> It's late, Lord.

> I've lived so long inside the walls.
> But in my new gained freedom,
> the casualties of my fears,
>> *strewn round the perimeter of my defences,*
>> *stir into life.*
>
> Joy and adventure,
> long alien to me,
> reach out and welcome.
> I feel the sunshine,
> hear the birdsong of renewal.
> See your face again.[94]

Finally, we note in passing some of the ways in which Ephesians might continue to speak to the world of today. Of all of the NT letters Ephesians is perhaps the most relevant for the church as she moves rapidly into the twenty-first century. This can be seen on three separate, but overlapping, fronts. First, it gives us a theological basis for ecumenism via its central theme of the unity of the church of Christ; second, it provides a model for a ministry of bringing about peace and reconciliation between warring factions via the emphasis on the creation of a new Humanity out of what were previously two incompatible groups (Jews and Gentiles); third, it offers an opportunity for those committed to ecological issues and those committed to theological beliefs to talk to one another via its vision of the whole of the cosmic order being brought together and finding its purpose in God's divine plan.

APPENDIX 1: MAPS

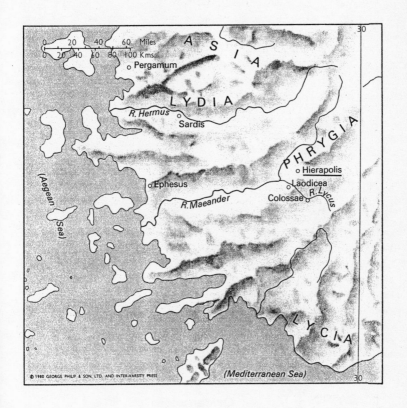

Western Asia Minor and the Aegean Coast

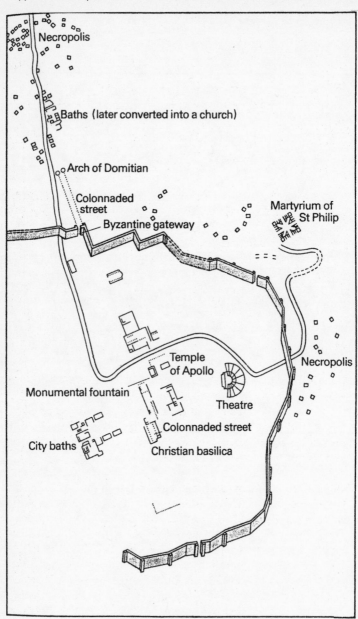

The City of Hierapolis

APPENDIX 2: THE PLUTONIUM OF HIERAPOLIS IN ANCIENT SOURCES

The following passages which mention the Plutonium in Hierapolis are taken from the Loeb Classical Library volumes published in London by the Harvard University Press: Strabo *Geography* (8 volumes), translated by Horace L. Jones (1917–1932); Pliny the Elder (10 volumes), translated by H. Rackham, W. H. S. Jones and D. E. Eichholz (1938–1963); Dio Cassius *Roman History* (9 volumes), translated by Earnest Cary (1914–1927); Ammianus Marcellinus *History* (3 volumes), translated by J. C. Rolfe (1935–1940).

1. Strabo *Geography* 12.8.17 and 13.4.14 (pertaining to a visit made by Strabo to the region in 19 CE):

> I might also say that the whole region in the neighborhood of the Maeander is subject to earthquakes and is undermined with both fire and water as far as the interior; for, beginning at the plains, all these conditions extend through that country to the Charonia, I mean the Charonium at Hierapolis and that at Acharaca in Nysais and that near Magnesia and Myus (12.8.17).

> When one crosses over the Mesogis, between the Carians and the territory of Nysa, which latter is a country on the far side of the Maeander extending to Cibyratis and Cabalis, one comes to certain cities. First, near the Mesogis, opposite Laodicea, to Hierapolis, where are the hot springs and the Plutonium, both of which have something marvellous about them; for the water of the springs so easily congeals and changes into stone that people conduct streams of it through ditches and thus make stone fences consisting of single stones, while the Plutonium, below a small brow of the mountainous country that lies above it, is an opening

of only moderate size, large enough to admit a man, but it reaches a considerable depth, and it is enclosed by a quadrilateral handrail, about half a plethrum in circumference, and this space is full of a vapour so misty and dense that one can scarcely see the ground. Now to those who approach the handrail anywhere round the enclosure the air is harmless, since the outside is free from that vapour in calm weather, for the vapour then stays inside the enclosure, but any animal that passes inside meets instant death. At any rate, bulls that are led into it fall and are dragged out dead; and I threw in sparrows and they immediately breathed their last and fell. But the Galli, who are eunuchs, pass inside with such impunity that they even approach the opening, bend over it, and descend into it to a certain depth, though they hold their breath as much as they can (for I could see in their countenances an indication of a kind of suffocating attack, as it were), – whether this immunity belongs to all who are maimed in this way or only to those round the temple, or whether it is because of divine providence, as would be likely in the case of divine obsessions, or whether it is the result of certain physical powers that are antidotes against the vapour. (13.4.14)

2.   Pliny the Elder *Natural History* 2.208 (Pliny died in the eruption of the volcano Vesuvius in Naples on 24 August 79 CE, so his account of the Hierapolis Plutonium must precede this date; it is unknown if he ever visited the city of Hierapolis himself):

(There are) places called breathing holes, or by other people, jaws of hell – ditches that exhale a deadly breath; (including) the hole at Hierapolis in Asia, harmless only to the priest of the Great Mother.

3.   Dio Cassius *Roman History* 68.27.3 (difficult to date, but perhaps pertaining to a visit made by Dio Cassius while he was in charge of the cities of Pergamum and Smyrna in 218 CE):

I saw … an opening … at Hierapolis and tested it by means of birds; I also bent over it myself and saw the vapour myself. It is enclosed in a sort of cistern and a theatre had been built over it. It destroys all living things save human beings that have been emasculated. The reason for this I cannot understand; I merely relate what I saw as I saw it and what I heard as I heard it.

4. Ammianus Marcellinus *History* 23.6.18 (written circa 293 CE):

A similar opening was formerly to be seen (as some say) at Hierapolis in Phrygia. And from this also a noxious vapour with a penetrating stench came forth and was destructive to whatever came near it, excepting only eunuchs; and the reason for this may be left to natural philosophers to decide.

NOTES

1 *Ephesians* (NTG; Sheffield: Sheffield Academic Press 1993), p. 95.
2 This is an important subject for the study of Ephesians and, fortunately, it is one for which a number of recent books are available. Three of the most accessible are: David G. Meade, *Pseudonymity and Canon* (Tübingen: J.C.B. Mohr 1986), pp. 139–157; James D.G. Dunn, *The Living Word* (London: SCM Press 1987), pp. 65–85; Donald Guthrie, 'Epistolary Pseudepigraphy' in *New Testament Introduction* (Leicester: IVP 1990, 4th edition), pp. 1011–1028.
3 All of the Pauline letters are alluded to in Ephesians with the exception of the Pastoral epistles and II Thessalonians. This is not surprising given that these are all commonly regarded as post-Pauline documents and probably were written after Ephesians.
4 J.N. Sanders, 'The Case for Pauline Authorship' in F.L. Cross (ed), *Studies in Ephesians* (London: Mowbray & Co. 1956), p. 11.
5 *The Literature of the New Testament: The Pauline Epistles* (Edinburgh: T. & T. Clark 1909), p. 183. Scott goes on to contrast Paul the apostle with the author of Ephesians by saying (p. 186), '(Paul) is a gnarled oak tree, while this other writer's emblem is the stately pine or palm.'
6 An interesting variation on this is Charles P. Anderson, 'Who Wrote "The Epistle from Laodicea?"', *JBL* 85 (1966), pp. 436–440, who argues that the letter we know as Ephesians was written to the church of Laodicea by Paul's fellow-labourer Epaphras. The suggestion that Epaphras is the author remains a real possibility and is perfectly compatible with the suggestion being put forward in this commentary.
7 The Greek term for the cavern was the Charonion, named after the ferry-man Charon who was responsible for transporting the dead across the river Styx. Both Strabo and Cassius Dio note that the eunuch priests of Cybele who served in the area were seemingly immune to the effects of the poisonous gas. Both also relate how they witnessed the deadly effects of the grotto's vapours upon other living creatures, including bulls and birds. Strabo's evidence is particularly suited for our discussion since he visited the city in circa 19 CE.

According to the Roman historian Ammianus Marcellinus, writing in circa 393 CE, the entrance to the Plutonium was no longer accessible (see his *History* 23.6.18). William Ramsay, *The Cities and Bishoprics of Phrygia* (Oxford: Clarendon Press 1895), p. 87, thinks that this was 'the action of Christians, who deliberately filled up and covered over the place, the very dwelling-place of Satan'. The site has since been rediscovered. W.C Brice, 'A Note on the Descent into the Plutonium at Hierapolis of Phrygia', *JSS* 23 (1978), pp. 226–227, relates how he visited Hierapolis in 1950 and descended into the fissure.

8 As Arthur G. Patzia, *Colossians, Philemon, Ephesians* (GNC; San Francisco: Harper & Row 1984), p. 214, notes in his comment on 4.9: 'Since the apostle does not clarify what he meant, one assumes that his readers must have known to what he was referring.'

9 It is likely that the geo-thermal conditions of the area are in part responsible for the imagery used to describe the church of Laodicea in Revelation 3.14–22. In particular, the reference to the church being 'neither hot nor cold' may imply that the Laodiceans can offer to a weary traveller neither cold water (as could Colossae) nor hot water (as could Hierapolis). For more on this see M.J.S. Rudwick and E.M.B. Green, 'The Laodicean Lukewarmness', *ExpT* 69 (1957–58), pp. 176–178; Stanley E. Porter, 'Why The Laodiceans Received Lukewarm Water (Revelation 3.15–18)', *Tyndale Bulletin* 38 (1987), pp. 143–149.

10 Jim Grenfell, a retired missionary who served for many years with the Baptist Missionary Society, tells of a remarkable parallel to this which is drawn from his experiences in Africa. He worked in north-central Angola where the Nkanda hills overlook the Mbrize valley below, and comments that in the KiKongo language the names given to villages of the area reflected the local geography. Grenfell explains (in a private letter): 'Early in the day the hill villages were frequently shrouded in mist which looked like clouds to the folk who lived in the valley. To go up the hills to the villages at the top was always referred to as going *kun'ezulu* (lit. "to the sky" or "to heaven"). The two principal towns up the hills were Mongezulu (lit. "Hill in the sky") and Kizulu (lit. "Heaven place").'

11 'Reasons for Ephesians', *Evangel* 14 (1996), pp. 8–14. Moritz thus follows the lead of Michael D. Goulder in reviving the thesis of Marcion concerning the origins of the letter. See Goulder's 'The Visionaries of Laodicea', *JSNT* 43 (1991), pp. 15–39, for more on this.

12 *The Pauline Churches: A Socio-historical Study of Institutionalization in the Pauline and Deutero-Pauline Writings* (SNTSMS no. 60; Cambridge: Cambridge University Press 1988), pp. 85–158. She sees both

Colossians and Ephesians as Deutero-Pauline documents which build upon the 'community-building institutionalization' found in the undisputed letters of Paul; a third stage is found in the Pastoral letters which is concerned with 'community-protecting institutionalization'. Not all agree with the sociological analysis underlying such an assessment, however, and question the extent to which the model of institutionalization might be legitimately applied to the New Testament. See, David G. Horrell, *The Social Ethos of the Corinthian Correspondence* (Edinburgh: T. & T. Clark 1996), pp. 285–291, for a discussion along these lines.

13 'Ephesians and Acts' in L.E. Keck and J.L. Martyn (eds), *Studies in Luke-Acts* (London: SPCK 1968), pp. 288–297. Also see Ralph P. Martin, *Reconciliation: A Study of Paul's Theology* (London: Marshall, Morgan & Scott, 1981), pp. 157–198, who adopts this interpretation of the setting.

14 *Reconciliation, Law and Righteousness: Essays in Biblical Theology* (Philadelphia: Fortress Press 1986), pp. 182–200.

15 Ralph P. Martin, *Reconciliation: A Study of Paul's Theology* (London: Marshall, Morgan & Scott 1981), pp. 157–198, is another example of someone who adopts this interpretation of the setting of the letter.

16 For full details of the inscription see Emil Schürer, *The History of the Jewish People in the Age of Jesus Christ III. 1*, revised and edited by Geza Vermes, Fergas Millar and Martin Goodman, (Edinburgh: T. & T. Clark 1986), pp. 27 and 89. The inscription, which probably dates to the second century, is frequently discussed as evidence for the presence of a Jewish community in Hierapolis, but to my knowledge it has never been applied to a study of the provenance of Ephesians. The most recent study of the larger issue of Jewish populations within the province is Paul Trebilco, *Jewish Communities in Asia Minor* (SNTSMS no. 69; Cambridge: Cambridge University Press 1991).

17 See R.A. Wilson, ' "We" and "You" in the Epistle to the Ephesians' in F.L. Cross (ed), *Studia Evangelica II* (Berlin: Academie Verlag 1964), pp. 676–680, for an intriguing discussion along these lines. Nils Alstrup Dahl, 'Gentiles, Christians, and Israelites in the Epistle to the Ephesians', *HTR* 79 (1986), p. 33, says that 'The alternation of first and second person plurals may reflect a combination of epistolary style and devotional language.'

18 It goes without saying that the same would hold if the Writer was a member of the church at Laodicea and that church was in fact the 'mother-church' of the region. I am assuming that the Writer was from the church of Colossae simply because this would in theory give him greater access to Paul's letter to the church there upon

which he is so reliant. One can but speculate as to where the Writer is when he composes the letter. My own guess is that he is in Ephesus itself and that this is ultimately the reason why the letter comes down to us as one associated with 'the Ephesians'.

19 Note the following examples of texts from Ephesians which are cited in Origen's work: in *De Principiis*: 1.4 is cited in 3.5.4; 1.21 in 1.5.1; 2.2 in 2.11.5; 2.7 in 2.3.5; 4.13 in 1.6.2; 4.27 in 3.2.4 and 6.2–3 in 2.4.3; and 6.12–13 in 3.2.1, 4; in *Contra Celsum*. 2.2 is cited in 7.52; 2.3 in 4.72; 2.20 in 8.19; 4.10 in 1.35; 4.14 in 5.18; 5.1 in 6.73; 5.16 in 6.53; 5.31–32 in 4.49; and 6.11–12 in 8.34; 8.55; 8.73.

20 Full details of most of these passages, and several others, can be found in C. Leslie Mitton, *The Epistle to the Ephesians: Its Authorship, Origin and Purpose* (Oxford: Clarendon Press 1951), pp. 160–169.

21 *Ephesians* (NTR; London: Routledge 1994).

22 *Paul's Letters From Prison* (NClB; Oxford: Oxford University Press 1976), p. 31.

23 This is how the verses are set forth in the United Bible Societies 1st edition (1966). Other Greek texts, such as the United Bible Societies 4th revised edition (1993) and Nestle-Aland 27th edition (1993), divide it into four sentences (verses 3–6, 7–10, 11–2 and 13–14).

24 *St Paul's Epistle to the Ephesians* (London: Macmillan & Co. 1928), p. 19.

25 Markus N.A. Bockmuehl, *Revelation and Mystery in Ancient Judaism and Pauline Christianity* (WUNT no. 36; Tübingen: J. C. B. Mohr [Paul Siebeck] 1987), p. 202, describes this as 'a change in emphasis ... from a christological (Galatians 1.12, 15) to an ecclesiological focus'.

26 Martin Kitchen, *Ephesians* (NTR; London: Routledge 1994), pp. 35–42, contains a useful discussion of the Greek word and its meaning. Also see Erik Osborn, *The Emergence of Christian Theology* (Cambridge: Cambridge University Press 1993), pp. 146–152; Robert M. Grant, *Irenaeus of Lyons* (Routledge: London 1997), pp. 50–51.

27 C. Leslie Mitton, *Ephesians* (NCB; London: Marshall, Morgan & Scott 1976), p. 62, points out that in modern Greek the term has come to be used for an engagement ring.

28 The first three United Bible Societies editions (1966, 1968, 1983) all take the passage to consist of one sentence. Meanwhile, the United Bible Societies 4th revised edition (1993) and Nestle-Aland 27th edition (1993), divide it into two sentences (verses 15–19 and 20–23).

29 It is wise to use 'exaltation' or 'enthronement' in discussing Ephesians and reserve the term 'ascension' to Luke-Acts.

30 *Ephesians* (WBC no. 42; Dallas, Texas: Word Books 1990), p. 62.

31 As cited in Veronica Zundel, *The Lion Book of Famous Prayers* (Tring: Lion Books 1983), p. 51.

32 Paul uses similar compound verbs in Romans 6.4 ('co-buried'); 6.6 ('co-resurrected'); 6.8 ('co-exist'); Galatians 2.19 ('co-crucified'); Colossians 2.12 ('co-buried' and 'co-raised'); 2.13 ('jointly brought to life'); 3.1 ('co-raised'). Is it significant that Ephesians does not refer to the believer's 'co-crucifixion' with Christ?

33 Such ideas of 'corporate personality' have been sharply criticized in recent years by both OT scholars and NT scholars alike. In any case, it is difficult to see how an idea, which was originally posited for *ancient* Israel, could persist into the Graeco-Roman empire of Paul's day.

34 *Ephesians 1–3* (AB no. 34; Garden City, New York: Doubleday & Co. 1974), p. 241.

35 Although Buist M. Fanning, *Verbal Aspect in New Testament Greek* (Oxford: Clarendon Press 1990), p. 319, argues that too much stress can be placed on the idea that the action of the verb began in the past. He says that the phrase is a periphrastic one 'focusing on a condition with an implication of the occurrence which produced it'.

36 *Principalities and Powers: A Study of Pauline Theology* (Oxford: Clarendon Press 1956), pp. 80–81. Similarly, T.K. Abbott, *The Epistles to the Ephesians and to the Colossians* (ICC; Edinburgh: T. & T. Clark 1909), p. 49, likens the sense of *este sesōsmenoi* to 'persons rescued from a wreck, but not yet arrived in port'.

37 It is worth noting that the *only* reference to Ephesians in E.P. Sanders' pioneering *Paul and Palestinian Judaism* (London: SCM Press 1977) occurs on p. 449, and there in a footnote. Sanders is discussing the fact that in Paul future or present tense forms of *sōzō* are generally used and casually remarks: 'The perfect tense of Ephesians 2.5, 8 thus represents a distinct theological development.' In his follow-up work *Paul, the Law, and the Jewish People* (London: SCM Press 1985), Sanders again gives little attention to Ephesians. The only mention of the letter occurs on p. 172 in connection with 2.11–22 and offers what is, in all probability, a misinterpretation of 2.19, arguing that *'fellow* citizens' means Gentiles are given the same citizenship as Jews. For more on this issue, which is crucial for the interpretation of Ephesians, see the discussion of 2.19–22 below.

38 *The Epistle to the Ephesians* (London: Pickering & Inglis 1961), p. 52. The JB also uses 'work of art' here.

39 Words taken from *Hymns and Psalms* (London: Methodist Publishing House 1983), no. 267.

40 It is worth noting that Camus himself was a *French* Algerian, a fact which helps set up the exploration of estrangement which is so powerfully pursued within the story.

41 In fact the gender of the phrase rendered 'both' is not consistent in

the passage. In verse 14 it is neuter plural (*ta amphotera*), while in verse 18 it is masculine plural (*hoi amphoteroi*).

42 Foote relates this idea within Ken Burns' award-winning documentary entitled *The Civil War* which was produced by the Public Broadcasting System (PBS) in the USA. The series of nine one-hour episodes was broadcast in the UK in 1991 and received a BAFTA award for Best Foreign Television Programme in 1992.

43 In addition to Barth's commentary, note the discussion of this in his *The People of God* (JSNTSup no. 5; Sheffield: Sheffield Academic Press 1983), pp. 45–49.

44 J. Armitage Robinson, *St Paul's Epistle to the Ephesians* (London: Macmillan & Co. 1928), pp. 160–161, gives the Greek text of the inscription together with a discussion of the ancient sources which mention such a dividing-wall. A black-and-white photograph of this stone can be seen in J.D. Douglas (ed), *The Illustrated Bible Dictionary Volume 3* (Leicester: IVP 1980), p. 1529. A colour photograph of one of the other smaller 'warning' fragments discovered in 1935 and now on display in the Rockefeller Museum in Jerusalem is contained in Richard M. Mackowski, *Jerusalem: City of Jesus* (Grand Rapids: Eerdmans 1980), p. 121. Colour photographs of the fragments are also contained in Alan Millard, *Discoveries from the Time of Jesus* (Oxford: Lion Books 1990), p. 83.

45 Jordan was a member of the Southern Baptist Convention (SBC) in the USA but found that his stance on such matters as racial equality, wealth and possessions, and pacifism made him unacceptable to the constituency which he sought to serve. He was eventually kicked out of the SBC as a dangerous renegade. It is worth mentioning that Jordan's translation of the Pauline Epistles is set in the form of their being letters addressed to modern equivalents in the American context; thus Romans is *The Letter to the Christians in Washington D.C.*; the two Corinthian epistles are addressed *To the Atlanta Christians*; Galatians is addressed to *The Churches of the Georgia Convention*, etc. The Letter to the Ephesians is described as *The Letter to the Christians in Birmingham, Alabama*.

46 This useful distinction is made in his *The Moral Teaching of Paul: Selected Issues* (Nashville: Abingdon Press 1985, second edition).

47 A.T. Lincoln, 'The Church and Israel in Ephesians 2', *CBQ* 49 (1987), p. 612, similarly remarks: 'This is the "third race" which is different from both Jews and Gentiles.' In his later commentary (1990), p. 134, Lincoln slightly alters this statement. There we read, 'The concept of the Church here is, in fact if not in name, that of the "third race," neither Jewish nor Gentile.' Peter Richardson, *Israel in the Apostolic Church* (SNTSMS no. 10; Cambridge: Cambridge University Press

1969), pp. 147–158, also contains a valuable discussion of this theme. It may well be that this idea of a 'third race' represents a *necessary* development within Christianity in a post–70 CE setting and there are indications that it was not restricted to those writing from within the Pauline tradition. Similar interpretations of Matthew (generally dated to about 85 CE) have been put forward which follow the same line of argument. For example, G.N. Stanton, *A Gospel For a New People* (Edinburgh: T. & T. Clark 1992), pp. 11–12, remarks: 'The evangelist considered his readers to be a "new people" – in effect a "third race" (*tertium genus*) over against Jews and Gentiles.' Descriptions of Christians as a 'new people' (*kainos laos*) or a 'new race' (*kainos genos*) appear frequently in the period of the Apostolic Fathers.

48 To push the metaphor to its limits, we could say that the Writer here is suggesting that the new life in Christ is such that a new birth certificate has been issued, one which serves as the basis for the issuing of a new passport. Whether we should associate this new birth with the rite of baptism, and thus give a setting for the letter as a whole, must be left open.

49 Words taken from *Baptist Praise and Worship* (Oxford: Oxford University Press 1991), no. 393.

50 Words taken from *Baptist Praise and Worship* (Oxford: Oxford University Press 1991), no. 474.

51 *Ephesians 1–3* (AB no. 34; Garden City, New York: Doubleday & Co. 1974), p. 323.

52 Although Jerome D. Quinn, '"Seven Times He Wore Chains" (I Clement 5.6)', *JBL* 97 (1978), pp. 574–576, suggests that this refers to the seven NT documents which speak of Paul's imprisonment (II Corinthians, Acts, Ephesians, Philippians, Colossians, Philemon and II Timothy).

53 *Ephesians* (NTR; London: Routledge 1994), p. 30. What is particularly interesting about this way of interpreting 3.1–13 is that it allows one to make sense of the pseudepigraphical nature of the passage and offers a reason, as well as an historical setting, for its composition.

54 Somewhat inconsistently, the REB translates *diakonos* as 'deacon' in I Timothy 3.8; 12–13 and as 'servant' in 4.6.

55 *Commentary on the Epistle to the Ephesians* (NICNT; Grand Rapids: Eerdmans 1957), p. 73.

56 *Ephesians* (Edinburgh: T & T Clark 1991), pp. 141, 143.

57 *The Letters to the Galatians and Ephesians* (Philadelphia: Westminster Press 1976), p. 126.

58 Cited in Friedrich Kerst and Henry Edward Krehbiel (eds), *Beethoven: The Man and the Artist as Revealed in His Own Words* (New York: Dover Publications 1964), p. 105.

59 *The Message of Ephesians* (BST; Leicester: IVP 1989), p. 134.

60 Words taken from *Mission Praise* (London: Marshall Pickering 1990), no. 295 (the italics are mine).

61 *The Iona Community Worship Book* (Glasgow: Wild Goose Publications 1991), p. 13. These lines work well sung to the Gaelic tune entitled 'Bunessan'.

62 'A Life Worthy of the Calling: Unity and Wholeness', *RevExp* 76 (1979), p. 517.

63 *Ephesians, Colossians, and Philemon* (Interpretation; Atlanta: John Knox Press 1991), pp. 46–47.

64 Rudolf Schnackenburg, *The Epistle to the Ephesians: A Commentary* (Edinburgh: T. & T. Clark 1991), p. 168, calls the seven 'a manifesto of Christian unity'.

65 Words taken from *Baptist Praise and Worship* (Oxford: Oxford University Press 1991), no. 393.

66 Words taken from *The Baptist Hymn Book* (London: Psalms and Hymns Trust 1962), no. 264.

67 A more detailed argument is found in Caird's 'The Descent of Christ in Ephesians 4, 7–11' in F.L. Cross (ed), *Studia Evangelica II* (Berlin: Akademie Verlag 1964), pp. 535–545.

68 R.P. Martin, *Ephesians, Colossians, and Philemon* (Interpretation: Atlanta: John Knox Press 1991), p. 51, gives a useful diagram which sets out the various options of 'incarnation', 'descent into hell' and 'descent at Pentecost'. The most comprehensive treatment of the passage is W. Hall Harris III, *The Descent of Christ: Ephesians 4.7–11 & Traditional Hebrew Imagery* (Leiden: E.J. Brill 1996). Harris offers a thorough survey of critical scholarship on the cryptic passage before concluding that the author had Christ's subsequent descent from heaven at Pentecost in mind, building on prevailing Jewish traditions about the ascent of Moses at Sinai and the subsequent giving of the gift of the Law to the Jewish people in the process. Thorsten Moritz, *A Profound Mystery: The Use of the Old Testament in Ephesians* (NovTSup no. 85; Leiden: E.J. Brill 1996), pp. 56–86, remains unconvinced of the necessity to turn to such Jewish legends about Moses. Instead, he sees the passage to be a Christian polemic against a Torah-based misuse of Psalm 68.18, and suggests that the close relationship between Christ and YHWH is deliberately being set over against the relationship between Moses and YHWH as part of the Writer's argument.

69 Used with permission of Wild Goose Resource Group, Iona Community, Glasgow.

70 Cited in J. Armitage Robinson, *St Paul's Epistle to the Ephesians* (Macmillan & Co.: London 1928), p. 112.

71 See Nils Alstrup Dahl, 'Addresse und Pröomium des Epheserbriefes', *TZ* 7 (1951), pp. 241–251, and J.C. Kirby, *Ephesians: Baptism and Pentecost* (London: SPCK 1968), for more along these lines.

72 Geza Vermes, *The Dead Sea Scrolls in English* (Harmondsworth: Penguin Books 1968), p. 124.

73 Ibid., pp. 75–76.

74 Words taken from *Baptist Praise and Worship* (Oxford: Oxford University Press 1991), no. 404.

75 'Ephesians' in Carol A. Newsom and Sharon H. Ringe (eds), *The Women's Bible Commentary* (London: SPCK 1992), p. 341.

76 Brian Sibley, *Shadowlands: The Story of C.S. Lewis and Joy Davidman* (London: Hodder and Stoughton 1985). See also Lyle W. Dorsett, *Joy and C.S. Lewis: The Story of an Extraordinary Marriage* (London: HarperCollins 1993).

77 A similar idea is found in *Didache* 4.11 where the slave is ordered to obey his master 'as a type of God'.

78 Neil Elliott, *Liberating Paul: The Justice of God and the Politics of the Apostle* (BS no. 27; Sheffield: Sheffield Academic Press 1995), goes so far as to suggest that our picture of Paul as a social conservative is a distorted one because we have misunderstood his teaching about the emancipation of slaves in I Corinthians 7.21. The verse he suggests has been misinterpreted because it is caught in 'the force-field of the pseudo-Pauline writings' (p. 39). In effect, Elliott argues that our reading of the genuine Pauline letters which deal with the issue of slavery, notably Philemon and I Corinthians 7.20–24, has been contaminated by the teaching on the subject contained in the *Haustafeln* of the pseudo-Pauline epistles. He takes *both* Colossians and Ephesians to be pseudepigraphal writings.

79 R. Hobbs, 'The Language of Warfare in the New Testament' in Philip F. Esler (ed). *Modelling Early Christianity: Socio-scientific Studies of the New Testament in its Context* (London: Routledge 1995), pp. 259–273, discusses this at some length, pointing to Isaiah 59.17; I Maccabees 3.3 and Wisdom of Solomon 5.17–23 as literary antecedents to the passage while remarking that the idea of a soldier donning his armour 'is found in works from the *Iliad* to the films of Ingmar Bergman' (p. 263).

80 (Fort Washington, Pennsylvania: Christian Literature Crusade 1957). The details of Nee's life and ministry in pre-communist China are sketchy, but his writings have had an enormous impact in conservative circles in both the UK and the USA.

81 Nigel Wright, *The Fair Face of Evil* (London: Marshall Pickering 1989), pp. 17–31, offers a good introductory discussion on this very point.

82 Also worth consulting on the subject are the popular treatments of

Clifton E. Arnold, *Powers of Darkness* (Leicester: IVP 1992), and Tremper Longmann III & Daniel G. Reid, *God is a Warrior* (Carlisle: Paternoster Press 1995), pp. 165–179.

83 Also note the discussion on p. 174 above, where the possibility of interpreting Ephesians 6.5–9 as a denial of the Pauline vision in Galatians 3.27–28 of the abolition of slavery is discussed.

84 *The Pilgrim's Progress*, edited with an Introduction and Notes by Roger Sharrock (London: Penguin Books 1987), p. 51.

85 Words taken from *Hymns and Psalms* (London: Methodist Publishing House 1983), no. 719.

86 Words taken from *Hymns and Psalms* (London: Methodist Publishing House 1983), no. 378.

87 Cited in Paul Oestreicher, *The Double Cross* (London: Darton, Longman & Todd 1986), pp. 63–64.

88 *Long Walk to Freedom* (London: Little, Brown and Company 1994), p. 750–751.

89 'Ephesians' in Frederick Carl Eiselen, Edwin Lewis, David G. Downey (eds), *The Abingdon Bible Commentary* (London: Epworth Press 1929), pp. 1224–1225.

90 'The Quintessence of Paulinism', *BJRL* 4 (1917–18), p. 285.

91 *Table Talk*, 25 May 1830.

92 Neil Elliott, *Liberating Paul: The Justice of God and the Politics of the Apostle* (BS no. 27; Sheffield: Sheffield Academic Press 1995), p. 25.

93 'Ephesians' in Carol A. Newsom and Sharon H. Ringe (eds), *The Women's Bible Commentary* (London: SPCK 1992), p. 341.

94 *Breaking the Rules* (Brentford, Middlesex: The Leprosy Mission International 1992), pp. 26–27. Used by permission.